Conversations
With
Uncommon
Women

Insights From Women Who've Risen Above
Life's Challenges to Achieve
Extraordinary Success

Ellie Wymard, Ph. D.

AMACOM
American Management Association

New York • Atlanta • Boston • Chicago • Kansas City • San Francisco • Washington, D.C.
Brussels • Mexico City • Tokyo • Toronto

Special discounts on bulk quantities of AMACOM books are available to corporations, professional associations, and other organizations. For details, contact Special Sales Department, AMACOM, an imprint of AMA Publications, a division of American Management Association, 1601 Broadway, New York, NY 10019. Tel.: 212-903-8316 Fax: 212-903-8083

This publication is designed to provide accurate and authoritative information in regard to the subject matter covered. It is sold with the understanding that the publisher is not engaged in rendering legal, accounting, or other professional service. If legal advice or other expert assistance is required, the services of a competent professional person should be sought.

Library of Congress Cataloging-in-Publication Data
Wymard, Ellie
    Converstaions with uncommon women : insights from women who've
    risen above life's challenges to achieve extraordinary success /
    Ellie Wymard
        p.   cm.
        ISBN 0–8144–0520–7 (alk. paper)
        1. Women in the professions—United States Interviews. 2. Women in
    politics—United States Interviews. 3. Women in public life—
    United States Interviews.   4. Successful people—United States
    Interviews. 5. Women in the professions—United States Biography.
    6. Women in politics—United States Biography. 7. Women in public
    life—United States Biography. 8. Successful poeple—United States
    Biography. I. Title.
    HD6054.2.U6W96 1999
    331.4′0973—dc21   99–34078
                                                                          CIP

Printing number

10 9 8 7 6 5 4 3 2 1

For my husband, Joseph Michael Wymard,
and our grandchildren,
Thompson Parker Wymard
and
Elizabeth Reid Wymard

Contents

Remarkable Voices vii

Acknowledgments xiii

Introduction xvii

Chapter One
Women in Politics: "I Had to Go Out There and Fight" 1

Chapter Two
Women and Policy: Entrepreneurial Advocates for Social Change . . . 53

Chapter Three
Women in the Law: Soundings From Bench and Bar 95

Chapter Four
Women in Journalism: "Hire This Girl" 135

Chapter Five
Women and Business: Negotiating the Culture 171

Chapter Six
Women in Arts Management: Out on Thin Ice 223

A Coda
"You Aren't What You Do" 245

Index 247

Remarkable Voices

Agee, Mary Cunningham, Founder and President, The Nurturing Network, Carmel, CA   76

Agosti, Deborah, Judge, Reno, NV   98

Anderson, Susan, WBBM-TV, Chicago, IL   142

Arsht, Roxanna, Judge, Wilmington, DE   96

Avery, Byllye Y., Founder, National Black Women's Health Project, Atlanta, GA   72

Balser, Barbara, President, Management Compensation Group, Inc., Atlanta, GA   176

Barnes, Teveia Rose, Esq., Associate General Counsel and Senior Vice President, Bank of America National Trust and Savings Association, New York, NY   131

Belton, Sharon Sayles, Mayor of Minneapolis, MN   33

Berglin, Linda, State Senator, Minnesota State Legislature   25, 50

Bickett, Mary Kay, Executive Director for the Texas Center for the Judiciary, Austin, TX   108

Bogart, Anne, Director of the Saratoga International Theatre Institute, Saratoga Springs, NY   231

Born, Brooksley, Esq., Partner, Arnold & Porter, Washington, D.C.   118

Braver, Rita, White House Correspondent, CBS News   142

Bunda, Sue, Executive Producer, *CNN and Co.*   166

Campbell, Nancy Duff, Esq., Co-President, National Women's Law Center, Washington, D.C.   116

Coleman, Maxine, Vice President of Personnel and Organization, KAL KAN Foods, Inc., Vernon, CA   217

Cranston, Mary C., Esq., Partner, Pillsbury, Madison & Sutro LLP, San Francisco, CA   133

Cromer, Diane, Political Consultant, Washington, D.C.   15, 29, 47

Danburg, Debra, State Representative, TX   28, 48

Davis, Susan, President and Founder of Capital Missions Company, St. Charles, IL   175

De Bolt, Jo, Executive Director, MON Valley Initiative, Homestead, PA   53

De Demonic, Patty, Founder and CEO, PDQ Personnell Services, Inc., Los Angeles, CA; President of the National Association of Women Business Owners 1994–95   186

DeLauro, Rosa, (D., CT) U.S. House of Representatives   1, 39

Dominguez, Cari, Under Secretary of Labor, Bush Administration   10

Domitrovich, Stephanie, Judge, Erie, PA   95, 134

Donnell, Caithlin, Esq., Founder, Colorado Women's Bar Association, Denver, CO   119

Elliott, Kate Ford, Judge, Superior Court of Pennsylvania   105

Evans, Gail, Executive Vice President of CNN and Executive Producer, Atlanta, GA   166

Fanning, Katherine (Kay) Woodruff, editor, *The Christian Science Monitor,* editor and publisher *Anchorage Daily News,* Pulitzer Prize   159, 161

Fertel, Ruth, Founder and CEO, Ruth's Chris Steak House, New Orleans, LA   171

Friedlander, Carolee, Founder and President of Carolee Designs, Inc., Greenwich, CT; President, Committee of 200   209

Godfrey, Marian A., Program Director for Culture at the Pew Charitable Trusts, Philadelphia, PA   229

Goodman, Ellen, Syndicated Columnist, *Boston Globe;* Pulitzer Prize, Boston, MA   137

Grant, Lee, Actor and Documentary Film Director; Academy Award, Obie, and Emmys, New York, NY   227

Gray, Cynthia, Esq., Director of the American Judicative Society's Center for Judicial Conduct Organization, Chicago, IL   101

Greenberger, Marcia D., Esq., Co-President of the National Women's Law Center, Washington, D.C.   114

Grogan, Barbara, Founder and President of Western Industrial Contractors, Denver, CO   218

Gutman, Roberta W. (Bobbi), Vice President and Director of Human Resources Diversity, Worldwide, at Motorola, Inc., Schaumburg, IL   187, 202

Harris, La Donna, Founder and President of Americans for Indian Opportunity, Bernalillo, NM   68

Hernandez, Antonia, President and General Counsel of the Mexican American Legal Defense and Educational Fund, Los Angeles, CA; Counsel to Senate Judiciary Committee   49

Hoeksema, Mary Jo, Legislative Aide, U.S. Senator Jeff Bingham (D., NM)   38

Hopkins, Karen Brooks, Executive Vice President, Brooklyn Academy of Music, Brooklyn, NY   223

Hutchison, Kay Bailey, (R., TX) U.S. Senate   33

Ifill, Gwen, NBC Correspondent   144

Jones, Dr. Anita K., Director of Defense Research and Engineering, The Pentagon   8

Kadushin, Karen D., Esq., Dean, Monterey College of Law; President, San Francisco Bar Association, San Francisco, CA   123

Kaye, Judith S., The Chief Judge of the State of New York   110

Kimberling, Sandra A., President, Music Center Operating Company, Los Angeles, CA   236

Kneale, Jean, Esq., Hicks, Anderson, Blum, P.A., Miami, FL   133

Lake, Celinda, Political Consultant, Washington, D.C.   9

Lichtman, Judith L., Esq., President, Women's Defense Fund, Washington, D.C.   112

LoRé, Linda, President and CEO of Giorgio, Beverly Hills, CA   179

Macaskill, Bridget, President and CEO of OppenheimerFunds, Inc., New York, NY   190

MacLennon, Linda, Anchor, WBBM-TV, Chicago, IL   157

Manning, Sherry, Founder and President of ECCI, The Education Communications Consortia, Inc., Charleston, WV; President, Colorado Women's College   198

Masloff, Sophie, Mayor of Pittsburgh, PA, 1988–1994   40

McCabe, Jewell Jackson, Chair, National Coalition of 100 Black Women, New York, NY   87

McGartland, Grace, author *Thunderbolt Thinking* (Bernard Davis); President, National Association of Women Business Owners, 1992–93; Founder and President of GM Consultants, Toronto, Canada, and Pittsburgh, PA   208

Milligan, Lynda, President and Cofounder of The Great American Quilt Factory, Inc., Denver, CO   205

Minner, Ruth, Lieutenant Governor, Delaware; Majority Whip, Delaware State House   26

Mizeur, Heather, Legislative Aide, Joseph P. Kennedy (D., MA)   11

Molinari, Susan, (R., NY) U.S. House of Representatives   10

Morella, Constance M., (R., MD) U.S. House of Representatives   16, 20

Murray, Therese, State Senator, MA   28, 37, 51

Myers, Sondra, Special Assistant to the Chairman for Institutional Relations, National Endowment for the Humanities   234

Normandin, Jeannette, S. S. A., Founder of RUAH House, Cambridge, MA   88

Norton, Eleanor Holmes (D., D.C.) U.S. House of Representatives   19

Nugent-Head, Marie, Director of Development, New York City Ballet, NY   239

O'Connor, Sara, retired Managing Director of the Milwaukee Repertory Company; President, League of Resident Theaters (LORT)   233, 242

Odel, Kathleen Ann, Esq., Sherman & Howard LLC, Denver, CO   121

Ott, Sharon, Artistic Director of the Seattle Repertory Theatre; Artistic Director of the Berkeley Repertory Theatre   232

Overholser, Geneva, Ombudsman, *The Washington Post;* editor, *Des Moines Register*   159

Phillips, Alicia, Director, Metropolitan Atlanta Community Foundation, Atlanta, GA   64

Pudlin, Helen C., Esq., Vice President and General Counsel, PNC Bank Corp., Pittsburgh, PA   129

Reuthling, Ann, President, Chinaberry Book Services, Inc., San Diego, CA   213

Reynolds, Barbara, senior columnist, *USA Today*   153

Richards, Ann, Governor of Texas, 1990–1994   43

Roberts, Cokie, *This Week*, ABC; analyst, NPR   139

Rothman, Clare L., President of the California Forum, Los Angeles, CA   173

Rowe, Sandra Mims, editor, the *Oregonian*, president, American Society of Newspaper Editors   159, 164

Savocchio, Joyce, Mayor, Erie, PA   44

Tarr-Whelan, Linda, President and Executive Director of the Center for Policy Alternatives, Washington, D.C.   42, 58, 171

Temin, Carolyn Engel, Judge, Philadelphia, PA   100

Tiernan, Kip, Social Activist, Boston, MA   57

Todhunter, Marcia C., Esq., private practice, San Mateo, CA   126

Toretti, Christine, President, S. W. Jack Drilling Co., Indiana, PA   197

Torre, Marie, WILM Newsradio, Wilmington, DE; KDKA-TV, Pittsburgh, PA; Columnist, *The New York Herald Tribune*   148

Totenberg, Nina, Legal Affairs Correspondent for NPR   135, 149

Turner, M. Caroline, Esq., Vice President and General Counsel, Coors Brewing Company, Golden, CO   128

Wald, Patricia M., Chief Judge, United States Court of Appeals for the District of Columbia Circuit   103

Walker, Liz, coanchor, *Eye Witness News*, WBZ-TV, Boston, MA   155

Walsh, Alice C., President and COO Alaska Center for the Performing Arts, Anchorage, AK   225

Walsh, Holiday, Esq., Partner, Allswang, Smith & Walsh, San Francisco, CA   122

Weister, Linda, President, Cleany Boppers, Inc., Baltimore, MD   202

Whitman, Christine Todd, Governor of New Jersey   30

Widnall, Dr. Sheila E., Secretary of the Air Force   4, 37

Wilson, Betsy, President, "Let's Face It," Concord, MA   81

Wilson, Marie C., President, MS Foundation, New York, NY   65

Woods, Harriet, Lieutenant Governor, MI; Democratic Nominee, U.S. Senate; President, National Women's Political Caucus   8, 24

Woods, Sandra, Vice President and Chief Environmental, Health and Safety Officer of Coors, Brewing Co. Golden, CO   192

Yancey, Jean, Jean Yancey Associates, Denver, CO   245

Acknowledgments

This book is the result of the encouragement of many men and women, some who are family and friends, others whom I have never seen.

I am grateful to Dr. Grace Ann Geibel, R.S.M., president of Carlow College, for suggesting that I write a book on women and leadership, and then releasing me from teaching so I could do it.

I am grateful to Dr. Marianne Alexander, director of the Public Leadership Education Network, Washington, D.C., for encouraging my research and gaining the enthusiastic support of PLEN colleges: Agnes Scott College, Decatur, GA; Bennett College, Greensboro, NC; Carlow College, Pittsburgh, PA; Chatham College, Pittsburgh, PA; College of New Rochelle, New Rochelle, NY; College of Notre Dame of Maryland, Baltimore, MD; College of St. Catherine, St. Paul, MN; Columbia College, Columbia, SC; Douglass College, New Brunswick, NJ; Hood College, Frederick, MD; Mount St. Mary's College, Los Angeles, CA; Newcomb College, Tulane University, New Orleans, LA; Pine Manor College, Chestnut Hill, MA; Randolph-Macon Woman's College, Lynchburg, VA; Sweet Briar College, Sweet Briar, VA; Trinity College of Vermont, Burlington, VT; Trinity College, Washington, D.C.; Wells College, Aurora, NY; Wesleyan College, Macon, GA; and PLEN Associate Schools: George Washington University Women and Power Program, Washington, D.C.; Goucher College, Baltimore, MD.

I am grateful to the 150 women I interviewed for graciously interrupting their workday to spend time with me. I also appreciate their administrative assistants for juggling schedules to arrange our meetings.

I appreciate the efforts of many individuals for arranging and/or suggesting interviews: Marianne Alexander, Washington, D.C.; Nancy Alexanderson, Concord, MA; Happy Barranco, Washington, D.C.; Susan Bohn, Pittsburgh, PA; Carol Brown, Pittsburgh, PA; Diane Cromer, Washington, D.C.; Betsy Crone, Washington, D.C.; Charlie Day, Pittsburgh, PA; Dorothy Davis, Pittsburgh, PA; Susan Davis, Chicago, Ill; Judge Stephanie Domitrovich, Erie, PA; Caithlin Donnell, Denver, CO; Gail Evans, Atlanta, GA; Dan Fallon, New York, NY; Carolee Friedlander, Greenwich, CT; Janice Friedman, Pittsburgh, PA; Marcia Greenberger, Washington, D.C.; Barbara Grogan, Denver, CO; Mary Catherine Conroy Hayden, Pittsburgh, PA; Karen Johnson, Washington, D.C.; Sandra Kimberling, Los Angeles, CA; Lydia Lewis, Chicago, Ill; Judith Lichtman, Washington, D.C.; Linda MacLennon, Chicago, Ill; Jewell Jackson McCabe, New York, NY; Grace McGartland, Toronto, Canada; Woodene Merriman, Pittsburgh, PA; Patricia G. Milligan, Pittsburgh, PA; Sara O'Connor, Milwaukee, WI; Judge Carol N. Park-Conroy, Falls Church, VA; Margaret Rieck, Pittsburgh, PA; Mary Alice and Vincent Stanton, Cambridge, MA; Marie Torre, Wilmington, DE; Jan Walker, Washington, D.C.; Marie Wilson, New York, NY; Josh T. Wymard, Washington, D.C.

I wish to thank students and staff at Carlow College for helping me, at different times, in important ways: Diane Cook, Christy Hillegas, Elizabeth Lawler, RoseAnn Opferman, Jenny Veleko, and Beth Walter. I am indebted to my daughter-in-law, Bonnie Barrett Wymard, for her very careful research. I am happy to acknowledge Donna Sivvy for her computer skills and cheerful, prompt response to my arbitary deadlines.

I am eternally grateful for the professional advice of Judith Applebaum, Sara Blackburn, Florence Radovic, and my good friend, Mary Ann Eckles. I must mention that the day-to-day involvement of Mary Devlin, Joan Dorgan, and Ellin Wymard meant a great deal to me.

My warm thanks to Cathleen Ouderkirk for her cover design; Jon Tibbetts and Lynn Steines for their careful attention to production, and Jeanne Patterson for her precise copy-editing.

I am blessed with friends and family—all the Wymards and Grigassys—who were with me on this project from beginning to end. My husband, Buddy, lived every word. Our two sons, Josh and Peter, and their wives, Ginger and Bonnie, consistently offered encouragement.

I am grateful to my editor, Ellen Kadin, for enthusiastically welcoming this book, and for always being available and intelligently involved in its every detail.

Introduction

You are cordially invited to meet one hundred women of achievement who will tell you how they got where they are today. They are leaders in their fields: women who are affecting policy, bringing their influence to bear in business, creating their particular styles of communicating in the media, and transforming our culture in the arts. In the pages of this book, they talk about what questions and problems they have had to confront, about how they deal with difficulties, about their personal and professional goals, and about their desire to make a difference.

All of these women agreed to report on their own life experiences because all of them want to support other women and to provide practical guidance and realistic examples for those who are entering or reentering the job market, those who are changing jobs or thinking of doing that, and those who want to accomplish more. Like Secretary of the Air Force Sheila E. Widnall, they feel a responsibility to serve as role models. "I guess the reason I'm talking to you is that throughout my career, I have consciously taken on additional assignments that I thought would lead to increased visibility," Widnall told me during a lengthy conversation. "In terms of my own time, family responsibilities, and professional responsibilities, it would have been very easy to say no," she explained, "but I didn't say no very often because I told myself, 'We want to see more women doing these things.'"

The stories you will read here are culled from face-to-face and telephone interviews and focus on six major fields: politics, public policy, law, print and broadcast journalism, business, and the arts. Within each field, women from markedly different backgrounds report on markedly different undertakings.

Through snapshot autobiographies, personal anecdotes, and lingering images, these high-achieving women have much to tell us. My hope is that the interaction of their voices will help each of you create your own pathway toward a fruitful, satisfying life. Somewhere here, I believe, are the right words for each reader.

Chapter One

Women in Politics:
"I Had to Go Out There and Fight"

Rosa DeLauro (Democrat, Connecticut) says that even the benefits of growing up with a ringside seat at politics do not alleviate the tensions of running for office. Until 1990 when she was elected to Congress, DeLauro was drawn to the idea of "working behind the scenes." She had seen politics from the inside out as the only child of activist parents from New Haven's Wooster Square: Her father Ted was an alderman, affectionately called "the mayor of Wooster Square"; her eighty-two-year-old mother Luisa is the senior active member on the New Haven Board of Aldermen, where she has served for more than thirty years. In 1933, at the age of nineteen, Luisa was the secretary of New Haven's Tenth Ward Democratic Club when she wrote a letter to the other members: "We are not living in the Middle Ages when a woman's part in life was merely to serve her master in her home, but we have gradually taken our place in every phase of human endeavor and even in the heretofore stronghold of the male sex: politics."

> *We have gradually taken our place in every phase of human endeavor and even in the heretofore stronghold of the male sex: politics.*

With her mother as a trailblazer, Rosa DeLauro came naturally to political advocacy. As we talked in her Washington office, DeLauro ignored the ringing telephone and the insistent aide in her doorway and spoke passionately about her mother's influence: "My mother didn't have a college education; she worked in shirt shops and dress shops, and old sweatshops. I remember waiting

1

for her after school, watching her and the other women bent over those machines.

"It always saddened me to realize how few opportunities they had without an education. My mother showed me how important an education was," she said. "In Italian culture at the time, women were not sent to school the way young men were, but it was very clear that I would go to college and have a profession."

He would say that I had a wonderful theoretical knowledge of politics, but if I wanted to really be engaged with what politics was all about, I needed to understand street politics and get involved at that level. And he was right.

DeLauro has a strong academic preparation in politics: a bachelor's degree in political science from Marymount, a year of study at the London School of Economics, and a master's degree in International Politics from Columbia University. Yet she credits her father with giving her the best advice: "We would have these lofty arguments. He would say that I had a wonderful theoretical knowledge of politics, but if I wanted to really be engaged with what politics was all about, I needed to understand street politics and get involved at that level. And he was right."

Being Out Front

Still, DeLauro never thought about running for office herself. Instead, she worked for mayors and senators. She managed Frank Logue's campaign for mayor of New Haven in 1978. And after steering the first senate campaign of Connecticut's Christopher J. Dodd, she served as his chief of staff for six years. She also was the executive director of EMILY'S List, the national organization committed to recruiting and raising money for women running for elected office. "I was always ambivalent," DeLauro says. "I thought it would be great to run and would like to try, but I wasn't sure if maybe I should work behind the scenes."

But when Representative Bruce Morrison decided to run for governor of Connecticut and gave up his congressional seat, DeLauro was endorsed as a candidate. "My primary opposition pulled out as I was making the run," she reminisces. "I knew that whether I won or lost the race, this is what I wanted to be doing. I was ambivalent, but my decision was confirmed in running for the office. Even if I lost—and I don't like to lose—I knew I had made the right decision and should have done it sooner."

DeLauro's hesitation was based on issues that many women considering elective office face, including the daunting amount of campaign money to be raised and deep concern about the logistics of doing the job well. She also had to resolve a persistent stereotype about female roles and how to shape choices for herself. "Do you really want to be the person out front?" she asks rhetorically. "Just think about that. You have a great luxury in serving as a person behind the scenes. You can give all the advice, and you don't have to cast the vote and take the glory or the heat that results from that."

DeLauro decided that behind the scenes was no longer the place for her. "It's much better to be the person who casts the vote, who sits at the table and makes the decision. You take the heat when some people don't like what you do. But I've always found that if you really believe what you've done is the right thing and have based it on research and by talking with people, then others might disagree with you, but they'll also have a certain amount of respect for you. The job has exceeded its expectations."

Even though DeLauro's life had been devoted to politics, entering the field of action demanded a leap. Just as her mother had pointed the way for her, DeLauro says that women must be dedicated to serving as guides for each other. She is candid about her hesitance in running for office because she hopes other women won't regard their own indecision as a portent against being "the person out front."

A New Generation

Young women have long been on Capitol Hill, but, until the 1970s, most were expected to remain as clerks and secretaries until they married and left. When DeLauro was chief of staff to Senator Dodd, working behind the scenes on the comprehensive child care legislation passed by Congress, fewer than ten women held the same position in other senate offices. Today the halls of the Senate and House office buildings are filled with women in their twenties who are as focused on their career goals as the young men who hurry beside them. As more women are elected to Congress, their numbers will continue to grow.

Rosa DeLauro says, "People always ask me, 'Isn't this a male bash?' Women can get marginalized in Congress. We are a small number, very diverse and bipartisan. Our strength is in coalesc- ing with men and women who have like ideas and putting forth legislation and public policies that we believe are the right thing about a whole variety of issues. Otherwise, you're never going to get anywhere in this body. Some would like to relegate women to specific areas that are more stereotypical. But we deal with an American agenda . . . a public agenda that includes foreign pol- icy, budget, the economy, environment, whatever it is! I'm very interested in what we can do about getting people jobs in my state. Healthcare is also of critical importance. But within health- care I take a large role in women's issues because I'm a cancer sur- vivor. So my perspective is to be an advocate of the people. Some- times women pigeonhole themselves or allow themselves to be pigeonholed. I think it's crazy. That's not why I'm here."

The Hot Seat

Dr. Sheila E. Widnall, the first female Secretary of the Air Force, says women in leadership positions should never be offhand about their accomplishments. "Women have to be more willing to step forward and admit that they are putting themselves on the line," she says. "Women need to see other women acknowledge themselves as risk takers . . . letting people know that something is important to them."

Women need to see other women acknowledge themselves as risk takers . . . letting people know that something is important to them.

Within months of our conversation, Widnall proved her words. The buck stopped at her desk in the highly publi- cized case of First Lieutenant Kelly Flinn, the Air Force's first female B5 pilot, who faced a court-martial for lying about an affair with a married man and disobeying an order not to see him. In a no-win situation, Widnall, a civilian, negotiated a general discharge instead of a court-martial or an honorable discharge. Her decision was that she had "to protect the Air Force core values" and that Lieutenant Flinn's "lack of integrity" and "disobedience to orders" were more serious to the Air Force than the adultery charges were.

Presence Is Clout

Widnall says that her appointment has given important visibility to all women in the military. "I get a lot of comments" she says, "from female officers from all the services who indicate they are pleased that a woman is serving in this position."

Women's groups throughout the 1970s argued that the discriminatory practices and traditions of the armed forces would be altered if the numbers of women increased, particularly in leadership roles. Twenty-five years later, advances in the military academies and in the services are noteworthy, Widnall asserts: "When you work in the fields of aeronautics and aerospace, there's no business more rewarding than the Air Force. And no more exciting time for women to be a part of it. . . . And that's all our women have asked for—the chance to compete; a level playing field."

Widnall is candid in noting that "sexual harassment has been a front-page issue that all the services have had to deal with. I'd like to think my appointment sends a signal that we do treat those issues very carefully, and that I have special skills to help us work through them." When she visits bases, for example, Widnall is concerned about the treatment of women in their units: "If nothing else, I send a message that I expect that everybody will behave themselves and get along and work productively together and form teams and fundamentally deal with these issues as professionals." In general, she intends to improve the living conditions for families regarding base housing, education, and day care. The Air Force will benefit by "putting people first," she says, and giving them the training and education necessary for building strong careers that will also enhance their family life.

Sheila Widnall considers herself to be an integrated person, addressing problems as a woman, an aeronautical engineer, and an educator. She fits well with her position because the Air Force is at the leading edge of aeronautical technology and has a special focus on education and training for its people. And 20 percent of the Air Force today is composed of women. "So being a woman and secretary is not totally an unusual idea as far as the Air Force is concerned," she observes. Nevertheless, she says that being the first female service secretary in history is a dream come true for her.

Engineering Feats

Widnall is accustomed to being at the cutting edge of change. She was one of only twenty women who matriculated at the Massachusetts Institute of Technology School of Engineering in 1956, when women constituted less than one percent of the engineering profession. Once she earned her undergraduate and graduate degrees in aeronautics and astronautics from MIT, she became the first woman to join the faculty at its School of Engineering. She is internationally known for her work in fluid dynamics, specifically in the areas of aircraft turbulence and spiraling airflows, called vortices, created by helicopters. Before she assumed her position as Secretary of the Air Force, she was the first woman provost at MIT.

As a child, Sheila Widnall knew she was good at math. She is the oldest of three daughters and had a close relationship with her father, "building things and doing things that fathers normally do with sons." Her energetic mother worked as a probation officer with delinquents and troubled families, and Widnall knew clearly by the eighth grade that she herself would have a career and work outside the home.

At a Catholic all-girls' school in Tacoma, Washington, the Dominican nuns encouraged her to succeed in math and science and sent her to the local public high school for a physics class. Although the male teacher "was taken back a little bit, he joined the train very quickly," Widnall remarks. "He was extremely supportive and thought it was great that I was in the class."

The mild surprise registered by this teacher more than thirty-five years ago seems to be the closest to a stumbling block that

Widnall will acknowledge in her pursuit of success in this distinctly nontraditional field for women. One stage in the recruitment process for MIT required her to go to Seattle with a group of twenty students, all boys, to meet with a committee of twelve (male) scientists and engineers who represented the alumni council of the Seattle-Tacoma region. "Their purpose in getting us all together was to pick the one individual that would win the Seattle Alumni Scholarship. They chose me, which I thought was really extraordinary, out of all those people."

She and the nineteen other women who matriculated into the MIT class of 1960 barely even qualified as a minority among their 900 male classmates, but Widnall credits "the environment with providing a lot of leadership opportunities. The women students were always getting organized and trying to solve problems, and the administration and faculty always reacted positively when we put forth coherent requests."

I always had a very supportive environment, so I worry about bringing on the next generation and making sure that they have similar experiences to pick up the flag for the next generation.

When I asked if she missed not having had a woman faculty mentor, Widnall responded: "I don't think an aeronautical engineer expects that. . . . I don't know. It's not an experiment that I can run against."

She expresses a deep feeling of responsibility for encouraging women and minorities to see themselves in new roles. "I always had a very supportive environment, so I worry about bringing on the next generation and making sure that they have similar experiences to pick up the flag for the next generation." In her speeches to various groups of leaders, she urges them "to keep mentoring, role-modeling, and opening doors."

Being willing to make gutsy calls by using the power of her office is a distinguishing trait of many women in government today. It is a record that is relatively young, for, as late as the 1950s, the brilliant humanitarian and diplomat Eleanor Roosevelt was still being ridiculed for making the role of first lady into a position of influence.

Evolving

"Many women still continue to justify their civic involvement on the basis that it's good for someone else," remarks Harriet Woods, retired president of the National Women's Political Caucus and former lieutenant governor of Missouri. "[Too many] don't take the next step and run for office. . . . I think this is partly because women still sense they should be meeting other priorities and have to explain taking time away from family. They can't say that political office will give them more power to get things done."

"Yes, Sir"

Dr. Anita K. Jones, a civilian, is Director of Defense Research and Engineering at the Pentagon. She does not mind when members of the armed forces unconsciously answer her with "yes, sir": She figures that "yes" is a positive acknowledgment of whatever is being talked about and "sir" is merely the traditional form of respect.

The relationship between language and sexism is a nonissue for Anita Jones. She likes the fact that at the Department of Defense people are treated according to their offices within a hierarchical structure. "It's particularly easy to come in as a minority because of the line organization. Everybody knows who they work for, whether your office ranks higher or lower than another. When you speak from your office, it's the office speaking."

Since respect is based on rank and position, Anita Jones accepts "sir" as an affirmation of her leadership and does not worry that it overshadows any individual identity. She believes that her job at Defense is the best because "it's as high as you can get and still be wholly concerned with science and technology."

Pentagon Responsibilities

Dr. Jones is responsible for the management of science and technology programs and oversight of in-house laboratories, university research initiatives, and the Advanced Research Projects Agency. She directs an annual budget of roughly 8 billion. Twice a month she chairs a "Breakfast Club" for the executives from the agencies and military services, who report through their own organizations, but whose budgets she supervises. Her agenda for these meetings is to arrive at consensus so that programs will be executed with compatible goals. A staff of five reports directly to her, but "when you trace those charges down, personnel measures in the hundreds."

In seeing herself as a collaborative leader within the rigid hierarchical system of the military, Anita Jones shares the enthusiasm that many women express for exercising leadership within the more formal structures of government as opposed to politics. "It's the office speaking," a fact that women continue to employ creatively and often with a special talent as agents of change.

Clout

Celinda Lake, a leading political strategist for the Democratic Party and a pollster to *U.S. News & World Report*, believes that old stereotypes about female behavior remain stronger within the informal network of politics than in the prescribed worlds of government or corporations. To be called "sir" at the Defense Department may seem inconsequential if one is making critical decisions regarding a budget of $8 billion dollars. On the other hand, a congresswoman may have the facade of power yet receive little recognition or support from her party leaders in terms of her general political clout or her potential as a legislator.

According to Lake, "politics is personalized and operates in one-on-one subjective relationships, and stereotypes are stronger in informal arenas than in formal ones. When women run for Congress they are entering a man's world, not just taking one step up the political ladder." In this way, the sturdy structure of the Pentagon may offer a more comfortable setting than the more fluid but relatively unpredictable province of Congress.

When women run for Congress they are entering a man's world, not just taking one step up the political ladder.

Women who are appointed to positions in government are given an opportunity to lead because they have demonstrated their authority in a particular area. Cari Dominguez, former assistant secretary of labor in the Bush administration, says that serving as an appointed official is very different than being elected to office: "If appointed, you serve at the pleasure of the president and you are depending on the pleasure of the cabinet secretary, so your personal philosophy and policies need to fall within the parameters of their views and directions, and you have to complement their initiatives. The focus is more narrow and managerial. For example, I administered ninety-two laws within the Department of Labor. I had the Fair Labor Standards Act, the Worker Comp law, the EEO laws, immigration, child labor, etcetera. And sometimes I had to make current and interpret laws that were forty and fifty years old. So there's more of a management focus in appointed offices. You're also working within a certain Administration, so you have to be very sensitive to the political nuances that are going on, regardless of your personal views."

In comparison, women have more flexibility in promoting legislation because they are serving the interests of a broad community. But their power also relies a great deal on interpersonal relationships. Women inside Washington politics frequently have mentioned to me that Geraldine Ferraro's (Democrat, New York) tight relationship with House Speaker Tip O'Neill, as compared with Patricia Schroeder's (Democrat, Colorado) history of impressive legislation, won Ferraro, not Schroeder, the Democratic vice-presidential nomination in 1984.

To Run or Not to Run

Deciding to run for office is a tough enterprise in itself. "To go public with your ambitions and to lay your credentials out to everyone, as opposed to just one person in management or to the CEO of a company, really requires a certain amount of confidence and fortitude in order to go through all that," says former Representative Susan Molinari (Republican, New York).

Even though she had lived through many political campaigns as the daughter of former Representative Guy Molinari, now Staten Island's borough president, she felt uneasy about throwing her own hat into the ring. "I always thought I would be the person behind the scenes, managing the ads. I saw myself as a pretty typical female, I guess, as opposed to having the power; I thought I'd help someone else to access power."

When a seat became open in the New York City Council, the odds were against a Republican winning, Molinari explains. "It was a good time to challenge myself—I run on the philosophy that if you want to do something and you're afraid to do it, then you have to do it." Only twenty-seven when she was sworn in, Molinari became the body's minority leader because she was the only Republican on the council. Thrown into prominence, she did not have the luxury of learning her role over the years. "I had to absorb it quickly—within a week!" Laughing, she confesses that her term often seemed far longer than the four years she actually served. Molinari went on to be elected to three terms in the U.S. House and delivered the keynote address at the 1996 Republican Convention. Then she resigned to become coanchor of *CBS Saturday Morning.*

Considering her service in the House, she says, "There clearly is a void in the United States Congress when it comes to women, but that helps you to become outspoken on issues. Women bring a different priority. . . . We may all see equal merits in the legislation we vote on, but when you can incorporate it into your life, or your own experiences, it's just natural to pursue that legislation with a greater passion and sense of understanding. Any of the issues which deal with women's health or women's choice, certainly crimes against women, are ones that have not been given full discussion. Women in Congress in each political party have to shake the sensitivities of the men around us regarding the importance of these issues."

Mizeur Moves

Heather Mizeur, twenty-five, says that she has wanted to run for office since she was eight. She knows how it feels to lose, she explains, because she was a legislative assistant in the Washington office of Representative Marjorie Margolies-Mezvinsky, a freshman Democrat from Pennsylvania's Thirteenth Congressional District, who cast *the* vote that ensured passage of President Clinton's budget in the House. It was on the evening of August 5, 1993; the tally was 217 to 217; and Clinton needed one more vote to give him the majority. According to R. W. Apple, Jr., in *The New York Times*, Margolies-Mezvinsky said to the President: "Frankly, I think I lose my seat on this one. I think I fall on my sword."

L eadership is about being able to make decisions and take a direction despite the fact that others feel that it may not be a good choice.

Mizeur says that the image of Margolies-Mizvinsky's casting that deciding vote will always remain an inspiration to her. A few weeks before the election, the congresswoman said to her—as she did to me in our interview —: "Leadership is about being able to make decisions and take a direction despite the fact that others feel that it may not be a good choice. It's being able to close the door after you've gotten all the facts and say, 'I'm going to vote this way or that way.' It's being able to go down there and decide not to vote to stay, which is, I think, a very difficult choice, because it's an interesting job."

When Margolies-Mezvinsky indeed lost her bid for a second term, Mizeur says she felt numb as she drove back to Washington from Philadelphia's Main Line. But within days she updated her résumé in order to "hit the ground running" with the new Congress. She knew the stats: There were thirteen new members, three thousand Democrats out of jobs, and only one hundred positions to compete for. Recognizing that she was on the "low end of the totem pole in terms of experience," Mizeur plotted her strategy by working as a volunteer in the orientation center, where she had direct access to the newly elected members of the House. By mid-December, she was hired by Representative Sheila Jackson Lee from Houston, Texas. In July 1995, Representative Joseph P. Kennedy (Democrat, Massachusetts) hired her as a legislative aide and named her his top legislative director within a year.

Kennedy's Top Aide

Mizeur conceived and drafted twenty-one of the thirty-five bills Kennedy introduced in the first session of the 105th Congress. "Joe expected his staff to be legislative entrepreneurs," Mizeur says. "He's passionate about causes. Sometimes I felt pushed to my limits continually thinking up ideas." She often worked fourteen to eighteen days in a row. "I loved the job. It was always my goal to be in Kennedy's office because Bobbie and JFK were my teenage idols. I loved drafting legislation and speeches, and organizing news conferences, and had no intention of leaving."

But, out of the blue, Mizeur got a call from the National Association of Community Health Centers, a nonprofit Washington-based organization providing affordable healthcare to low-income and often uninsured patients. She was offered the position of Director of State Affairs, traveling nationwide on behalf of child health insurance and tobacco legislation. "I knew if I were going to run for office, I had to broaden my experience beyond being a congressional staffer," Mizeur says, "but I didn't think I'd face the decision so soon."

Mizeur hated to interrupt Joe Kennedy's Christmas holiday to say she would be leaving, but "after praying over it," she did call him in Vail. The very next day Michael Kennedy was killed in a skiing accident. "If I had waited, I would never have made the move, and added to Joe's burden," she says. "But I really went through a lot of discernment to change jobs when I did. Policy work is very transferrable. It's a different focus than being on the Hill, and it's the kind of experience I need now."

A few months later, Kennedy announced he would not seek another House term.

On Track Early

As a third grader in the small rural town of Blue Mound, Illinois, Heather Mizeur was drawn to politics when she read a biography of John F. Kennedy. "I thought, oh my gosh, this guy has so much charisma!" Smiling ruefully as we sat at a table in a House meeting room, she said: "I really didn't know what that word meant then, but I knew

I really didn't know what that word meant then, but I knew I had a feeling for what Kennedy embodied, how he was able to move people with his words.

I had a feeling for what Kennedy embodied, how he was able to move people with his words."

Her enthusiasm for President Kennedy kindled her interest in the 1980 presidential election debates to the point where she regaled her family with the little position papers she wrote. She also set up mock elections, which she continued to do for every election throughout grade school and high school. She signed a scrapbook for a third-grade friend: "To David, my best friend in the world. I love you very much even if you do like Reagan!" Meeting her recently, the same David observed, "Heather, you've been political since birth."

Mizeur's mother and father are baffled about her acute interest in politics, but they have never discouraged her. During election campaigns, her mother always drove her to the Macon County Democratic headquarters so that she could be in the thick of it all, stuffing envelopes, walking the precincts with candidates, and planning for upcoming parades.

Labor as Force

Building on her experience in practical politics, Heather Mizeur became a political science major at the University of Illinois in Champaign-Urbana. She wanted to study labor issues and union management because her father, who worked as a welder at Caterpillar, always talked about "strikes and layoffs and scabs at the dinner table. I was raised in an atmosphere where labor-management problems were always discussed, and I kept trying to figure it out. And it was like, well, if Dad goes back to work we start getting money again. We can buy groceries; it just wouldn't make sense to me why he wouldn't cross the line. So I would read things on my own. But my father and I were always close, and as I grew older I realized the financial difficulties that were caused by strikes. My father's sweat and toil have meant a lot to me over the years. I've seen the hell he's gone through."

This strong work ethic continues to draw Mizeur to issues of healthcare, poverty, and the environment. At the age of fifteen, she worked with Penny L. Severens, an Illinois Democratic state senator, who remained her mentor until her death from cancer at the age of 46 in 1998. "She taught me to give 100 percent to serve the needs of my community. When I throw my hat into my own race, she will still be right there with me, running all the way."

A mentor herself, Mizeur was one of four honored by President Clinton at the White House for distinguished service in the AmeriCorp national service program. In addition to her full-time job in Kennedy's office, she tutored low-income minority students and served as project coordinator for a chapter of the I Have A Dream Foundation.

A Harry S. Truman Scholar, Mizeur intends to study law in the Northeast before returning home to Illinois and making a run for Congress. "I would probably like to move from the House to the Senate. I can really never say what my final goal is because I just keep taking steps where I need to. . . . But I say this truly from the heart. I'm very people-oriented and want to be in the true service of the people. I would be involved in government or policy-making or Congress for no money, no name recognition, no power, because I've been able to witness from a very young age that public policy can do good things for people if you have the right person pushing the policies and getting things done with the right intentions. I'm going into politics because I feel called to it. To me, public service is a lifestyle. It's the very fabric of who I am."

Heather Mizeur's ability to chart her political career is a recent phenomenon: Most of the women I spoke with have made their way into public office by spending years of hard work for deeply held causes. Those who have done so place great value on what they were able to bring to politics as a result of these rich and varied experiences, and they hope that young women starting out will be able to integrate similar passions into their own early careers, even if paths to office are more streamlined.

Hitting the Road

Diane Cromer, the founder of Diane Cromer Enterprises, is a Washington political consultant who affirms that issues are what matter and says that they have to be tangible. She says that a young woman preparing for a political career needs to be directly in touch with the lives of the women she will be representing: A degree in political science is no match for personal contact.

Cromer uses herself as an example. In the early seventies, she served on the first staff for the Pennsylvania Coalition Against Domestic Violence and took a second job at the local Dunkin' Donuts because she wanted to save money to buy a house. Her routine was that in the middle of the night she baked muffins at Dunkin' Donuts, and toward dawn she left for her office at the state capitol. And she learned far more, she says, about the suffering caused by domestic violence from her coworkers at Dunkin' Donuts than she did from reading all the studies about it in Harrisburg.

Every woman I worked with had been abused on some level. They were either abused by their husbands, or victims of incest, or they came from families with alcohol problems. I really gained insight into the people who go to the polls.

"It was the only time in my life," Cromer says, "that I ever had to clock in and clock out. I never told anyone there that I had a college education because I wanted to fit in. Every woman I worked with had been abused on some level. They were either abused by their husbands, or victims of incest, or they came from families with alcohol problems. I really gained insight into the people who go to the polls. Today when I try to help a client of mine communicate, I imagine my coworkers and the variety of people at the counter at Dunkin' Donuts. Candidates for political office have to know the texture of life, see it from the bottom up, not just the top down."

For this reason, Cromer believes that candidates who are elected to full-time legislative positions without having worked hard at something do not have the skills or the conviction of women who have held jobs, led grassroots causes, or run businesses and households.

A Springboard Into Politics

As a young woman, Constance A. Morella (Republican, Maryland) never considered a political career. Before she was elected to

Congress in 1986, she had been an English professor at Montgomery College for fifteen years. Though she had held various offices in student government from grade school through Boston University, she never ran for president "because women didn't really do that in the fifties."

Connie Albanese's parents expected her to be a "secretary, marry, and have a nice family. To be a politician was unheard of!" she says. She married Tony Morella and earned a master's degree in English from American University then helped some friends in their local campaigns. "In the early seventies, the women's movement put the movement into me," Morella says. She was appointed to the first Montgomery County Commission for Women in 1972 and testified on the need for women to win equity in the realms of credit, education, housing, and employment. One of her first goals as its president was to revise the gender language in the *Annotated Code* of the State of Maryland. She also endeavored to make affirmative action work in the educational system, so that women were able to advance to the positions of principals and supervisors. For the first time, she began to see herself as a candidate.

"That was my springboard for seeking office. I decided that since I was testifying and moving things forward, I could do more in a legislative position. I thought I would have more influence on the other side." With pride, she adds: "We also got the Equal Rights Amendment passed in the Maryland Legislature."

Morella lost her first race for the Maryland House of Delegates, but she won her second in 1978 and served for eight years. Then she was elected to Congress as the representative of Maryland's Eighth District. In all these endeavors—as a volunteer, in the state legislature, and in Congress—her name has been synonymous with legislation that continues to make a positive difference in many areas of women's lives. *McCall's* named her one of the "10 best politicians for women" and the "best Republican in the House" for her pioneering work in acquired immune deficiency syndrome (AIDS) legislation and for pushing the National Institutes of Health to increase research on human immunodeficiency virus (HIV) in women. She has sponsored bills to expand apprenticeship opportunities for women in nontraditional jobs like construction, and to advance opportunities for women in engineering and science. She was one of the rare Republicans in the House voting against the impeachment of President Clinton.

Advocating for Women

Connie Morella is a complex blend of gentleness, determination, altruism, and ambition. "Forgetting about being modest," she says, "and being very candid with you, I have made a big difference in terms of women's issues, but I think it's my efforts to make people more aware of domestic violence that stand out."

I have made a big difference in terms of women's issues, but I think it's my efforts to make people more aware of domestic violence that stand out.

Shameful Secrets, an ABC movie aired in prime time, dramatized the custody problems of women trying to keep abusive ex-husbands away from the children. It was inspired by a resolution sponsored by Morella and passed unanimously by the House and Senate. House Concurrent Resolution 172 entreats the courts to consider a parent's history of spousal abuse when deciding a child custody case. The resolution argued that "evidence of spousal abuse should create a statutory presumption that it is detrimental to a child to be placed in the custody of an abusive parent." When Morella introduced the resolution in 1989, only twelve states and the District of Columbia allowed or required the court to hear such evidence in determining custody. To date, thirty-seven states include the resolution in their statutes. Morella was also a major sponsor of the Violence Against Women Act and the Domestic Violence Hotline.

Inseparable from the educational and domestic issues that Morella addresses is the fact that she is an educator and a mother who has raised nine children, including her late sister's six children. "Young women are fortunate that they can work toward their political aspirations earlier than my generation could," Morella notes. "Many women my age started ten years later because they spent that time thinking about families, but that also opened up other issues for them. At least until now, women have been driven to seek office by virtue of problems that they wanted to do something about. Men have just said, 'Hey, I think I want to grow up and be a member of Congress.' Now women are saying some of the same things, but I still think they will bring something unique."

Special Responsibilities

When Eleanor Holmes Norton (Democrat, District of Columbia) was seven years old, her grandmother, who lived in the next block, sent her to the corner butcher to buy three lamb chops. On principle, Eleanor rejected the first two, but returned with three nicely trimmed chops, wrapped in brown paper. Trivial as it may sound, Norton considers this incident as a defining moment in her life. That evening as neighbors passed by the porch, her grandmother told the story again and again: "I sent this child to the Safeway today. First time she went by herself. The butcher tried to give her one set of lamb chops but she said she wanted other ones. She's the smartest child in the world. Yes, indeed."

Norton calls her grandmother an intuitive psychologist for giving her responsibility for a task and then rewarding her for carrying it out. "Right in front of me, over and over again, she praised me, and continued to praise me throughout my childhood." This early dose of self-confidence was basic, Norton claims, to her success in politics.

Norton is also firm in her conviction that gender is important in the process of decision making, and that women represent distinctively female experiences. "Your experience colors how you look at public issues, so that if you are a *conscious* woman—another name, in my judgment, for feminist— you bring to the table what has very seldom been there in politics, and that is the different experiences that come from being and growing up female." For Norton, the goal in a democracy should be to have as many experiences as possible represented. "If too many

Your experience colors how you look at public issues, so that if you are a conscious woman— another name, in my judgment, for feminist—you bring to the table what has very seldom been there in politics, and that is the different experiences that come from being and growing up female.

people are left out," she contends, "then they look for other ways to influence government, and some of these are dangerous, or you get the kind of apathy that can drain a society."

In order to act effectively on her values in public office, a woman has to be confident that her personal experience offers a crucial perspective to the legislative process. Many women, like Constance Morella, are galvanized to action during adulthood when social concerns pull them into the political system. As the lamb-chop anecdote demonstrates, Eleanor Holmes Norton was instilled with confidence about taking responsibility as a child. "My family always rewarded me for taking responsibility. And I think that is part of the parcel of what leadership is made of: self-confidence to go ahead and do something because somebody had made you feel you could."

I think that is part of the parcel of what leadership is made of: self-confidence to go ahead and do something because somebody had made you feel you could.

Throughout her childhood, Norton was groomed to accept responsibility by her parents, grandmother, and aunt. "I was conditioned toward leadership as the oldest of three daughters. There was a clear ideology that the oldest had special responsibilities. I remember very clearly feeling as though there were things that I was supposed to do that Portia and Nellie were not. I was left in charge; I was the spokesman for the group. It's a clear case of how kids measure up to what you expect of them."

Political discussions at the dinner table also prepared young Eleanor to be accountable for her opinions. Near the end of the Truman administration, while she was attending the Columbia Scholastic News Conference at the Waldorf Astoria as editor of her junior high newspaper, she was invited to be on the *Edward R. Murrow Show*. "I was the only black child," she says, "interviewed with about five white kids. They all said, 'I like Ike,' or something similar. I remember my teacher said, 'When you're asked about the elections, Eleanor, what are you going to say?' And I said, 'Oh, my goodness. I would have to support Mr. Stevenson, wouldn't I?' When my time came, I was clearly at variance with every one of the white children who wanted Ike. And I could not have had that kind of conviction without the conversation that went on at our dinner table." With laughter in her voice, Norton adds: "My father believed that it was the beginning of the end of the world when I was back home and he could actually see me on television on Sunday night."

Race, Gender, and Forging Common Cause

Asked her views about being a leader, Norton says that standing for one's convictions is only one of its aspects. Another is "being willing to move forward when others will not." She distinguishes between "leadership responsibility" and "tests of leadership," noting that as an African American it was easy to denounce racism and to demand full right for blacks. "While I regard standing forward on racism as a leadership responsibility, it would not be my definition of the test of leadership. Tests of leadership come in moments when it is more difficult to step forward," she says.

Norton was faced with such experiences during the late sixties and early seventies when the civil rights movement was winding down and the women's movement began to "march forward in justifiable imitation." Black women were reluctant to identify with feminism, she says, because of "confusion about whether people who had suffered as much as blacks did ought to be promoting white women." During this period, she felt a profound responsibility for explaining that "feminism was built less on black people, but that black people had taught feminists."

The issue posed itself most dramatically for her during a 1980 convention of black Democrats who were meeting to discuss issues to prepare for the presidential election year. "I will never forget," Norton says with deep feeling, "sitting in a room filled to the brim with mayors and Jesse Jackson. And in a speech Jesse made a passing remark about feminism, that as far as he was concerned, in slavery there were not only slave masters, but also slave mistresses. Well, the remark brought down the house! It was just that bigoted."

"I have got to find the brother. That cannot go uncorrected," Norton promised herself. Spotting Jackson in an elevator that was about to close, she told him, "'When you go at white feminists, you're going after me!' The doors were closing, but he heard me. The next week he called and we had a long conversation. The upshot was that a huge march was set for Chicago, because Illinois was the last of the states that we had any hope of getting the ERA [Equal Rights Amendment] through. Jesse came out and gave a great ERA speech. . . . When he thought about it, Jesse changed absolutely, and has been an extraordinary feminist ever since. Before that, he had never been challenged, and blacks were still trying to find their way around feminism."

Caring Toleration

The values that compelled Norton to confront Jesse Jackson are centered in her personal experience. "As a child I had an instinctive reaction against racism until I was able to formulate a philosophy that repudiated it. When you have thought about racism with any sort of rigor, it's very difficult not to analogize it to other groups. I have a hard time understanding how it is possible to apply principles that repel bigotry to yourself without applying them to everybody else who is similarly situated . . . if there is black anti-Semitism, for example, somebody black has got to say that's wrong."

When she addressed some incidents of anti-Semitism generated by black extremists in 1994, Norton thought hard about a way to respond "convincingly and responsible . . . because another important ingredient of leadership is how you exercise it. It's important to bring people with you." As the District of Columbia's congressional representative, she decided to mark the anniversary of the assassination of Dr. Martin Luther King, Jr., by addressing a letter to every Washington church, synagogue, and mosque, plus its superintendent of schools and the presidents of its colleges and universities, calling for a citywide promotion of "caring toleration and concern for equality."

Norton explains her rationale: "If somebody is criticizing black people, they figure you're supposed to be on the side of black people. Regarding my constituents, I couldn't drive them to the other side of the ship; so here again I used analogy. Even though Washington was segregated by law when I was growing up, I first learned lessons of toleration and respect from church and in the public schools of D.C."

Because of the opportunities offered her, Norton insists that she has never paid a personal price for holding strong convictions. Instead, she thinks of the leaders in the early civil rights movement, all the feminists ahead of their time, and the individuals accused of Communism during the McCarthy era as "really suffering for their beliefs. Even within segregation," she points out, "I was able to have the best education the country afforded at Antioch College and Yale Law School. I got to be a lawyer and have had one gratifying professional experience after another. Being black and a woman has allowed me to live an exciting life and have an opportunity to make a contribution here, there, from the time I was a youngster. I don't understand the notion of being a black victim or a female victim."

> *Being black and a woman has allowed me to live an exciting life and have an opportunity to make a contribution here, there, from the time I was a youngster. I don't understand the notion of being a black victim or a female victim.*

Recognizing the River Kwai

Norton says she has always called upon her positive inner confidence to see her through difficult situations. Drolly, she mentions that her drive for perfectionism sometimes reminds her of Colonel Nicholson, the Alec Guiness character in *The Bridge on the River Kwai*, who is so determined to build the best bridge that he forgets to remember that he is in servitude to the enemy. "My own standards always kick in and say if you're going to do it, do it very, very well," she observes. "But then I have to catch myself and say, wait a minute. Is this the bridge on the River Kwai? Should I invest as much as this?"

Setback or New Frontier?

Like Eleanor Holmes Norton, women in politics generally see themselves as problem solvers and believe that there are always ways to move ahead. Even in defeat, they learn to plot strategies for taking significant action.

Harriet Woods, the first woman ever elected statewide in Missouri, served as its lieutenant governor from 1985 to 1989. She had been a city council member and then was elected state senator, an office she held for eight years. Woods was the Democratic nominee for the U.S. Senate in 1982 and again in 1986, when she lost a close race. "I never brood at all about the past," she says. "I hope it's not Pollyannish, but there are always other frontiers and ways to move ahead. In fact, I have a hard time remembering unpleasantries. I like to take something where I see a problem and figure out answers to it."

Justice Thomas's Confirmation

Shortly after she was elected president of the National Women's Political Caucus, Woods testified before the all-male Senate Judiciary Panel during the confirmation hearings of Judge Clarence Thomas for the Supreme Court. She was the only one to raise the issue of why she really needed to be there, she says: "Women are so underrepresented in the legislative bodies that we have to seek justice in the courts, and therefore, we have to be worried about who is on the court because we are not making the laws."

Women are so underrepresented in the legislative bodies that we have to seek justice in the courts, and therefore, we have to be worried about who is on the court because we are not making the laws.

Her statement helped to focus women on the need to elect more women and train others to "get inside so that we can make decisions." Not only did she help to launch the "year of the woman" in politics; she headed the Clinton administration's Coalition for Women's Appointments and submitted names of more than six hundred women qualified to fill key policy posts within it.

Assume Expertise Standing on Tiptoe

Despite their increasing numbers, women in political office say that they still must prove themselves each step of the way in a male-dominated legislative process. "There's the long-standing saying,"

Woods notes, "that any young man coming out of law school is automatically qualified to run for office, but a woman has to run every tax campaign in town, over and over again, before she's perceived as being capable. . . . Men don't have their own campaign training; they don't have organizations like ours—men get elected because the whole system is theirs. The official party automatically works for them—to the extent that it works for anyone—but women are newcomers who are trying to pry open the door. So they feel that they have to learn everything and get all this training before they'll take risks within the political system."

There's the longstanding saying, that any young man coming out of law school is automatically qualified to run for office, but a woman has to run every tax campaign in town, over and over again, before she's perceived as being capable.

Study Male Behavior

Linda Berglin, a member of the Minnesota state legislature who spearheaded healthcare reform in the state, says women in politics often think they have to be supercompetent before they assume leadership on an issue. "What I learned very quickly, and what I think is very important for women to know, is that there are an awful lot of very, very, very incompetent men who by virtue of holding office or having a title are assumed to have competence. Women shouldn't be intimidated about having to know everything before trying to do something."

. . . there are an awful lot of very, very, very incompetent men who by virtue of holding office or having a title are assumed to have competence. Women shouldn't be intimidated about having to know everything before trying to do something.

What women do need to know, Berglin adds, is "that for some men the merits of issues are not always as important as trading votes or making deals with each other. I'm not suggesting that women need to imitate this behavior to be successful, but they need to understand how some men operate in order to know what they need to do."

Berglin was not in the Minnesota state house for very long before she advanced the issue that veterans' preference was making it very difficult for women and minorities to be hired for state government jobs. She brought together groups representing women and minorities, plus public employees who were being passed up for promotion because they were not veterans. "The more diversity and the more kinds of groups you can pull together to have a common interest on an issue, the more successful you're likely to be," she says.

"Don't Lead: They May Not Follow"

Ruth Minner, the former majority whip of the Delaware state house and the state's first female lieutenant governor, concurs that the most galling realization women face in all levels of political office is that they still have to work harder than men. "We always have to be ready," she sighs. "Men can simply say, 'Well, I don't know; maybe I'll do that tomorrow,' and they accept that among themselves, but not from women: A woman who doesn't have something done is said to be lazy. That's the hardest part for women—knowing they always have to be prepared."

Minner dropped out of high school at age sixteen to marry her first husband, Frank Ingram. But Frank died when she was thirty-two, leaving her with three sons, the oldest of whom was only fourteen. After his father's death, young Frank told his mother not to worry, that in two years he too could quit school and help her raise his brothers. "That remark forced the issue with me," Minner says. "I wanted my sons to continue their education and make a better life for themselves. And to prove it to them, I went back to school." She earned her general equivalency diploma (GED) and continued with courses at the University of Delaware.

From early in her marriage, Ruth Minner had been a gofer for the Democratic party in Delaware, eventually becoming an attache for the state house of representatives. There she researched bills, drafted some legislation, answered letters, and organized agendas. In 1973, she became a receptionist in the office of Governor Sherman Tribbitt and learned how legislation is put into effect. Within a year, Minner was persuaded to run for an opening in the house by a male politician who said: "Remember all those times that you prepared our notes and we delivered them poorly and you complained? Well, now *you* can deliver what you've prepared, and you can do it to the best of your ability."

Her bid was a success, and in her third term in the house, she was elected majority whip. "I earned leadership because of all the work I had always done. My philosophy has always been 'Don't lead, they may not follow; don't follow, they may not lead.' Just work together and try to solve the problem. Leadership is about being able to work together with people to accomplish something. It's not about making demands that people *have* to follow."

> *Leadership is about being able to work together with people to accomplish something. It's not about making demands that people have to follow.*

Not Settling for Worker Bee Status

Minner says that women are too ready to accept themselves as "worker bees" when they should be valuing their ability to "take the lead and make a difference." She spreads this message by visiting schools and persuading potential dropouts to get their diplomas. She also talks with groups of homeless, battered, or confused women, nudging them to move forward. As Delaware's lieutenant governor, she uses her clout to get closer to people, not to distance herself. "Sometimes I meet with women individually and have them come visit me. Some of them are like I was. I was in a terrible position, but I had choices to make if I was going to have a better life for myself and my sons. Not everybody has the ambition to do that, nor do they make the right decisions. One of the things I can do is to help them along the way."

Ruth Minner's experience as a struggling widow was more than a personal episode in her life. It is integral to how she acts as an elected official, relating to people one-on-one and helping to solve problems.

In order to be ready for the unexpected, women politicians often inform each other across party lines in informal caucuses. One representative says: "I've seen with my own eyes that if a woman gets on the mike and says something stupid, all the guys will say, 'Oh you women don't know anything about parks and wildlife.' Whereas if a guy said an equally stupid thing, nobody would ever generalize about all men. So there's definitely mutual support that women inform each other about our bills to make sure that we know what's coming up."

Risky Business

State Senator Therese Murray of Plymouth is a risk taker who quarterbacked welfare reform in the Massachusetts house during her first term in office (1992–1994). She describes a frustrating day she spent watching the ups and downs of the state's welfare bill as it made its way through the legislative process. "When you're looking for something to happen, and it doesn't happen, it's like stepping through Alice's mirror, and it gets more and more curious. Nothing is as it seems. My chief of staff was screaming, 'It's not going to happen if leadership doesn't want it to happen.' I said, 'Well, it's the boys again.' And he said, 'Yeah, it's the boys, and that's the way it goes'. . . .

"'Well, who says?' I asked. 'I'm not going to accept that. I don't like to lose, and I'm not going to lose.'"

Murray's brand of determination and patience are still requisites for women elected to state houses and the U.S. Congress.

Smart Strategies

Debra Danburg, a lawyer and state representative in Texas for fifteen years, says women have to work especially hard in building coalitions they need. They can stay motivated to do this if they have a "vision and keep chipping away at moving toward that vision," she asserts. A pragmatic approach is also key. Building a coalition means compromising on issues that are irrelevant to being classified as a conservative or a liberal, Danburg points out. "Log roll, help people with what they're doing in other districts, and call in some chits later."

Danburg recalls energetically supporting a colleague on a bill regarding hoof-and-mouth disease, an issue that was without relevance for her district. "Now I can go to him when I need his vote," she says, "but I also have to cover him later. Don't ask people to do things that are going to backfire on them or bite them in the tail. I don't hide things in bills. You have to be clear about what the side impacts are going to be and how to explain it to their folks that they voted with this liberal feminist from Houston."

The Value of Coalitions

When Danburg was a young college graduate "hanging out to see what to do with a sociology degree," she was given her first lesson in building coalitions as assistant director of Texans for ERA, a lobbying group composed of women's groups of every political stripe. "Even if we disagreed on any number of side issues, that didn't stand in the way of our committed stand on the ERA. If you make people feel like they are part of your coalition on one issue, they'll trust you on some other issues," she advises. "It's a matter of constantly reaching out to as broad a group as you possibly can."

Building coalitions can be daunting for women in state houses with multi-issue agendas. Political consultant Diane Cromer describes the standard style of male representatives as "two elks locking horns: I get the power and I fight the rest of you back as you come up the hill to me, until I get too old and you finally knock me down."

Making Things Happen

Political consultants and politicians agree that because women have been outsiders to elected office, their usual leadership style is to urge wide participation from constituents in the legislative process. In order to demonstrate their political clout and substitute support and eloquence for the power of money and status, women traditionally have organized advocacy groups and coalitions to influence public policy.

Political consultant Diane Cromer expresses hope that as more women are elected to public office, they will continue to be as resourceful in building coalitions as they have had to be because they lacked traditional insiders' clout. "If women carry on their legacy of including rather than excluding people from the process of making decisions, better legislative decisions will result for everyone," she says.

A Governor's Perspective

Christine Todd Whitman, governor of New Jersey, says that women will always be issue-oriented as they move into the political system because this has been their consistent hallmark. "Women go into politics because they recognize something bigger than themselves. They are not in it just for the glory, but to accomplish something, and that's what the process is supposed to be about," she says.

Women go into politics because they recognize something bigger than themselves.

In her first inaugural speech, Governor Whitman said candidly: "I believe that the best decisions are based on consensus . . . I did not run for governor to conduct 'business as usual.' I'm not one of the boys. It is going to be different around here."

When we spoke together, she affirmed that she "believed very much in consensus building. I think you have to know what it is you want to accomplish and you have to have a base set of standards and goals. Then you bring as many people into the process as possible to help present them in the way that is going to get the most support so that you can actually accomplish them."

Whitman maintains that she learned this style of leading long before she became governor, "that it has always been true" of her. "But women in general prioritize differently and problem solve differently. They are just more inclined to build consensus than many of their male counterparts. They are not as afraid to reach out and say, 'I don't have all the answers. Let's see what we can come up with together.'"

Special Strengths

Women in politics generally say they have a perspective that gives priority to people. In 1999, in the 106th Congress, women held sixty-seven of the 535 U.S. House and Senate seats—only 12.5 percent of the total, an increase of 2 percent since the last Congress and only 7 percent in their representation thirty years ago. Even with these small numbers, women have always brought special strengths to the legislative process.

During the seventies and early eighties, women members of Congress did much to illuminate issues of child care, healthcare, and education. Representative Shirley Chisholm (Democrat, New York) for example, advanced the cause to assure a minimum wage for household workers. As a member of both the Post Office and Civil Service Committee and the Armed Services Committee, Patricia Schroeder (Democrat, Colorado) secured important pension rights for the ex-spouses of foreign service and armed forces employees and improved working conditions for military personnel. Margaret M. Heckler (Republican, Massachusetts), as a ranking member of the Veterans' Affairs Committee, supported the installation of centers for the aged in Veterans' Administration hospitals, and the creation of counseling facilities for veterans of the Vietnam War. In 1971, she was an early advocate of child care for working parents and spoke against President Nixon's veto of a comprehensive child development program. She joined with Elizabeth Holtzman (Democrat, New York) to lead support to extend the period for ratification of the ERA.

Issues to the Table

Bipartisan coalitions of women have given vitality to quality-of-life issues on all levels of government. Congresswomen today are even expected to champion the cause of women they represent, but that is a new freedom, according to Esther Peterson, who has a long memory as executive vice chairman of the president's Commission on the Status of Women under the chairmanship of Eleanor Roosevelt. Peterson went on to serve as assistant secretary of labor in the Kennedy and Johnson administrations. In "The Kennedy Commission," an essay published in 1983, she pointed out the very different expectations that were placed on these women appointed to cabinet positions over a forty-year period.

The first woman to hold a cabinet post, Frances Perkins, was appointed secretary of labor by President Franklin D. Roosevelt in

1933. Another twenty years passed before President Dwight D. Eisenhower chose Oveta Culp Hobby to head the Department of Health, Education, and Welfare. The third appointment was not made until President Gerald Ford named Carla Hills as secretary of housing and urban development. By then, Peterson said, the "women's movement had established the right for women to hold such offices." But with no such structure to support her, "Frances Perkins had to prove that she could be as good a secretary of labor as a man. [She] "had to make it a point to use her office on behalf of *all* working people. Had she done otherwise, she would have sacrificed her legitimacy."

"Women's Issues" Are Everyone's Issues

Since Perkins forged her position, women no longer have to be silent on equal employment, comprehensive child care, domestic violence, and welfare reform in order to establish their credibility as legitimate voices in government. Nonetheless, the pressure to focus on nontraditional female interests in order to reinforce the perception of their competency is the flip side of the problem that faced Frances Perkins. To compensate for the lack of a common standard, campaign strategies endorsed by EMILY's List advise female political candidates to obtain experience in areas that are considered untraditional for women, such as taxes and foreign policy.

Diversity Makes a Difference

A legislative body functions best when it includes a variety of perspectives, differing points of view that make it truly representative. For that reason, women are an essential part of an effective democratic government. . . .

Senator Kay Bailey Hutchison (Republican, Texas) observes that she brings a different perspective to public policy, but does not consider gender to be the determining factor of her political philosophy. "A legislative body functions best when it includes a variety of perspectives," Hutchison maintains, "differing points of view that make it truly representative. For that reason, women are an essential part of an effective democratic government. . . . It has always bothered me that our tax code punishes women who chose to be homemakers, whether as a life's work or for a few years. I, like other women, have been in and out of the workforce and have experienced the discrimination of not being able to continue providing for my retirement security during a period when I was not employed. I am cosponsoring a bill to correct that inequity with Senator Barbara Mikulski (Democrat, Maryland). This is the sort of initiative that nearly every male senator supported once it was explained, but which none of them had thought about before two women raised the issue."

Grassroots Activists

As we have seen, women often win political office after they successfully organize advocacy groups for grassroots causes that then influence the legislative agenda and produce new policies. These journeys usually begin in their organizers' own neighborhoods, and the women who embark on them seldom have their eye on elected office. Eventually, their self-gained expertise and confidence in carrying out their deeply held convictions translate into their being recognized as effective political leaders.

Sharon Sayles Belton, the first woman mayor and first African American mayor of Minneapolis, always thought she would be effecting change from the outside because she truly enjoyed her life as a political activist. Then, during a rally in the state capitol in January 1983 in support of Martin Luther King Day, a group from South Minneapolis asked her to run for city council because she came from their neighborhood and had lived through their problems. Her run was successful, and at the end of her third term, Sayles Belton became the first African American elected president of the Minneapolis city council. She decided to run for mayor in 1994, and her platform stressed diversity and inclusiveness: "Public policy is better when the people it's designed to affect are making it."

Before she joined the city council, Sayles Belton was a grassroots activist. As a student at Macalester College, she had a "life-changing experience" when she went south during the civil rights movement to help with voter registration in Jackson, Mississippi: When she and a girlfriend stepped from the bus, two policemen told them to "go back to where you came from. We don't like your kind down here." For a few days, they stayed at the home of a white professor, but his safety was threatened and they feared for their own lives. They moved to the home of a black minister, and he was beaten after their arrival. From there, they moved to a deserted house on the outskirts of town, where they worked without using any light in order to escape surveillance.

Do Something

Sayles Belton says she has always considered herself to be a leader. Why? Because her mother observed her playing with her childhood friends and told her early in life, "You're a natural-born leader." Today Sayles Belton says a leader is a person who can help diverse people discover what they share in common as they sit down to find solutions to problems.

A leader is a person who can help diverse people discover what they share in common as they sit down to find solutions to problems.

She says she first learned the satisfaction of working for a cause at the age of sixteen when she complained to her stepmother about a problem she cannot even remember. But her stepmother's response remains vivid: "Whining and complaining aren't going to change anything. If you want to change, you have to do something. What are you willing to do?" That same summer, Sayles Belton volunteered as a candy striper at Minneapolis's Mount Sinai Hospital, where the lesson was reinforced that "I could help somebody and make a difference for someone, even though I wasn't being paid."

That was the beginning of her community volunteering. She tutored grade-school children and worked with the National Association for the Advancement of Colored People's (NAACP's) summer program for troubled inner-city youth, and found herself steadily developing a sense of personal power as she contributed her time to supporting and alleviating the problems of the people she worked with. On an academic internship from Macalester, she worked as a volunteer with women who were on parole and probation from prison. The assignment became the foundation of her first professional job as a parole officer for the State of Minnesota. Supervising women on parole convinced her that she needed to work with men if she were going "to make the world better for women." She became one of the first women in Minnesota to oversee adult males on parole.

"Most women on parole," she explains, "were hooked up with men who were living an antisocial life. You could never get women to decide to let those things go unless you could get the man in their life to agree to let them. So I made a very conscious decision to go after the source." Sayles Belton knew all the available community resources for helping a man get on the right track. Her message was always "it's your choice. You can do the right thing or end up back in prison. Not because of something I do, but what you don't do."

Propelled by what she saw as a parole officer, Sayles Belton became an advocate for women who were victims of sexual abuse. She put herself on the line as a feminist at a time when most African-American women saw the women's movement as representing class privilege. "They thought I was selling out and identifying more with white women than with black people," she recalls.

White feminists in the Minnesota region were indeed addressing sexual assault from their own perspective, but Sayles Belton was able to convince them that the discussion explicitly needed to include women of color. "It was clear to me that the victories of the women's movement needed to be shared by all women, so I said let's change this and make it work for all women, because I'm tired of being excluded."

As a result, the Minnesota Program for Victims of Sexual Assault was expanded and revamped to address violence in the context of African Americans. As its assistant director, Sayles Belton also extended efforts to include the Native-American, Hispanic, and Asian populations in Minnesota. If they understood the specific cultural issues surrounding rape and sexual violence, she reasoned that they would start programs in their own communities.

Hard Knocks

Mayor Sayles Belton's commitment to public service and her vision for Minneapolis were shaped not only by her experiences as a volunteer and a professional, but by her personal history. When she was a student at Macalester, her first daughter was born mentally retarded as a result of a lack of oxygen. She carried her in a basket to finals because there was little community support for a handicapped child. Sayles Belton refers to this sadness in her life as a growth experience that caused her to develop leadership skills. "I had to go out there and fight," she explains, "to find the things that I needed so that my daughter could have a halfway decent life. It caused me to develop conviction and drive and determination."

No matter how good the parks, the schools, or the teachers, kids go home. There's an African proverb, 'the ruin of a nation begins in the homes of its people.'

As mayor of Minneapolis, Sayles Belton has sponsored Success by Six/Way to Grow, an innovative program created by a partnership forged between city government and the private sector. It is designed to make sure that mothers receive prenatal care and that children, from day one, have the physical, mental, and emotional nurturing necessary for becoming productive students. Sayles Belton wants to go a step further: "My personal view is that I've got to help a woman access whatever it is—a GED, college tuition, a training program—so that she can be self-sufficient and have self-esteem. And not be dependent upon Uncle Sam or anybody to take care of herself and her child." The key question she wrestles with as a policy maker is how to develop responsibility in adults. "No matter how good the parks, the schools, or the teachers, kids go home. There's an African proverb, 'the ruin of a nation begins in the homes of its people.'"

Sayles Belton brings empathy and drive to the office of mayor because of her years as an activist for social justice. Her hope is that political leaders will continue to come out of the ranks of community activists and grassroots workers because they know from firsthand experience the realities of suffering and inequity, and how lives can be improved with legislative action.

I Will Win

State Senator Therese Murray of Massachusetts also endorses grassroots activism as almost a prerequisite for responsibly holding public office. Like Secretary Widnall, she is a leader who accepts responsibility for initiating action. She describes herself as a "bologna-and-cheese Democrat who's concerned about people." Murray never plotted a political career, she says; it was her involvement in a variety of community organizations and agencies that prompted her admirers to encourage her to run for the Massachusetts legislature in the early nineties.

"I really surprised myself by going into this," she admits. "In fact, after I agreed to it, I actually panicked and said, why am I doing this? What if I don't win? But, really, I always think that if I'm going to do something, that I will win."

Politics as a Way of Life

Murray grew up in a hardworking, Boston Irish-Catholic family that always argued politics around the dinner table, even though no one expressed personal political aspirations. In her office, only a short distance from Plymouth Rock, she laughs when she says she had never met a Republican or known a Protestant until she was a teenager. Both her mother and father encouraged their five daughters to be independent, so shortly after graduating from high school Murray worked in small businesses and volunteered with community service agencies.

Her pull toward politics began when she served as director of the Municipal Women's Project in Boston, a program that advocated work and educational equity for women. "Out of the blue," she says, "a physician telephoned to say that insurance companies were not covering his patients for reconstructive surgery after mastectomies on the basis that it was cosmetic, but men were covered for testicular reconstruction." Murray had experience in organizing women around issues of employee rights, but to confront the enormous injustice of this problem she called together other women's organizations and state legislators to form the Betsy Coalition, a name inspired by the demonstration model for breast self-examination.

Blitzing the Media

To pressure insurance companies to change their policies on reconstructive breast surgery, the Betsy Coalition blitzed the media and put together a bill with State Representative Barbara Graves as sponsor. Murray says the Coalition won its point when shortly before the bill was to be filed, Blue Cross/Blue Shield announced a change in its policy.

Her passionate commitment to social issues has consistently driven Murray's political career. As the freshman Democrat from Plymouth, she presided over hearings on welfare reform throughout the state of Massachusetts. She authored welfare reform legislation that was drawn to help women reach a greater level of independence and self-sufficiency. "We need to give people a helping hand to get out of the hole they're in," she says; teenage pregnancy and violence are symptomatic of a welfare system that is not working, she maintains.

No Style—No Content

As a newcomer to Massachusetts politics at the age of forty-five, Murray expresses concern about those young women who move into politics without the advantage of having had diverse life experiences, a deficit that makes it difficult for them to work with each other and form coalitions. "Some of the women I work with are going forward in their careers, but there's something missing that's hard to get hold of. It's all surface," she says, carefully choosing her words, "and there doesn't seem to be much beneath it. There's nothing wrong with competition and being assertive, but you don't have to cut yourself off from the feminine side where you can go to another woman and work with her on an issue and understand it from all aspects, not just what the bill does legally, or what the ramifications are in the way it's written. Emotion . . . passion. That's what I see missing," she says.

Making a Difference

One of the many young women in political life who defies this profile is Mary Jo Hoeksema, age twenty-seven. She is already a seasoned legislative aide, having worked in the offices of Senator Jeff Bingham (Democrat, New Mexico) and Representative Rosa DeLauro. More important, Hoeksema speaks with passion, conviction, and optimism about a political agenda that ranges from gun control to healthcare for senior citizens.

Hoeksema first came to see the power of politics as public service when she took a summer job with an Easter Seal camp. Many of the children there were wards of the state, and the adults were dependent on supplemental security income (SSI). Her interest in politics crystallized as a student at the University of New Mexico. There, organizing students in support of Dukakis for president, she endured public ridicule in an atmosphere where most students were either politically conservative or simply apolitical. She went on to become state coordinator of the campaign. "It took courage on that campus," she explains, "not only to be a Democrat, but to speak out for a candidate that even the Democrats weren't sure they could support. I was an easy target."

From there, she secured internships and graduate fellowships that enabled her to work in various Washington agencies and programs on issues around peace, justice, and arms control. As a legislative correspondent in the office of Senator Bingham, she moved from the sidelines and used her position to advocate the importance of the Brady Bill to Bingham, who was not yet a strong advocate. "I wouldn't let up on him," she said, "but kept giving him articles and bringing people in to meet him." When Bingham announced his vote in support of the bill, other senators went with him. Hoeksema says she will always remember Jim Brady shaking her hand at the celebration party: "He was crying and said, 'We needed a western Democrat. I can't thank you enough.' That really made me feel that I had made a difference."

Mary Jo Hoeksema wants a career in public service, but she is debating whether she should return to New Mexico and run for office at the state level or complete her doctorate and work in public policy for a nonprofit organization. She represents the new breed of young women who believe that they need to get academic credentials as well as practical experience in the workings of day-to-day politics to build a solid career base.

Politics Is Local

Sophie Masloff, mayor of Pittsburgh (1988 to 1994) learned politics in her neighborhood. "Book knowledge alone doesn't do it. You have to volunteer and help other candidates; then your turn comes."

Sophie grew up in Pittsburgh's Hill District, a stone's throw from downtown. The youngest child of Romanian parents, she learned responsibility early: Her father died when she was two, and her mother did not read or write. She wrapped money in a handkerchief and sent young Sophie to pay the water bills in city hall, where Sophie liked to watch the big-time politicians. It was the Great Depression, and the rest of Pittsburgh seemed bleak.

Fresh out of high school in 1936, Sophie was thrilled to work in the office of county commissioner John Kane. The Democratic party was in its infancy, and Sophie loved the chase. From the beginning, she volunteered in every campaign, participated in the Democratic Women's Guild, and then became president of all the guilds in Pennsylvania.

Forty years after her first political job, Sophie's turn came when a seat opened on the city council. "I never had any ambition to run for office, but I won and stayed for twelve years. I became the first female president of council," Masloff says with pride. When Mayor Richard Caliguiri died in 1988, Masloff served out his term, and then won a full term in 1990.

It's not easy being a woman in politics. You need to have staying power.

"It's not easy being a woman in politics," Masloff says. "You need to have staying power." She learned staying power from her mother. "There wasn't welfare at the time, so to raise us she worked long hours in a tobacco factory. Then she bought a house and signed the deed with an X. She rented the second and third floors and worked as a janitor."

Staying power helped Sophie to gain political leadership, face issues, and ignore sexism. "It may be a coward's way out, but I always acted like I didn't notice slurs. I held my own and went back to the issues. Women weren't very welcome at the Duquesne

Club where so much of the city's business goes on, but I just entered with an attitude that you have to accept me."

A Little Revenge

Four male candidates challenged Masloff in the 1990 mayoral primary. In a public debate with them, she was in "complete despair. They took every opportunity to put me down, and I wasn't fairing well at all." But when Frank Lucchino turned and said, "Mrs. Masloff, you are running a very negative campaign," her adrenalin kicked in.

"Mr. Lucchino, that's like being called ugly by a frog," she responded.

The audience roared. The media latched on to the line, and cartoonists drew Masloff leapfrogging over her opponents. "Lucchino gave me an opening and it saved my day," Masloff chuckles. "Little else was reported."

Mr. Lucchino, that's like being called ugly by a frog.

For a woman to survive in politics, "a sense of humor is absolutely necessary," says Masloff. "You take so much abuse that you are doomed—you can die!—without it. I always took my job seriously, but not myself."

Masloff shows little humor about Pittsburgh's current efforts to build new sports stadiums. In her last year as mayor, Masloff had city architects draw plans for a baseball stadium for the Pirates. She was ridiculed in headlines, at watercoolers, and on talk shows. "The city went bananas. They laughed at me for a combination of reasons: The idea was innovative, and it was hard for people in a sports town like Pittsburgh to imagine a woman coming up with an idea about a sports stadium."

A sense of humor is absolutely necessary. You take so much abuse that you are doomed—you can die!—without it. I always took my job seriously, but not myself.

Since then, news commentators have apologized to her. City government now wants to build not one, but two stadiums for the Pirates and Steelers. Watching from the sidelines as politicians, club owners, and corporations scramble for funds, Masloff rues, "a stadium would have been built by now at one-fourth the cost."

Ties That Bind

When she stepped into the arena of Pittsburgh politics, Sophie Masloff had no women to learn from. To this day, Eleanor Roosevelt's visit to the city in 1936 remains a highlight of her life. "I literally fell in love with her. She had such a quiet dignified presence and manner." Mrs. Roosevelt came to dedicate the Bedford Dwellings in the Hill District, the first public housing project in the country, not far from where Sophie grew up. The staying power of her mother and the idealism of Mrs. Roosevelt were always her inspiration.

"Thank God, women are no longer so alone. Women can now be elected to anything, but they still need to know the ground rules," Masloff warns. "You can't expect things to be handed to you. Education isn't the whole story. You have to start at the bottom at the neighborhood level, join a political party, and work within the guidelines. Get in there and contribute. Get name recognition before you expect to see your name on a ballot."

Don't Get Trapped

Asked about how they became leaders in their field, pragmatic insiders like Linda Tarr-Whelan, president and executive director of the Center for Policy Alternatives, agree that women of all ages learn leadership by plunging into issues. Tarr-Whelan, who was a deputy assistant to President Carter in the White House, says:

If there is an open seat, there ought to be a woman in it. If you don't think you're capable of running, look at the boys who are talking about running and decide whether the electorate will really be better off.

"Leadership is about putting yourself on the line and trying things. Young women interested in politics have got to get a taste of the rest of the world . . . find out what it's really like and play a role in it."

She is also adamant that women should never let an office be vacant in any community. "If there is an open seat, there ought to be a woman in it. If you don't think you're capable of running, look at the boys who are talking about running and decide whether the electorate will really be better off. But if you want public office for its perks or to be more privileged," she warns, "then you will get trapped into behavior that is different from entering office to make something good happen."

Tarr-Whelan says women have exerted enormous influence as role models. "If women were more self-conscious about themselves as change agents, they would achieve even more change than they do already. If they consciously thought about how to teach younger women to do the same thing, you could make the cycle work faster."

Experience Wins Votes

Ann Richards, governor of Texas (1990 to 1994), says the future of women in politics is in the "pipeline, and it's hard to know how long it'll take." She participated in thirty campaigns during the elections of November 1998, and was heartened by the level of sophistication of women candidates and their staffs: "They were very experienced, articulate, credible, and organized."

While women are getting better at running for office, "you can't really tell someone how to do something," Richards insists. "Experience is the best teacher. A candidate has a better chance of winning when her staff is experienced, but the best way to learn is by doing. And all that takes time. The other issue is that women in politics have to be better than men, not just as good. And I don't know how long that's going to go on."

. . . women in politics have to be better than men, not just as good. And I don't know how long that's going to go on.

Richards believes women should imitate men in passing on their know-how. "The best way to be a role model is to take a young woman into your office and have her travel with you and carry your bag. That's the male system. Over the years I've wached young men just standing by and handing a fountain pen once in a while, and I'd think, isn't that a waste of time! Then it finally hit me that men learn from each other that way; just standing by and watching. Women don't do that for each other. Asking someone to serve in a subsidiary role seems demeaning and makes us uncomfortable."

Asked if this is the way she mentors, Richards bellowed, "NO. I've never done it. It slows you down. Causes trouble, but that's the way I should do it."

Like other trailblazers, Richards had no female politicians to imitate. At an early age, she was told she was smart and could be whatever she wanted, but translated that meant "stewardess, nurse, or teacher." She received double messages for admiring Eleanor Roosevelt: "People would say 'Isn't it remarkable the things she does, but she has no business doing them.'"

Role models or not, Richards does not believe there is a clear-cut way for women to succeed in a political career. "Anyone who says so is just making it up," she challenges. "None of us knows how we got where we are. There are no patterns or formulas to lay down. Who can say if you do this, then you'll get that?"

We learn by our failures, not our successes.

For Richards, the only answer is trial and error. "We learn by our failures, not our successes," she reminds. In the future, more women will be in the big political jobs because more women will be qualified to hold them, and more women will be skilled in helping them to get there. Simply counting on women to vote for women is not Richards' way of winning or bringing change.

"I Looked Like Changes"

Joyce Savocchio was elected the first woman mayor of Erie, Pennsylvania, after her predecessor, Louis J. Tullio, had been in office for twenty-four years. Savocchio was a strong candidate from the Erie city council, but she was the underdog in the primary. Articulating a clear platform, she was able to win media endorsement—and the election. Now in her second term, Savocchio assesses her first campaign: "People were ready for a change and wanted a change. . . . Simply because I was a woman I symbolized that change. I was *physically* that change. I looked like change. Other women in Erie and the

People were ready for a change and wanted a change. . . . Simply because I was a woman I symbolized that change. I was physically that change. I looked like change.

environs were elected to offices that year. . . . The election was a very cleansing experience for Erie because voters really took the opportunity to study the candidates."

Her second campaign was very different from the first, she says, because she had to combine the old politics with the new politics to prove that she could deliver. Savocchio emphasizes that the big issue for a woman candidate is to say *how* she is really going to make a difference. "The old politics is going around to bars . . . and door to door, which I believe in very strongly. The new politics involves really putting out what your program is, and just what you've done. . . . It was important to get the message out through the media . . . not the person, but the message."

Before she ran for the Erie City Council, Savocchio spent twenty years as a social studies teacher. But she knew in grade school that she wanted to be in politics. Her father, Daniel Savocchio, never held office, but, she says, always worked very hard for Democratic candidates. Joyce grew up surrounded by politicians, though she never saw a woman in elected office. Her sense of public service comes from her parents, who lived upstairs of the mom-and-pop grocery store they owned.

"The store was just part of being home," Savocchio says. "My mother had a tremendous love for people and was very much a mother figure for the entire neighborhood, always concerned about how everyone was doing." And because her father wanted little Joyce to safely cross the busy street in front of the store, he became Erie's first school crossing guard.

"I can still picture him in his butcher apron, stopping cars," Savocchio reminisces, "so the police said we might as well give him a badge and a hat."

Joyce liked the energy and commitment of politicians and always volunteered at Democratic headquarters. As a high-school student in 1960, she read profusely about John F. Kennedy and studied hard to be his stand-in for a mock debate with Richard M. Nixon. Two boys were selected instead, but one cancelled, so the history teacher turned to her: "I don't think you can do it, Joyce, but we're desperate." Savocchio says his negativism actually spurred her on. She not only won the debate, but was galvanized to think about entering public life.

From Classroom to City Hall

Savocchio attended Mercyhurst College, where she was moved by the intellectual life of the nuns on the faculty and their commitment to social issues. After graduation, she went on to a master's degree in education at the University of Pittsburgh. She wrote her thesis on the history of Erie politics, and a councilman she interviewed during her research said, "'You'd really like to run for office, wouldn't you, Joyce? Erie won't be ready for a woman for twenty more years.' And he was exactly right," she adds.

From 1965 to 1985, Savocchio was a teacher and assistant principal in the Erie School District. She was also a member of Erie's city council from 1981 until she ran for mayor in 1989.

Her experience in the school system gave her a valuable handle on community problems; she decided to run for city council because there "wasn't any direction. People almost made fun of city government, and I love Erie. I thought I could help kids and families more on council than I could as an assistant principal."

Seeing firsthand the hopelessness of young people looking for jobs after graduation, Savocchio was committed to creating more jobs in the city. She wanted to improve job training and help people reclaim their neighborhoods from crime. In her office as an assistant vice principal, she had witnessed the pain of children living in severely dysfunctional families. Consequently, she wanted city government to enter into partnership with the private sector to develop more programs to help children and families, and to stimulate the economy.

In short, she was determined to make the city "better and empower the people. I know that's a buzzword, a trite word, but that's what's happening here and that's what government's about. . . . Partnership, that's another buzzword. And people from the private sector looked at me and said, 'Mayor, what you're saying is you want our money.' And I said, 'Yes, that's right.' But I also said, 'The money only buys you the ticket into the party. Then it's how involved are you going to become, and what are you going to do to be a participant in it?' And they've been wonderful. We have had a real sense of partnership, where people will come to me and say, 'We want to be a partner with you.' So it's really not a trite word anymore."

Basic Principles

According to strategist Diane Cromer, certain principles are basic to running all political campaigns. And the more a candidate strays from them in a mistaken effort to show how she is "different," the greater her chance for losing, Cromer warns. After sizing up the uniqueness of an election in terms of issues, geography, and demographics, a candidate has fundamental choices regarding political strategy and techniques. The challenge for a woman candidate, therefore, is to emphasize the issues she cares about so that the electorate will listen to her. Cromer recommends that a candidate present herself as being in touch with the issues that are important to the voters, without sounding as if she is "different" or in the superior position of educating them. "Nothing is ever won," says, "by running an election as if it were one of the Crusades."

Nothing is ever won by running an election as if it were one of the Crusades.

Typically women in grassroots efforts have been elected to office because they have listened to the voices of those whom no one really wanted to hear. Not pretending to have all of the answers, they have formed coalitions in order to bring their new agendas to the relevant political leadership. Women candidates who have won their first election on the basis of grassroots support often try to apply the same campaign techniques when they want to make the next step up the political ladder. Political advisors point out, however, that the difficulty and the level of campaigning intensifies dramatically with the size of the race.

For example, if a woman has won a seat on a city council by spending $8 thousand and having eight of her friends make phone lists, phone calls, and neighborhood visits, this does not mean she can win a race for mayor by spending $64 thousand and getting eight others to work in the broader constituency. Cromer notes that some female aspirants to office assume that if they do a good job on social issues, they will be rewarded by moving into higher legislative positions. This is not to imply that women should change their focus, only that they must become skillful at using the communication techniques of modern campaigning so that they become widely known by the public. Once their visibility has been established, they will be in a strategic position to take advantage of an opportunity, whether it is to move into leadership within a legislature or to vie for the next legislative office.

Beyond the State House

"A glass ceiling still exists for women in politics," Cromer says. "Women made it off the school boards, went into county commissions, and they are moving into leadership positions in the city and in state houses. The next steps for U.S. Senate and to governor are tough. They're every bit as tough as it was to make it to mayor and to president of the city council. But there are too many good women in the legislatures not to have it happen."

There's a big difference between trying to do what you can where you are and only using it as a stepping stone for something else.

According to Debra Danburg, a Texas legislator, many women are successful in the state house precisely because they are not seeking higher office and want to make a difference where they are. The women she meets in state houses across the country "are not generally looking at service as a credential for their résumés for some sort of a job deal, but I really think that a tremendous number of men see it as that. It's like their wives put them through graduate school, then the legislature, and then they can make their fortunes from the contacts that they make. I don't see that with any of the women," Danburg observes. "There's a big difference between trying to do what you can where you are and only using it as a stepping stone for something else."

Because the legislature has traditionally been a place for men to groom themselves for higher office, more women are truly making leadership gains there. The national average for female legislators is 22 percent. Washington State has the country's highest percentage of female lawmakers—41 percent, with 60 of 147 seats. Other states where women comprise close to one-third of their legislators are Arizona, Colorado, Connecticut, Kansas, Maryland, Minnesota, New Hampshire, Nevada, Maryland, Minnesota, and Vermont.

The experience in state houses is valuable for learning the legislative process and the skills required for making it work. Legislators also are positioned to understand how issues affect a diverse population within a statewide constituency. Voting on these issues allows a legislator to generate a track record on which to run for higher office.

"But women still need to prove that they can do the job each step of the way," I heard over and over again from women who are seasoned politicians and political observers. As one state legislator says, "A lot of men, especially lately, can just kind of walk into a U.S. Senate seat without having any political experience. Women are not at the point where they can do that."

"Touchdowns My Way"

Describing her work as an attorney with the all-male Senate Judiciary committee, Antonia Hernandez says: "Men deal with power like football; it's a competitive team sport. For me, it was understanding that, and then figuring out how I felt more comfortable making sure that I didn't get sidelined by their rules, but applied how I dealt with issues. I don't want to change the rules of playing football. I just want to make sure I don't get trampled on, and that I make the touchdowns . . . my way, not their way!"

Like other women in the public eye, Hernandez is very much at home in describing the power of ordinary moments in shaping her life. Now the president and general counsel of the Mexican American Legal Defense and

No one sent me to school to learn leadership skills. I learned them on the street.

Educational Fund (MALDEF), she says, "No one sent me to school to learn leadership skills. I learned them on the street."

On Fridays, Antonia and her mother stayed up all night making tamales for her father to sell. Early Saturday mornings, Antonia climbed into the car with him, balanced between huge pots, and delivered the tamales to garages and bars. At the same time, she also sold her mother's crocheted doilies.

"I was part of the economic unit of my family at an early age," she observes, "but I can articulate these things only now that I'm older. I somehow knew that if I offered a positive example, my brother and sisters would follow in my footsteps and go to college."

The Perils of Perception

Among the women I interviewed, separatist feminism was way out of date. Many of them acknowledge the support of male mentors and colleagues and affirm the importance of building gender-blind political coalitions. But all expressed their irritation at being judged on their style instead of their substance. A few of them gave the example of former President George Bush arriving in China during the Beijing World Conference on Women and remarking that he felt sorry for the Chinese with Bella Abzug running around the country. It was a remark that placed Bush firmly in the realm of the dinosaurs, but as these pages show, dinosaurs are still common denizens of political life today.

All expressed their irritation at being judged on their style instead of their substance.

Women are especially vulnerable to being judged on style when they are campaigning. This is particularly true when two women compete for the same office, which is still an unusual occurrence. From her experience of running against a woman in the 1994 Minnesota Democratic primary for U.S. Senator, Linda Berglin speculates that people are accustomed to "discerning even the most subtle differences between male

It will take more women running before people can get used to the experience of being able to compare them as candidates.

candidates . . . but they haven't done that with women. It will take more women running before people can get used to the experience of being able to compare them as candidates."

Advice

Massachusetts State Senator Therese Murray tells women who are new to politics not to be "babies. Women need to learn to imitate men by putting personal feelings aside after a heated debate," she asserts. "With men, when it's over, it's generally over. But that doesn't happen with women. Women have to develop a thick skin, especially when they catch a perceived political ally moving against them. See it as a learning experience, and don't harbor feelings. In the future you'll know that you don't need to like someone in order to develop an alliance on an issue you agree on."

The best legacy of gender inequity and women as outsiders in public life is their ability to identify with issues from the ground up and be inspired to take action on the basis of authentic concern and conviction. This is the quality that distinguished women currently in office say they most value and want to maintain, even as they pave the way for future women to become insiders.

Chapter Two

Women and Policy: Entrepreneurial Advocates for Social Change

From the sun-streaked woods of Concord, Massachusetts, to the rusted steel belt of Homestead, Pennsylvania; from Wall Street offices to the low-income neighborhoods of Oakland, California; women are major players in the drama of social change. They continually venture into uncharted territory to confront daunting problems of poverty, homelessness, employment, education, abortion, and healthcare. Free from layers of bureaucracy, these women have convictions and values that compel them to address burning issues and find solutions for them.

The Velvet Stiletto

Displaced steelworkers in Homestead, Pennsylvania, call Jo De Bolt "the velvet stiletto." As executive director of the Mon Valley Initiative, she characterizes her manner as "strategic, not strident." During a meeting, if a retired steelworker calls her "Honey," she says she writes it off as part of his culture. "I don't get bent out of shape. If you get so focused on that kind of thing, you lose the main point.

"The hardest thing I've had to learn," she observes, "is that it's okay if people don't like you sometimes, as long as they respect you. Respect is better than somebody saying, 'Isn't she swell!' You have to get things done that some people aren't going to like . . . but if you don't hold a grudge, people come around in time."

After the Mills Closed

The Mon Valley Initiative (MVI) is a coalition of seventeen development corporations that represent seventeen mill towns along the Monongahela River. The Initiative is committed to revitalizing the region after the demise of the steel industry in Pittsburgh. When the area's steel mills closed, the towns' neighborhood organizations and advocacy groups also shut down because they had been connected to the mills or otherwise tied to the large coal and steel corporations.

Only a few institutional organizations were independent from the steel industry, and these were overwhelmed with the enormous socioeconomic problems that the closings caused. Responding to the crisis, De Bolt and a few others helped to organize neighborhood groups and create the structures throughout the Mon Valley that would be needed to attract development funding from the major Pittsburgh foundations. The MVI is now recognized as a national model for similar organizations. The goal of their capital campaign was to raise $6 million in five years, but it took less than one year for them to raise $4.4 million in 1995.

"We believe that people who live and work in the Monongahela Valley have the right to determine their future," MVI's powerful mission statement proclaims. Jo De Bolt's job is to interpret that mission to members of the individual communities as well as to foundations, banks, businesses, and government agencies. The purpose is to develop businesses, generate jobs, construct affordable housing, rebuild commercial districts, and improve the quality of living in these mill towns now that they are no longer fueled by the steel industry that supported them for so many generations.

To have a woman at the helm of MVI is an important choice, for the towns traditionally have been intensely male-oriented: Politics was as hierarchical as the formidable smokestacks dominating the riverbank. One major aim of the MVI is to educate the townspeople and their local governments away from the dependency encouraged by the "big boss" and "empower them to help their communities," De Bolt says.

Back to Andrew Carnegie

In her office, eating a fish sandwich bought from the kitchen of one of Homestead's many ethnic churches, De Bolt gestures to the view outside: "No matter what the town looked like, the faces at council meetings were always male, white, and sixty to seventy years old. And they all had some connection to the mill, which allowed them to pick up the phone and get a stand built for a Fourth of July parade, or to get a work crew out of the mill to fix the borough building's roof. That relationship between the mills and local government goes way back to Andrew Carnegie and the Homestead Strike. There was never a place in leadership for a woman, or for a woman to develop her leadership skills, until now."

Asked about her conception of leadership, De Bolt says that she considered a leader to be the person "on top, or out front and isolated. But in my work I'm largely the person behind the scenes. As I get older and do this more, I'm convinced that leadership really happens out of groups working together and people pulling together. Then somebody takes on the tasks that have to be carried out in order to move things along. So in that sense I've provided a lot of leadership."

I'm convinced that leadership really happens out of groups working together and people pulling together.

After seven years in her position, De Bolt credits her success to listening to people and thinking carefully before she acts. "I know when I'm saying something that I'm representing the views of my organization, but I keep in very close touch with what people in the communities want. They know I'm not a hot dog out there doing my own thing. If I don't move forward four feet today, we'll go two feet today and two feet tomorrow. This is a complex organization made up of scattered communities, so my job is trying to figure out where the common elements are and to pull people together so they're motivated to take action."

For example, because the people depended upon the mills for employment, even longtime residents in the Mon Valley have not been accustomed to taking responsibility for what happens to their land. According to De Bolt, "U.S. Steel just bought property, tore things down, and expanded the mill, and nobody questioned it. Nobody ever did anything."

When citizens now speak up at zoning meetings, De Bolt says she "gets chills. Five years ago you couldn't get people to attend housing hearings in downtown Pittsburgh at 10 A.M. because they had to take the day off from work. We had to arrange car pools. But then they said, 'You bring the housing hearings to us in the evening,' and HUD [Housing and Urban Development] backed that up. For me to see people stand up for themselves after they have been consistently robbed of opportunities and gain a sense of their dignity is really the heart of this job and makes it all worthwhile."

The Real Experts

For the first time in generations, women now have a voice in Mon Valley decisions because MIV organizes groups for community development projects to represent whole communities. Having learned to articulate their ideas in these forums, women are now running for office, sitting on school boards, and serving on town councils. When De Bolt first visited communities, men and women expressed irritation that she would not advise them what to do. But she persisted in telling them that they were the real experts on their towns, and that she would listen. To witness these residents now define problems and take positions on issues that will make life better for them has been "really, really exciting" and satisfying, she says.

Mother's Example

De Bolt became involved with MIV in a "roundabout way." Married and divorced with young children, she had completed her undergraduate degree at Duquesne University and then received her master of business administration from the University of Pittsburgh. She passed up job opportunities in corporations and large accounting firms because every time she had an interview she felt "webbed in. I would walk away thinking '*This* is going to be a tough place to have to spend all day.'" So she organized the Small Business Development Center at Duquesne and began doing private consulting. Her clients were business districts that were hurting because the Pittsburgh economy was shifting away from steel. One of them was Homestead.

Plunging into work in the Mon Valley, Jo De Bolt's first fear was that she did not know enough about community organizing. "But then I thought that's what my mother did when she wanted the school to do something differently—she got on the phone and called other mothers and neighbors to get together to see the principal, or whatever. Community organizing was just getting everybody together . . . I knew what that was because I grew up with it. My mother and father were adamant that you are your brother's keeper and that you have to give back. . . . So it was just a great fit; I felt at home here. These communities and families are like those where I grew up. And I brought a lot of technical skills."

The Road to Influence

Jo De Bolt is often asked to run for political office, a tempting prospect when she becomes frustrated with government decisions. "If I were inside, I'd have a great way to fix up what I think is wrong, but I don't think I'd be nearly as effective. I'd miss the daily interaction."

Her position allows her many targets. She enjoys developing the political savvy of low-income residents by showing them how politics, industry, and business are interconnected in their lives. She is strengthening their organizational base so that experienced leaders will emerge from among them to replace vestiges of the old power relationships. With patience, she nurtures the leadership of others instead of jealously guarding her own ability to control. "What I love best," she says, "is seeing people testifying at hearings, going to their elected officials and demanding responsiveness, and I really believe that if we didn't have a presence in these communities to encourage and support people, that would not happen."

Door Open/Lights On

Kip Tiernan, co-founder of the Poor People's United Fund, a "small-change foundation" in Boston, lives in voluntary poverty in subsidized housing and refers to these conditions as her "preferred

When you know in the deepest darkest part of your heart that you have options, you're not taking a lot of risk.

geography." She maintains a low economic base with her partner, Fran Froehlich, in order to keep in touch with the people whom they serve. "And yet we can't," she says, "because we're white, we're middle class, so we always have options. When you know in the deepest darkest part of your heart that you have options, you're not taking a lot of risk."

The Poor People's United Fund, which subsists on small private donations, gives its member charities—all dedicated to helping the poor—enough money to keep the doors open and the lights on. Tiernan and Froelich established the fund when many social agencies had their federal monies cut in 1980. Volunteers at those agencies were kept busy writing grants when their time was desperately needed for more practical tasks like driving the elderly for medical appointments or serving in soup kitchens. "It's essentially a small-change foundation," Tiernan says, "where unfundables can be funded." The small donations raised are enough to keep unsung projects from folding. The makeshift office, located at the top of a steep stairway in The Old South Church, is filled with splintered furniture, bulging file cabinets, and cluttered bulletin boards.

Change From Outside

In contrast, the Center for Policy Alternatives, the nonprofit, nonpartisan progressive public policy center headed by Linda Tarr-Whelan in Washington, D.C., occupies an extensive space of comfortable suites with spacious windows and upgraded computers. But the dissimilar appearance of these two organizations camouflages their basic philosophic similarity. They agree that the best perspective for targeting and initiating change in socioeconomic policy is away from the corridors of power.

"Change happens because outsiders want change to happen," says Linda Tarr-Whelan. Policy Alternatives brings together grassroots activists with leaders in the fifty states to advance forward-looking policies on issues of ecology, equality, and social and economic justice. "The further inside you are, the more you have to lose, and therefore you conserve the status quo in order to preserve power . . . so in many cases, women are the outside force trying to make things change, to be different than they have been in the past."

Epiphany

Kip Tiernan, age 68, had her own advertising business on Long Wharf Road in New Haven in the 1960s. Busy and successful, she lunched in Manhattan when she felt like it, wrote checks *I never took any risks particularly. I was just there as another little warm, cute body.* for liberal causes, and marched once or twice with Dr. Martin Luther King, Jr. "I never took any risks particularly. I was just there as another little warm, cute body." With her raspy voice, heavy workpants and shirt, floppy tennis cap, and weathered skin, Kip Tiernan is hard to imagine as a "warm, cute body." But the rest is easy.

In the midst of Tiernan's comfortable and interesting career, Father Jack White, the pastor of St. Phillip Church in Roxbury, hired her as a public relations consultant. Her assignment was to bring attention to the fact that the diocese was closing his church. An event was planned at the church to publicize the news, and, as a final hurrah, he invited as a speaker Daniel Berrigan, the Jesuit peace activist. At the time, Berrigan was out on bail and facing federal charges of interfering with the Vietnam draft.

Tiernan remembers what happened next with novelistic vividness. As she walked down the aisle of the church, shepherding members of the media to front-row pews to hear Berrigan, she stopped suddenly and uttered, "'Holy shit.' I just passed through a door and there's no turning back. And I just looked around to see who said that, because I wasn't all that thrilled with that coming out of my mouth. But I thought, 'This is where the church should be.'"

The next day Tiernan had a call from White, asking her to join his new ministry team in Roxbury. "Poor people also need public relations and advertising," he said. "We can't afford it, and you'll have fun."

Tiernan says she hesitated: "Look, Jack, I'm a renegade Catholic."

But Jack White was "a graceful guy," she says, and he convinced her when he said, "We kind of think of ourselves as human beings with a Christian dimension rather than Christians with a human dimension."

Comforting the Afflicted and Afflicting the Comfortable

Tiernan soon became a popular figure in Roxbury. She immersed herself in the lives and problems of the poor for fourteen years: walking the projects, helping with housing problems, organizing and demonstrating against the cutting of beds at Boston City Hospital, getting people out of jail. But when she saw poor women in her neighborhood disguising themselves in order to get a meal at Boston shelters, which were open only to men, she was moved to act further.

Gender statistics on homeless people did not exist in the early seventies, and she was told that her sightings of homeless women were figments of her imagination. Consequently, she decided to do her own research. She set out to observe firsthand the situation of the homeless—in New York, Chicago, and Baltimore. At St. Joseph House in New York, she stayed for two weeks with Dorothy Day, cofounder during the Depression of the Catholic Worker Movement and its newspaper. The movement had inspired Houses of Hospitality in cities across the nation, offering beds, clothes, and food to impoverished men and women.

Twenty years later we're still fighting the same demons, only they're bigger.

Dorothy Day was always an inspiration to Kip Tiernan because of her "gift of being able to comfort the afflicted and afflict the comfortable. She was in the last stages of her life, old and fragile," Tiernan says, "but still tough and passionate. She was trying to start Mary House, but the city was giving her a hard time. I told her that I would probably open a place for women before she did. And that turned out. On Easter Sunday, 1974, we opened Rosie's Place in Boston, which was the first drop-in center and emergency shelter for women in the country. Twenty years later we're still fighting the same demons, only they're bigger."

Tiernan calls shelters the "burnt offerings of the twentieth century" because they are not answers for solving the problems of
poverty and homelessness. "We're looking for justice, not soup
kitchens and shelters. No matter how many I start, they are only alternatives, and I know that. We have to change the world, not fix it."

Compassion Fatigue

Michael Dukakis was governor of Massachusetts, and Tiernan confronted him at a public meeting. She told him that twenty-two sub-
committees existed on homelessness, but not one existed for homeless people who were also sick. Tiernan delights in repeating his
response: "'Well, Kippy, start one.'" The recommendations from this
small group became the basis for the first funding in Massachusetts
for Health Care for the Homeless. But Tiernan laments that advocacy efforts are not resolving the issues that lead to abject poverty.

"We need change," she grimaces. "Substantive, distributive
justice! . . . not incremental this and incremental that. . . . Our
accommodation has resulted in a world of shelters and soup
kitchens rather than an increased standard of living for everyone.
And now people are tired of poor people and have compassion
fatigue. . . . They're making it even harder for people to get into
shelters. Maybe they think they'll die on the streets, and then can
say we've got the housing problem all solved. . . . I think what I
have is a kind of creative fury that keeps me alive and dancing in
the streets. . . . I've learned to embrace the inscrutable darkness.
I've certainly learned to embrace the gray."

Within seconds, Tiernan can shift from speaking passionately
into employing the language of public relations. Her life in advertising has been an asset in her mission to broadcast the disgraces of
poverty. "Since I was in advertising before I was in the streets," she
says, "I use the same skills that I used to sell perfume to communicate about social policy."

Urban Prophet

Besides Rosie's Place, successful alternative programs begun by
Tiernan are the Boston Food Bank, Health Care for the Homeless,
and Up From Poverty, a campaign to raise financial assistance for

women on welfare. In addition to the Poor People's United Fund, she has started two other foundations "for people who are left out of the loop": Boston Women's Fund and Communityworks.

One philosophy all of these groups have in common is the belief in grassroots organizing and the power of a single person to act positively in the human interest

Sending liberty to those who are oppressed is the hardest thing that I'll ever do in my life . . . because we're all shrieking for the same dirty little piece of pie

"One philosophy all of these groups have in common is the belief in grassroots organizing and the power of a single person to act positively in the human interest," Tiernan notes in a 1992 essay, "The Politics of Accommodation," published in the *New England Journal of Public Policy.* Her cause, she stresses, is to bring *justice,* not *charity:* "Justice means having options, charity means not having options . . . charity makes us feel good about sheltering the hungry. Charity alleviates suffering, but justice eliminates its causes. Feeding the hungry and clothing the naked   are really easy. Sending liberty to those who are oppressed is the hardest thing that I'll ever do in my life . . . because we're all shrieking for the same dirty little piece of pie. . . . The next problem is the dismissal of people like myself as idiotic idealists or a pain in the ass. We could end homelessness, but we lack the political will."

In Dorothy Day's Footsteps

Tiernan put bite into her words with a four-day public fast at the Arlington Street Church in 1990 to beg the forgiveness of the poor people of Boston for what had been done to them "by our silence." She called her fast a "spiritual gesture of atonement" inspired by Yom Kippur. During the four days and three nights that she stayed in the church, she was visited by five hundred people. Poor people blessed her: "One woman said, 'I forgive you.' The fast was nothing," she says. "What got to me was the shingles and the fatigue."

Tiernan dismisses any talk about her being a prophet or visionary by noting that she is an "urban minister" and that her actions on behalf of the poor are based on research that supports her rage. She gives hundreds of speeches every year, writes *Urban Meditations* for The Poor People's United Fund, and often teaches courses at University of Massachusetts Boston on ethics, social policy, and moral principles. "It's important for students to know and articulate their ethics," she says, "because bad social policy follows bad ethics. So we begin by asking a question about people in shelters: '*Why* are they there?'"

Always dressed in workpants, a flannel shirt, and floppy hat, Tiernan continues to confront governors and mayors, testifies before legislatures, and brainstorms with economists. She was selected as a Fellow at the Bunting Institute at Radcliffe College in 1990. Harvard University awarded her the honorary degree of doctor of humane letters in 1989. But she says that Rosie's Place remains her "umbilical cord: It's my spiritual home which shows me the way. What a poor person tells you about poverty is different from a government economist."

Walking the Line

While she is recognized across the United States as a voice for the poor, Tiernan refuses to call herself a leader. "I've influenced some people, and that's fine. . . . It's not really false modesty on my part," she insists. "I have a tremendous ego and know where my skills are. . . . I have a great mouth and can articulate the torture that people have to go through, and I am committed to them for the rest of my life, but that doesn't make me a leader. . . . I've raised millions of dollars in this city . . . and have made some differences along the line in how poor people are treated. . . . I do an insane amount of research. I spend a lot of time with poor people and I spend a lot of time with middle-class people. I can walk that line, but that doesn't make you a leader. . . . Leaders to me are like Mother Jones and Dorothy Day and Mother Theresa. Then there are a lot of unsung people like myself who have been gifted with skills that we can use. . . . If there's a God, she's been good to Kip Tiernan."

Then there are a lot of unsung people like myself who have been gifted with skills that we can use. . . . If there's a God, she's been good to Kip Tiernan.

With Tiernan, what you see is what you get. Her most visible attribute is authenticity. She identifies with the pain of the suffering poor and brings pain to those who lack empathy for them.

Atlanta's Daughter

"You can't have just a handful of leaders in a community," says Alicia Phillips, director of the Metropolitan Atlanta Community Foundation. "You need tons and tons of leaders, from all parts of the community, and it's part of my responsibility to help make that happen."

Phillips became director and the only staff member of the twenty-six-year-old nonprofit foundation in 1977, when she was only 23. Her vivid enthusiasm and intelligence persuaded the search committee that she knew Atlanta well, as she had been the executive director of Central Atlanta Progress, a group composed of chief executive officers (CEOs) and business leaders. At the time, the foundation had a $7 million endowment. From its beginning as a one-woman organization, it is now the fifteenth largest in gifts received and one of the fastest growing philanthropic community foundations in the country, with assets of $150 million and a staff of twenty-three.

"There were just too many needs to be met in Atlanta to be sitting around with a $7 million endowment," Phillips says, "so I wanted to harness more philanthropic capital." She thinks business leaders were responsive to her because they saw her as their daughter. "I wasn't trying to compete with them as peer to peer, but just presenting the facts; and they'd look at me and think, 'Gosh I'd want my daughter to be doing that kind of thing.'"

Growing the assets was key to Phillips if the foundation was going to stretch beyond supporting safe projects. So she focused on convincing the foundation's board members to risk new programs that targeted poverty, homelessness, and healthcare. Since 1983, which is early when compared with the rest of the country, the foundation has contributed to the Atlanta Gay Center, an organization that offers support services for AIDS patients. In the past six years, the foundation has also contributed more than a half million dollars to various Atlanta organizations on behalf of AIDS.

Givers, Not Takers

One of Phillips's most rewarding returns, she says, is in the province of neighborhood redevelopment. The foundation provides initial grants for citizen-developed start-up projects aimed at improving low-income neighborhoods. An example is the Edgewood Community Gardens in Atlanta, the fulfilled dream of a small group of neighborhood women who wanted to plant a community garden, "which would give them fresh vegetables and where their kids could work." Besides underwriting the garden, the foundation paid for assistance for the planners to develop the leadership skills necessary to execute and sustain the project.

"In most cases, it's mainly single women at the grassroots level who are trying to make a difference for their families, but they need some very practical skill-building tools, like how to talk in front of a group or organize a meeting," Phillips says. "Then they pass on these skills to others, so you're building a cadre of leaders at a neighborhood level for other projects and issues."

The garden has been so successful that the organizers donated their excess harvest to the Atlanta Community Food Bank. For Phillips the bonus was to see "people using their skills not only to get good things for themselves, but to give back to others. How great for people who have never had the opportunity to be givers because they never had excess money or excess time. To have the opportunity to be givers is a great reward. All of us want to be givers and not just takers."

> *To have the opportunity to be givers is a great reward. All of us want to be givers and not just takers.*

Policy Making or Legislating?

Marie C. Wilson is the president of the Ms. Foundation, the only multi-issue women's fund in the United States. She describes herself as a grassroots activist who chose policy rather than politics; in 1983, she was the first woman elected to the Des Moines city council, as a member at large. Her focus there was to make Des Moines a community that supported families through its housing and workplace policies.

"I love politics," Wilson says, "but it was a long road in city council or legislature to make real, substantial economic change for women. . . . You could use it as a bully pulpit . . . and talk to developers about a child care center as a part of their housing needs, but getting money into the hands of women was hard." In fact, Wilson chose to run for city council because it meant working with a smaller group than in the state legislature, where "you have to move scores of people to get anything done, and it takes too long." The Ms. Foundation is an excellent match for her goals and temperament.

Wilson defines herself as an "entrepreneurial leader" because she likes to identify issues, raise money, and take risks to create solutions for them. From politics in Iowa to the Wall Street headquarters of the Ms. Foundation, she has expanded her concern for creating jobs and training programs for women into a national funding initiative. One of its aspects is the Collaborative Fund for Women's Economic Development, a major project of the foundation that directs $2.3 million to promote women's economic self-sufficiency by supporting innovative job creation projects.

Every Innovation Led to the Next Level

Marie Wilson's journey to the Ms. Foundation began when she was a Montessori preschool teacher. As the parents of five children themselves, she and her husband had little money, but as she tried to solve her own economic problems she began to find answers for other women too. Turning her experiences in education and motherhood into expertise about the large population she represented, she was hired by Drake University in 1979 to design programs for women. "I just kept setting up programs that would have been good for me and my friends," she says. "So many changes were occurring for women that just kept leading to the next step. . . . Every innovation led to the next level of responsibility. . . . If we were training women for management, then programs also had to be set up for organizations to do male/female training. You couldn't train women for management and then not fix the company so they could be successful!"

Wilson traces her commitment to social change to having been nurtured early by her religion. She first learned about justice issues in church because her mother and father were poor, and the "church helped them grow as people . . . and really did justice to my family." Because social change activists often find themselves fighting the restraints placed on them by organized religion, Wilson believes that many do not acknowledge that their convictions were originally instilled or supported by the church.

Given her own positive experiences there, Wilson says she "trusted the institution. When I went to church on Sunday nights and sang songs about justice and sharing and love, I believed it. And I also believed it because my mother and father were good working-class people who thought you could get something done if you got up in the morning and worked hard. A lot of social change work is vision, but it's also persistence, just like the guy from McDonald's. Persistence isn't only for the corporate world. This work takes enormous persistence. And I grew up seeing it. . . . My mother still works every day, all day long."

"I See That"

To create real change," says Wilson, "you need a public that says, 'I see that.' You have to make public what was private." Partly because her own independence has been supported by a strong work ethic, she was intensely troubled when Harvard scholar Carol Gilligan found that confident preadolescent girls lose self-esteem

To create real change, you need a public that says, 'I see that.' You have to make public what was private.

as they begin to experience physical changes and face society's expectations of them as women. After two years of brainstorming, consulting, and taking calculated risks, the Ms. Foundation sponsored and promoted the first annual "Take Our Daughters to Work Day" on April 28, 1993. The initiative was conceived as a means of counteracting this negative trend. "That's what entrepreneurial leadership does. . . . We did some things that didn't work, and some that only partially worked. There were also some failures."

Wilson says she is eager to describe the creative process that produced "Take Our Daughters to Work" because "people don't think about how an organization goes about such things." The method she used is not very different from the strategy she used for developing smaller-scale programs at Drake University: After reading Gilligan's research, she and Idelisse Malave, the foundation's vice president, decided to write each other a letter about what the conclusions meant to them personally and how they would go about focusing enormous public attention on the phenomenon of low self-esteem among teenage girls. Then for the next two years they talked with "everybody in the world" about how to create public awareness. They also paid $10 thousand for the development of a plan they discarded, but which proved helpful by convincing them of what they *did not* want to do. They invested time talking with representatives of national organizations for women and girls, which declined invitations to be partners with them. Pursuing further consultations, they finally arrived at the idea for "Take Our Daughters to Work Day."

That's the excitement about being able to change something, to achieve justice . . . that's what keeps me going.

Wilson says her desire to create a better world for her daughters has always been her basic motivation. "I always have wanted to build the kind of communities and organizations that I wanted to be part of myself," she explains. "I want to make possible for my daughters a world that never existed for myself and other women. That's the excitement about being able to change something, to achieve justice . . . that's what keeps me going."

Comanche Giveaways

La Donna Harris, founder and president of Americans for Indian Opportunity (AIO), describes an informal ceremony among the Comanches, called a "giveaway." Its purpose is to celebrate an individual's achievement while also revealing and affirming how her family and community have contributed to her strength and identity.

When her daughter Laura graduated from Stanford, Harris had a "giveaway" for her. In contrast with the Euro-American tradition, in which the celebrant receives gifts on such occasions, the Comanche practice is for the honored guest or host to give presents to those who supported her in accomplishing what she did.

La Donna Harris gave gifts to those "who had helped me become who I am, so that Laura was able to accomplish what she did. We are acknowledging that you are not by yourself; other people have also helped you get where you are. When something good happens, Comanches recognize that the support of the entire family and tribe—that means generations of fifth cousins on my Comanche side—was necessary to have brought it about. A giveaway is a kind of reconnecting to your roots, recognizing that it's not only my daughter, but *our* daughter who has accomplished something. That also ties her back to her responsibilities to the tribe."

Harris says that building coalitions and valuing consensus are intrinsic parts of her Comanche culture. "I never saw myself as a leader in the Euro-American sense," she says, "because one of the most important things in Comanche society is to get the right combination of people to work together in order that the right things can happen. So I never had to be up front, the high person on the totem pole, the first one that's considered. If you think of an idea, you bring together people who have the qualities that you don't have. And that's the role I've played throughout my life. . . . In Comanche society, you were not a leader until someone followed you. You weren't chosen by any group or hierarchy, but had characteristics that others admired and recognized as being important for what they wanted to do. . . . So that people who had skills were leaders in that area, and not over the whole body. Members of the tribe are then interdependent."

. . . in Comanche society, you were not a leader until someone followed you.

Harris adds: "Generosity is also stressed. You never possess anything that you can't give away. . . . So that a truly generous person is able to give things away, even ideas, and people can accept them as their own."

When she was very young, Harris learned from her Comanche grandmother to give back. "That's a value in many cultures," she says, "but it's very much ingrained in tribal societies where each person is expected to contribute their talents . . . and be responsive to their kinfolk, their clan, and their tribe. Once you get an extended family, then you just continue to expand that version of sharing and responsibility. We say in tribal societies that relationship is the most important thing, because the good things that you have done will come back to you, even though you don't expect it. The three Rs in Indian society are relationship, responsibility, and response. If people do good things for you, you have to do good things for others so that relationships keep in balance."

Tribal Values at Work

For more than thirty years, La Donna Harris has devoted her life to building relationships and coalitions that create change. As a child she lived closely with the values of two cultures. She grew up in the home of her maternal grandparents, an Eagle medicine man and a devout Christian woman, in Indian country on a farm near Walters, Oklahoma, during the Depression. She started grade school speaking only Comanche. "When I got more exposure during the 1960s, organizing Oklahomans for Indian Opportunity," she says, "I started saying a few words in English. But it wasn't until Washington that I started being able to put a whole sentence together and speak publicly, and it was quite difficult. One of the reasons was that Comanche was my first language, but I also protected myself like many young Indian people. People say, 'Indians are so stoic. They don't speak much.' Well, they are studying the character of the person who is addressing them so that they know how to deal with them. Going to Washington was quite a turning point for me."

Beyond "We've Got Problems"

As the wife of U.S. Senator Fred Harris, La Donna Harris was the first wife of a senator ever to testify before a congressional committee. She helped in the return of the Taos Blue Lake to the people of Taos Pueblo, and she assisted the Menominee Tribe in regaining their federal recognition. Her influence on both pieces of legislation led to landmark laws that set a precedent that still guides all Indian policy. In 1970 she founded Americans for Indian Opportunity (AIO).

One of AIO's current enterprises is the American Indian Ambassadors Program, designed for a young generation of Native-American leaders to reassess their tribal values and government. By studying these traditions, the participants are hoping to discover new ways of influencing current systems and addressing national and global needs for the next century.

For example, Harris has found that the tribal system of participatory government is a "good way of thinking about organizing ourselves socially and politically in cities. . . . We need to have a different kind of discussion than just to say we've got problems in the cities and inner cities. We're going to have to figure out some way of allowing people to participate so that they have some commitment to the outcomes; otherwise, they feel written off and then all kinds of things can happen. . . . I'm always trying to think of new ideas; trying to recognize what's not working. Tribal ways had a lot of strength and positiveness that might give us another way of connecting people to their communities. If you just have one way of looking at a system, then you can't come up with new solutions, and that's the idea."

Despite the serious problems that Native Americans have experienced, Harris points out that tribal people have both political and cultural autonomy. "Wherever cultural minorities struggle for autonomy, I think Tribal America, particularly through the Ambassadors Program, could make a positive contribution based on lived experience, without necessarily having answers," she observes.

How does she sustain herself personally in a position that is so consuming in terms of her energy and time? "It's hard sometimes if you feel as if you're always the giver and don't receive. That's what wears you out, so you have to stop and get nurtured or pamper yourself; do something good for yourself." Sensing when their mother is overextended, for example, Harris's two daughters tell her to stand in front of a mirror and practice saying *no*.

Tribal Myths Have Relevance

To illustrate how tribal wisdom has always valued an inclusive decision-making process, Harris recalls an ancient legend from the Oneidas, the tribe in upstate New York. The Oneidas called a meeting with all living things, including the animals, because the decision that had to be made would also affect them. Only the wolf was excluded, and no one at the meeting spoke for his interests. As a consequence, the wolf became the enemy of the Oneidas, threatening their lives and land. "Those people who are left out like the wolf," Harris says, "then create the problem. If you follow the tribal example of inclusiveness, you don't develop winners and losers; people come to an agreement because everyone is affected and sees it in their self-interest to have ownership in a decision."

Social activists like La Donna Harris often expand our imagery and understanding of the process of change. They are devoted to the understanding that people who are affected by social policy should be involved in designing it. They strive to bring a sense of collaboration to issues. They acknowledge that this is not always easy to do.

Byllye Y. Avery: Healthcare Activist

As a visionary and a grassroots realist, Byllye Y. Avery founded the National Black Women's Health Project in 1981 "out of passion and a need for black women to come together to make changes in our lives. I didn't found it because I wanted to sit on top of a bureaucratic structure, but I thought that black women needed to have more connection with each other about their problems."

Before she became a healthcare activist, Avery was a special education consultant at the University of Florida. From her work with autistic children, she borrows an image to suggest how she moves people and organizations forward: "Instead of sitting in front of the kids, I found it more effective if I sat to the side and put my arm around them and guided their hands. It felt a lot better than sitting in front and pulling their

Instead of sitting in front of the kids, I found it more effective if I sat to the side and put my arm around them and guided their hands.

hands. So it's a different way of guiding and moving people to the next level that I really like and that I'm really involved in."

Based in Atlanta, The National Black Women's Health Project is a nonprofit organization that addresses issues of physical and mental health among African-American women, largely through organizing self-help groups across the country. Along with working one-on-one with women, the Project interacts with healthcare providers, state agencies, colleges, and fund-raisers.

Avery became a healthcare activist when her husband, a young man with a Ph.D. and a promising career, died at the age of 33 from a massive heart attack, leaving her with two young children. "His education, my education," Avery says quietly, "didn't make any difference when it came to knowing about taking care of ourselves." He had suggested that she read *The Feminine Mystique*, she remembers, but she did not read it until he died. "I was in a state of shock trying to figure out how I was going to raise these two children," she says, "so anything that told me I was powerful was wonderful in my sight. I don't know how I would have received the book if he had still been alive."

Through her work at the University of Florida, Avery met the child psychologists Paul Adams and Judith Levy, who profoundly influenced her in perceiving herself as a feminist. She credits Adams, a Quaker, with encouraging her to think and dream and challenge the current status of healthcare for women. The three of them founded two women's health clinics in Gainesville, and Avery became more visible as a healthcare activist. Years before domestic violence became a topic for national conversation, Avery identified it as the major health issue for African-American women.

While she was preparing to present a paper for the annual meeting of the National Women's Health Network in 1981, Avery discovered statistics showing that African-American women had the poorest health of any group in the United States. Besides suffering physical abuse from violence, they were more likely to develop lupus, diabetes, hypertension and cervical cancer. In addition, the rate of African-American infant deaths was double the death rate of white babies. Behind the statistics she uncovered, Avery was able to see stories of personal tragedy. "I knew then that a paper was not enough, but that this information had to get out in a national conference, and we had to move on a plan of action."

Accepting Reality

With the help of Belita Cowan from the National Women's Health Network, Avery learned about funding. With her first proposal, she received a grant from the Ms. Foundation for a National Black Women's Health Project (NBWHP). From its beginning, the NBWHP has been run for black women by black women. For years, Avery has crossed the United States meeting with groups of women, encouraging them to talk with each other about their needs and problems. She is concerned that within families "people aren't talking about what they are really, really feeling. The number-one issue is to help people communicate, because they still believe in some ideal that doesn't exist anymore. . . . There's a high prevalence of cervical cancer among young black women. When you think about the unprotected sex that goes on, and the risk of HIV, and the lack of healthcare preventive services—these are serious problems. But people think magically, even the ones like me who know better, that 'well, my daughter doesn't need to start getting her pap smear until she's twenty-one.' But pap smears need to start with sexual activity. So mothers can't start their children with pap smears if they don't know or admit they are having sex. That's why the first priority has to be on communication and talking."

Consciousness Raising Continues

My white sisters thought that consciousness raising was a destination, when it is really an ongoing process.

Avery has consistently modified the practice of consciousness raising to the particular needs of African-American women. "When women start thinking about the changes that they need to make, they go through a transformation process which helps them to make decisions so that they will be in control of their lives. But they need to keep working at it and maintaining it," she contends. "My white sisters thought that consciousness raising was a destination, when it is really an ongoing process. Just think where we would be if we remained only doing consciousness raising," she muses.

She doesn't claim that the actual health conditions of African-American women have changed because of the NBWHP. "But what I do know," she says adamantly, "is that our perspective about who we are as black women has changed across the board. We have a greater sense of empowerment, and that we are in charge of our lives. We have given ourselves permission to move forward. . . . I can die because I know that has been accomplished."

Just as NBWHP was a spin-off from the National Women's Health Network, Avery is helping to start groups for other minorities as spin-offs from NBWHP. She has worked with the National Latino Women's Project and the National Asian Women's Health Project. "Just as America has to," she said, "we have to learn to galvanize and reach out to diverse populations. What we have learned is that we are really very, very connected. Black women in the United States have relatives who live somewhere else in the world; so our movement has to become more international in scope with a more global approach about health concerns. Their problems are our problems. We have to sit with other people and learn that there is diversity in leadership styles. Everybody doesn't do everything the same way."

As an example, Avery relates an anecdote about a self-help group composed of white and Native-American women. Asked to put together puzzles, the white women talked together and *Some of us get real crazy when our processes are not the same.* discussed their strategies. The Native Americans studied their puzzle without a word, and observers were uneasy that they would not have an answer. But just before time was called, they pushed all of their pieces into place. Both groups completed the puzzle, but in different ways. "Some of us get real crazy when our processes are not the same," Avery says, "not realizing that the end product is what we need to be looking at, and that there are different ways, as my mother used to say, to skin a cat. We end up bickering with each other instead of understanding and appreciating our diversity."

A realist and a visionary, Avery pictures a time when the National Women's Health Network will represent the health concerns of millions of women. Her image for bringing women together is to build bridges by listening and talking, building the trust required to cross over boundaries. She affirms and endorses the value of different ways of seeing. And she knows that the revolution she began must keep going.

The Personal Is Political

Mary Cunningham Agee created the Nurturing Network out of her own personal suffering when the anticipated birth of her first child ended in a second-trimester miscarriage. It was shortly after Christmas 1983 in Cape Cod, and, taking down the crib and putting away the quilts that she had made, Agee kept asking herself Why? Because she felt so much grief over a miscarriage, she wondered at the loss a woman must experience who has no alternative but to choose abortion.

Applying Industry Analysis

Her own sense of sadness compelled Agee to begin talking with women who had had abortions. She also researched the options available to women who had unwanted pregnancies. As a former vice president for strategic planning at Bendix, a $4-billion-a-year auto-parts maker, and earlier at Joseph E. Seagram & Sons, Agee believed that any project she would plan should be based on "industry analysis." Her conversations and surveys found that women between the ages of twenty and twenty-six, who had at least a high-school education, were very much in need of alternatives to abortion.

"There's an unspoken assumption," Agee says, "that a middle-class woman when faced with a crisis, much less a crisis of pregnancy, can look out for herself . . . but the woman who is in college or on her first job and has no savings account is completely confounded by a pregnancy. And her parents are often close to disowning her."

There's an unspoken assumption that a middle-class woman when faced with a crisis, much less a crisis of pregnancy, can look out for herself.

This population was the group that Mary and Bill Agee targeted when they used $300 thousand from the sale of their second home and opened the first Nurturing Network office in Osterville, Massachusetts, on Mother's Day in 1987. "I said to Bill," Agee recounts, "'We don't need a second home. How can I be asking somebody else to do something that I'm not doing?' And so that formed the capital from which we could open the doors."

The brochures for the opening of the Nurturing Network outlined a fresh approach to the problems of an unwanted pregnancy. This program's job opportunities and other supports were tailored for young professionals and students, the forgotten group that Agee identified as having little access to such services.

Matching Needs

"You can't attract a twenty-three year old into a program that offers to meet her needs if what you are suggesting is a home for unwed mothers. . . . But if I promise that there are employers prepared not only to give her something meaningful for her résumé but an environment where her choice to give birth to her child will be respected, that's important to her. Now she feels she has a choice. . . . She doesn't feel she has this choice if I point her in the direction of a home for unwed mothers. That might be all right for a fourteen-year-old wanting to finish high school, but not a twenty-year-old paralegal in Chicago. She might not even want her parents to know what is happening in the next six months, because she's choosing adoption. She's relieved when I tell her that the Nurturing Network can get her the same job in San Francisco in an excellent law firm, living with a family that pretty much parallels the one she grew up in, where the children have left and the parents are rattling around a big home, and have a lot of love to give. If I also tell her that we'll pay for the trip from Chicago to San Francisco and for as much counseling as she needs—well, that speaks to her, and that's what we do."

Calling Corporate Contacts

Agee began building the Nurturing Network by calling on contacts from her corporate days. She approached organizations, corporations, former business associates, private individuals, and foundations. She included doctors, nurses, and social workers. "I chose not to receive government funding, not a dime," Agee says emphatically, "because I really wanted us to stand as an example of what people can do at the grassroots level when they roll up their sleeves and put their values into action."

Agee is not publicly involved in the political or moral debate about abortion. In a statement that reflects her past as a Phi Beta Kappa graduate from Wellesley with a major in logic and philosophy, she told a *Wall Street Journal* interviewer (September 4, 1990) that the "life versus choice debate will go on forever, because they are not opposites."

*P*eople who are otherwise reasonable cannot even carry on a conversation about abortion, and I think that's tragic.

She characterizes the Nurturing Network as a "reasonable response to a significant crisis in our society. . . . People who are otherwise reasonable cannot even carry on a conversation about abortion, and I think that's tragic. Therefore, I tried to form an organization that would build bridges, not put up walls . . . that would make it possible for people who don't even use the same rhetoric to work side by side, roll up their sleeves, and help someone who may have learned last night that she's pregnant and has nowhere to turn. . . . *That* speaks to people who are pro-life and pro-choice. So the Nurturing Network is really the actualization of a dream that I've had for a long time that I cannot only minister to the needs of the woman who is suffering, but also to the needs of our society at large that is broken over this subject and needs to find a positive outlet for their energies, not more argument."

No Sermons

While young working women and college students are the primary clients of The Nurturing Network, no one is turned away and no one gets a sermon, Agee asserts, "on the sanctity of life. What women want to know is 'What do I do tomorrow? How do I put my right foot in front of my left foot?'" Women facing a crisis pregnancy therefore receive help that is shaped to their individual needs. The counselors at the Nurturing Network send Agee herself the toughest cases; she is the last call.

Since 1985, the Network has grown to nearly 20,000 members and is active in all fifty states. One thousand clients a year are served. Nearly 900 families offer their homes to women who want to relocate. Members throughout the country also extend help in employment, education, medical care, counseling, and finances. Numerous businesses and more than 400 colleges help young women to transfer to a school or college, or change jobs so that their career path is not interrupted. The Network's annual budget, according to Agee, "goes up about a hundred thousand a year," and is now well over a half million dollars.

A Practical Idealist

Asked about how she perceives herself in having launched and established such a major enterprise, Agee says her standard of success is to act as a "practical idealist." She knows people with MBAs from Harvard just like herself, she says, who are "wonderful pragmatists, but wouldn't dream of putting their time and energy into this kind of an effort." From day one, she says her life has been to walk a tightrope between being practical and idealistic, "finding pragmatic means for achieving an end which is idealistic, but never compromising my ideals along the way."

Looking back on her life, she observes a pattern. After graduating from Wellesley in philosophy and logic, she went on to Harvard Business School, where she was called "the poet." At the end of her second year, when asked what she was going to be, she responded "the CEO of an orphanage." Even as a five-year-old, she had always said she would be "taking care of other people's children. What a funny thing when I think back on that," she muses. "I suppose that meant running an orphanage or taking care of children that no one wanted."

The name of the Nurturing Network reflects Agee's practical idealism. She says she consciously did not choose "The Pregnancy Center" or "Something for Life," but preferred the gender-neutral "nurturing" and "network." *Nurturing* is the ideal," she explains, "and *networking* is the practical. That theme runs through everything I've done." For all of her life, she says, she has pulled back and forth between responding to quantitative challenges and her impulses toward idealism and creativity. "I probably became a strategic planner because you have to be creative with all of the pieces of the puzzle, but analytical in pulling out each piece to see what must be worked with. What are the resources? I've never allowed myself the luxury of being a plain old idealist, a plain old philosopher. But at Harvard Business School I also asked the philosophical questions that enriched my life: Why am I here? What am I doing? What have I accomplished just because I can push around some logic equation? Life is more than trying to be a CEO of some big company by the time you're thirty-eight."

The Shoals of Corporate Politics

Agee says the hardest times of her life were as an MBA candidate at Harvard and as a young executive at Bendix. "Both places were very similar because the dominant culture was pragmatic and tended to be cynical in the face of what I'm saying. They tended to look for 'what's the ulterior motive?'" she observes, "and I found that to be destructive and disheartening."

Dubbed a Fortune 500 *wunderkind* when she joined Bendix in 1979 at age twenty-eight as executive assistant to CEO William M. Agee and was promoted to vice president for strategic planning, Mary Cunningham resigned when the media speculated that her advancement was the result of a romance with Agee, whom she later married. She had been jubilant about her appointment to the chairman's council because she wanted to influence policy through strategic planning.

"What I underestimated," she says, "was how dominant the pragmatic culture was. How it was going to use me as a means of trying to push out the CEO, and I was a very convenient tool to do it . . . because I erred on the side of being an idealist. I had a blind spot a mile wide. That's why you have to walk back and forth between being practical and idealistic. It's not enough to work until two or three in the morning and do your best. You have to also have your eyes open if you're going to function in that corporate culture, or you can be devastated."

Agee refers to the psychological pain she went through at Bendix, and later with her miscarriage, as an "invitation to compassion and empathy." Asked how she perceives leadership, she observes that the leadership of women is distinctly marked by compassion for those who are suffering. "By virtue of the discrimination they experience and the pain they are asked to bear," she says that women uniquely identify with the suffering of others and consequently have the passion to want to eliminate it.

The Nurturing Network is based in Carmel, California, but Mary Cunnigham Agee spends little time playing golf or enjoying a life of leisure. "I can't get myself to the day where I can justify it," she says, "knowing that another woman is waking up worried about a pregnancy. Is that leadership? Is that fanaticism? I don't know what you call it, but I've had the privilege over the years of working side by side with some of the best in the arts, politics, and business, and what makes these women tick is an extraordinary capacity for empathy based upon a prerequisite amount of suffering in their own life."

Time for Introspection

At the end of her workday at Seagrams and Bendix, Mary Cunningham Agee recalls that she always asked herself "What have I done to alleviate the suffering of someone today?" Simply making sure that Seagrams sold more cases

. . . she always asked herself "What have I done to alleviate the suffering of someone today?"

of wine as a result of her strategic planning was never really fulfilling to her, she says. In fact, she says wryly, "the only viable alternative" she considered other than marrying her husband "was to go and work with Mother Theresa."

Let's Face It

Women are often strengthened by the tensions of their own lives to become change makers. They choose not to become victims of their suffering, but aspire to have their lives matter by making the world a better place. Their drive is compelling as they explore ways of making connections between the personal and the social, the private and the public. A prime example of this is Let's Face It, an independent nonprofit support network for people with facial difference. It was started by Betsy Wilson after her left lower jaw was removed because of a cancerous tumor.

From her little home in the woods of Concord, Massachusetts, Wilson distributes a hefty, comprehensive resource directory so that people who look different—because of surgery, accidents, or birth defects—can find ways to help themselves live with deviations that can be seen. Let's Face It is also intended to help their loved ones and the professionals who care for them. The organization is dedicated to the belief that "facial difference creates a ripple that affects not just the patient but those close to the patient as well. A healthy, productive life for the patient and family will only come about if all the circles in that ripple are acknowledged."

When I would come down for breakfast, the kids would say, 'Oh, here comes the victim,' because they wouldn't allow me to be a cancer victim.

Betsy Wilson underwent radical surgery at the age of 39 in 1972 when a malignancy spread along her facial nerves. Her young children accepted the change in her appearance with humor and candor. "When I would come down for breakfast, the kids would say, 'Oh, here comes the victim,' because they wouldn't allow me to be a cancer victim." But the adjustment was more difficult for Betsy's husband, and, in time, they divorced. Not only was she out of a marriage, but she was also out of a job. "I had nothing that I'd had before," she recalled as we drank tea on the sunlight porch of her cottage—which also doubles as the national headquarters for Let's Face It.

A Story That Begins With Reading

A childhood spent coping with learning disabilities steeled Betsy Wilson to deal with the ravages of cancer. When I asked how she started Let's Face It, she said, "I need to begin way back. . . . I didn't learn to read until the fourth grade . . . so the whole first experience of school was very, very painful. . . . I think I was forced to know myself in a certain way. That's a very adult thing to say, but it's just that. . . . In order to survive, I had to have a sense of humor. It was devastating because every Friday I was the last one chosen for the spelling bee because I just couldn't do it. . . . I could take you to the place in the school where over fifty years ago I recognized my first word. It was yellow. . . . Reading comes naturally, I guess, to most people."

When Wilson seriously considered creating Let's Face It, she was feeling isolated and lonely. Newly divorced with little money, she had just been turned down for a position in a pediatric cancer center. She was well-trained for the position, having earned a master's degree in education with a specialty in the needs of children in healthcare settings. "Ironically they [two women doctors and two social workers] didn't like my face, but I didn't realize that until about a year later," Wilson says, "because it never occurred to me that would be the reason in a hospital." The experience was not unique: She also was turned down from volunteer jobs at other hospitals.

At this low point in her life, a friend returning from a visit to London gave Wilson a copy of *Let's Face It,* a book written by Christine Piff, whom he had heard on the BBC, talking about having lost her palate and her eye to cancer. "I put it [the book] down in tears and at the end, when she started a support network called 'Let's Face It,' I said to myself that I wanted to start one here," Wilson remembers. For a year, she says, she talked about her dream, but hardly knew where to begin. Finally, she called her plastic surgeon and invited him to take her to lunch with a small group of people she thought would be interested in her project. By dessert, their enthusiasm had become contagious.

Confident that she had grassroots support, Wilson decided to visit Christine Piff in London. The decision was not easy for her. Even though she had traveled with her husband and children, the thought of crossing the Atlantic by herself was daunting. But "Christine's voice sounded nice on the phone," and she put aside her fears. And when they met, she recalls, Christine said, "'Just do it, darling! Just do it!'"

The Project Takes Off

"Christine didn't need to control what we were doing, and that was the key to our success. She was our inspiration by believing and trusting that we could find our own way," Wilson says. "And so I came back to the group who had lunch, and we tried to figure out how much money we needed to start. . . . I added up some things, and thought we needed a computer, a couple of desks and a coffee machine." All together, Wilson figured $25 thousand.

. . . I did have individuals who had worked with people who were different.

Using a very human measure, she identified her board. She invited mostly professionals in healthcare, people whom she felt understood grief. "I didn't have any other facially disfigured people," Wilson says, "but I did have individuals who had worked with people who were different. I wanted the avenues that they could take us down."

From her own experience, Wilson knew that people with facial differences carry a lot of sadness, to the point where they cannot grieve for every hurt they absorb. She wanted to count on a board that would appreciate that people who look different resolve their grief by communicating with others like themselves. Even though they know they will always be stared at or intentionally ignored, people with facial differences move on with their lives by knowing that others are coping with the same problems.

That wasn't the relationship I was after. Connections, yes, but not raising money.

With refreshing candor, Wilson talks about preparing for her first board meeting. "I was very nervous about sticking to the agenda and trying to be efficient. And I had read all of this stuff about boards of directors being fund-raisers, but that's not what I was going to ask them to do. That wasn't the relationship I was after. Connections, yes, but not raising money."

Her most earnest advice for starting a nonprofit support network counters conventional wisdom: "Don't depend on the board to raise money," for contributing companies and corporations will appoint representatives who lack passionate commitment to the cause, she says. If a board appointment is based on money and not a strong belief in its mission, "that's death to your spirit."

Serendipity

Betsy Wilson decided to assume responsibility for learning about funding and public relations herself. She began by attending seminars. She says it was "divine plan" when one day, after reading about grantsmanship in the Boston Public Library, she struck up a conversation with a woman sitting next to her on the bus. The woman happened to be a writer who was in the process of developing a business in desktop publishing; she helped Wilson write the letter she had been laboring over, requesting the $25 thousand start-up grant from an old family friend. This gift led to her writing other letters and receiving small grants from corporations, which set Let's Face It rolling.

Let's Face It runs on less than $40 thousand a year. If funding is down, then Wilson cuts back traveling to conferences. She is convinced that the most successful self-help programs run on little money, which forces them to be very creative. She lives frugally, without taking a salary, but she accepts help with rent and heat because her home is also her office. Franchising Let's Face It is a nonissue with her, although support groups have been formed throughout the country. "The power of Let's Face It is in the fact that I don't have to be concerned about control and fund-raising. I don't want to put my time and energy in raffling cars. All I need to be able to have is the money to make a phone call to connect a woman who has neurofibromatosis in Maine with another who has it in Atlanta. And I don't want to have to be concerned about calling when the rates are lower."

Answer the Call

No group is ever too small for Wilson to meet with. For example, when Christine Piff visited the United States a few years ago, she and Wilson spoke to professional groups throughout the country. Piff's tour ended with a "Boston Tea Party" in Concord, attended by numerous people with facial disfigurements. Among them was a young man who sold motorcycles and had undergone, at his own expense, many operations for facial reconstruction. "That chap needs a support group," Piff said. So he and Wilson and another young man, who was born without an eye, meet regularly for dinner in the cafeteria at Massachusetts General Hospital. Then they have dessert in the chaplain's office. "We've been doing that for six years," says Betsy.

Wilson's philosophy is always to answer the call. Wilson's philosophy is always to answer the call. "You have no idea where it's going to take you. . . . Some days I think we aren't really doing anything here, and then I'll get a letter or the telephone rings and something new begins to happen." She is highly aware of design and how chance meetings cross-affect each other: A producer from National Public Radio attending the Boston Tea Party for Christine Piff said Susan Stamberg might like to interview her for *All Things Considered.* "Imagine the power the Susan Stamberg interview gave me," Wilson says. "I got about seventy-five calls!" One of them was an invitation to spend a few days talking about healthcare at Bucknell University. The commitment included a visit to a fifth-grade class at a local public school. "I really didn't want to do it," Wilson says, "because I had no clue about what I was expected to do or say."

The students spoke to Betsy Wilson with an openness that startled their teachers. When time prevented her from talking with a little boy who was waiting patiently for a private conversation, she promised to call him that evening, she says. When he answered the phone, she asked him about his questions. He had a friend who was learning disabled and wondered why "some people learn slow and some people learn fast."

"That's a good question," Wilson responded, "but we just don't know. But then he blurted out, 'I wear Depends,' and I thought I had died and gone to heaven. This child was in such pain and he trusted me to talk. . . . I had gone into that school with the worst attitude, and it turned out to be one of the greatest experiences of my life."

For her, power is not an ego issue; she sees it as the ability to give up control. Wilson has the strength and the ability not only to pull herself through debilitating circumstances but to sustain others. No woman I interviewed was more confident about using the word power. For her, power is not an ego issue; she sees it as the ability to give up control. She does not want her own board members to be burdened with fund-raising and become trapped in competition; she wants them to be free to offer their best creative thinking on how people with facial differences can be helped in whatever way they need to be. She is clearly focused on the fact that public consciousness has to be changed to "value the person behind every face." For a society that places such high value on physical beauty as feminine power, her message is vital.

Validating

Jewell Jackson McCabe, chair of the National Coalition of 100 Black Women, lets people know who she is, what she can do, and what she wants. Without hesitation, she says: "I see myself as a policy advocate, and my strong suit is an ability to organize and make things happen. I am a doer. I am clearly a leader. I don't say that humbly either. . . . I'm direct and know how to take charge. . . . [Some women] are afraid to get into the game because of failure, but you can't let that stymie you. I am a pragmatic risk taker."

She is forthright in asserting that once African Americans are in leadership positions, they will bring "qualitative change" to the violence in black communities. "But gender equity," she says, "has never been on the agenda of civil rights organizations. It is ludicrous, but it's never been discussed. . . . The only black male leader without exception that has ever talked about a nonracial or nonsexist administration is Nelson Mandela. . . . Others will talk about brutality toward children and violence and child care only in the context of an agenda that fits their own design, but not in terms of the plight of women, and women as leaders within their own culture, which is a waste of talent."

But gender equity, has never been on the agenda of civil rights organizations.

McCabe is emphatic that men conceive of solutions, like martial arts and hierarchical military programs, that perpetuate violence and the need for control. "Subjugation and breaking the spirit are the characteristics of spousal abuse, or violence," McCabe says, "when the issue of nurturing is really at the root of the problem. The very core of the resolve and solutions has to come from a female experience, because we're still the mothers of these children; yet we're teaching young boys how to be tough and to stick it to somebody before he sticks it to you. Women in the black community who are poor and invisible become codependent on violent behavior. But they have to be validated in order to see this and bring a consciousness and a sensitivity to issues of violence. We need programs that truly deal with the psychological and emotional needs within our communities, but male leadership is atrophied on that because all they think about is demonstrating aggressive, militaristic behavior. . . . Women have got to be nurtured and cared for to develop a sense of self to recognize when they are being used at community board level, church level, or civil rights level. . . . Young black boys are taught to almost hate black women. It's demonstrated in those disgusting rap songs. Women would bring a qualitative difference to leadership so that black women don't buy into a sense of self-hatred."

Good People

"She's good people!" They may sound like the words spoken by a character in a Flannery O'Connor short story, but they were yelled by a woman locked in a prison cell, and Sister Jeannette Normandin, Sisters of St. Anne, received them as a personal blessing. In her first day as a volunteer at the Massachusetts Correctional Institute (MCI) at Framingham, Sister Jeannette was by herself on the maximum security unit.

"I took a very deep breath and just asked the Spirit to let me be who I was." This former administrator for the Sisters of St. Anne and spiritual director for the Paulist Seminary in Washington, D.C., understated her situation. "I had never been in that milieu, and I wanted to meet people where they were. The woman in the first cell roared at me. 'Who are you?' I heard the question as 'Describe to me who you are.' 'You know,' I said, 'that's a very good question. I hope I will be here long enough over the long haul that you'll be able to find out who I am but for starters, I'll tell you my name.'"

In a very quiet tone, Sister Jeannette continued her story. "I told her that I wanted to do some volunteer work. Immediately her whole presence changed, and the way she interacted with me was like a ministry to me. She said, 'Wow. Do you know anything about the Bible? Would you do a Bible study for us?'

"I said that I had been there for only fifteen minutes and didn't know what I could do, but if it were allowed, yes.

"Little did I know that this woman was the leader of that whole unit. She shouted down the tier to the other thirteen women inmates, 'She's good people. She's going to do a Bible study for us.' She was actually saying to the other inmates, 'Welcome her.'

"I consider that moment as the beginning of the rest of my life's work. I didn't know it then, but that was the start of my connection with everything in my future. I remain close to all of those women who are still living. The woman in the first cell now has AIDS."

> *I didn't know it then, but that was the start of my connection with everything in my future.*

Since 1970, Sister Jeannette has dedicated her life to the acute problems that affect the lives of women defendants and prisoners, particularly the abject poor. In her capacity as chaplain at MCI at Framingham, and later as an advocate in the Boston courts designing alternative sentencing programs for female offenders, she became alarmed at the increasing number of women infected with the HIV virus or AIDS. Many of those whom she had known at MCI–Framingham were sick and suffering. Those who were homeless had no place to go after serving their sentences. Even when the court accepted a proposal as a substitute for incarceration, a woman in need of medical treatment for AIDS generally landed back in jail for want of a place that would take her.

"Judges had to make awful decisions in those days," Sister Jeannette said. "Should they keep a woman without bail so that she could get medical attention, or send her to the streets? Homeless women with AIDS were going into shelters."

> *Should they keep a woman without bail so that she could get medical attention, or send her to the streets?*

But one heartrending case riveted Sister Jeannette's attention. For many years, she had watched Joanie float in and out of the prison system. She describes her as an African-American woman born in a state hospital and labeled as mentally retarded. In 1988, Joanie had AIDS and was given six months to live. On the day Joanie was charged with assault, Sister Jeannette was not in court. But visiting her in jail, she was startled to see her so sick. Joanie believed she was facing at least a six-month sentence, and she did not want to die in prison. If Sister Jeannette could find a place where Joanie would be supported for her drug addiction and provided with medical care for AIDS, the judge would substitute her sentence.

A difficult task faced Sister Jeannette. Drug treatment programs in 1988 did not have the medical component to accept persons with AIDS. After a three-month search, she found Chesed House in Westfield, the only residence in Massachusetts for homeless AIDS patients.

Living in the Light

Joanie brought light and inspiration to her, Sister Jeannette said. Watching her thrive at Chesed House, Sister Jeannette wanted other homeless women with HIV/AIDS to have similar opportunities. For example, when confronted by other patients that she had had a drug relapse, Joanie lied, but then confessed because she felt a loyalty not to disappoint them. She willingly went to Narcotics Anonymous for ninety days. She remains drug free.

To be with her, is like making a retreat.

"To be with her," Sister Jeannette said, "is like making a retreat. She has grown very intimate with her God, and has more common sense than the whole world. She's not retarded, but her developmental skills were slowed down because she could not read or write."

When the home in Westfield lost its funding, Joanie moved into a nearby apartment. Now she speaks to groups about HIV/AIDS and is enrolled in a literacy program. In 1994, together with civic officials, Joanie spoke at the renovation ceremony for Ruah House, a residence for homeless women with AIDS, spearheaded by Sister Jeannette. "For people like me," Joanie told

Ruah's supporters, "who've been in the dark so long, it means something to be in the light. Now I am living in the light."

The Victorian boardinghouse at 10 Russell Street, Cambridge, transformed into a bright and airy residence, opened with a great celebration. To arrive at this public ceremony was the fulfillment of a dream. Sister Jeannette's first course of action toward this goal was interior and private. After years of dealing with courts and prisons, she needed space for reflection. She divided a year's sabbatical by studying at the Ecumenical Institute for Theological Research in Jerusalem, learning Spanish in Guatemala, and relishing the art museums of Europe. She returned to Boston fortified to meet the challenge of opening a house that would provide holistic care for homeless women with AIDS to live in peace and dignity, and to grow in self-esteem.

But Sister Jeannette knew her goal would remain illusory without the support of women with diverse backgrounds, skills, and experiences. "I consider myself to be a leader," she remarks, "but the first thing is to admit

I consider myself to be a leader, but the first thing is to admit what you don't know and where you need help.

what you don't know and where you need help." From her office at the Jesuit Urban Center in the South End of Boston, where we talked, she gathered together twenty committed women known in the city as activists for social change. They wrote a mission statement and accepted Sister Jeannette's suggestion that the group be called Ruah, meaning "breath of life" in Hebrew. The twenty-woman board of directors, formed in 1991, met regularly to develop plans for education, outreach, programming, personnel, fund-raising, and public relations. They invited the advice of women with AIDS. Joanie recommended, for example, that Ruah House have a garden, land, and plenty of windows.

A Living Tithe

Their search for an appropriate house was long, hard, and often disappointing. But when a house was located in the spring of 1992, Ruah gained an important collaborator in the Women's

Institute for Housing and Economic Development. With the assistance of project manager Susan Davies, the Women's Institute helped Ruah obtain a financing package from various sources. The time was then right for Julia Smith, from the architectural firm of Buck, Smith, and McAvoy, to draw plans for the needed renovations, including an elevator and an addition. From a large base of individual donors, private funds from organizations, banks, corporations, and foundations, Ruah raised the $440 thousand necessary for rehabilitation costs. The only public funding, $250 thousand for staff, came from the Department of Public Health.

Sister Jeannette is always determined to make the future more human. She explains that the mission of the Sisters of St. Anne, founded over 150 years ago in Quebec, "is to be aware of a void and then respond to it. I have tried to live that."

She left British Columbia after years as a high school teacher, when family obligations called her back to Massachusetts. "The bishop in our diocese in British Columbia asked the people to tithe. I watched poor fishermen and their families answer that call. I wanted to tithe, too, and wondered how I could do it. After some reflection, I decided that I would contribute time each week to helping the poor, those on the margins of society. So when I returned to Massachusetts, I thought about how I would continue to tithe. My family's home was in the shadows of the Framingham prison, but in all of those years I had never been inside. After some soul-searching, I decided that's where I would give my time."

After some reflection, I decided that I would contribute time each week to helping the poor, those on the margins of society.

Restorative Bonds

The women here who pursue changes in public consciousness and social policy have little interest in themselves in being number one; they value power only for what it can accomplish. These women are in the strong tradition of nineteenth-and early twentieth-century leaders like Lucy Stone, Sojourner Truth, Mary Harris ("Mother") Jones, Jane Addams, and Ida B. Wells Barnett, who often faced ridicule and contempt to change the condition of the powerless. Their legacy is priceless, and their persistence and commitment are inspiring, especially when we consider that their groundbreaking work presaged constant renewal and expansion by new generations. Yet they have remarkable self-worth and a very clear sense of what they want to accomplish.

Chapter Three

Women in the Law: Soundings From Bench and Bar

As recently as thirty years ago, little girls had to depend upon their reading when they lacked opportunities for seeing women in nontraditional roles. As we talked in her chambers, Judge Stephanie Domitrovich, 38, the first woman elected to the bench in Erie, Pennsylvania, recalled her disappointment as a child when she discovered that her local library carried only a few juvenile biographies of women in professional careers. So at age 10, in order to imagine herself as a lawyer, she took a younger cousin by the hand, walked to the courthouse, and wandered into a trial. It was a sex abuse case; the judge halted the proceedings and had the children removed. But the visit gave Stephanie a sense of the courtroom so that she could continue to imagine herself there. Her anecdote reminds us that women have always found singular ways to locate the experience they need.

Domitrovich says she is always conscious of being an example for women lawyers each time she dons her judicial robes. "I know that what I do is going to be important for keeping the door open for the voters to put other women on the bench. I don't want to screw it up for the others," she adds.

One day in her courtroom, Domitrovich overheard a male prosecutor say to the woman attorney sitting second chair, "'Now, I'll whisper in your ear and you say just what I tell you.' She was just like a puppet!" Domitrovich exclaims. Her tipstaff and law clerk were equally outraged, and the judge called the young woman aside. "We all told her that she was terrific and could rely on herself. So she heard two different perspectives besides mine. It was like team building." Judge Domitrovich also spoke to the male prosecutor about his behavior and told him that she had talked with his associate.

When I asked women judges how they thought they had made a difference in the law, their most frequent first response was very basic: By their presence on the bench. Simply being there is important, they noted, because it encourages women attorneys to imagine themselves in that role someday. High-profile women in other careers do not place such importance on merely being visible, but women on the bench still have a short history. These judges have been strong advocates for women's interests before their appointments; now, many substitute responsibility they feel as role models and mentors for the personal involvement in other public issues that their judiciary positions no longer allow.

One of the First

Roxanna Arsht's journey toward becoming the first woman to be appointed to the bench in Delaware, for example, began when she started to volunteer in community organizations as a young lawyer. After graduating from the University of Pennsylvania Law School in 1939, she married, became pregnant, and passed the bar exam. But law firms would not hire a woman, Roxanna especially, it seemed, ostensibly because she was the wife of a local attorney and the firms claimed that her employment would create a "conflict of interest." So instead of practicing law, Roxanna Arsht devoted her time to her young family and to working on behalf of civic charities. Eventually, Delaware's governor began to appoint her to state committees.

"In 1942," Arsht says, "we couldn't buy a house where our social friends lived because Jews weren't allowed, but we did find a nice house in the country. Then the war started, and there was gasoline rationing. The house had a coal stove for winter cooking and heating, and a water pump down in the field, where I used to sit and cry: What the hell am I doing here? I went to college and law school, yet all I have to do is wash diapers. I can't even get in the car and go, and nobody will give me a job."

Eventually, Roxanna's husband suggested that she open her own law office. He offered to pay the rent for a year until she decided what to do. Friends encouraged her to specialize in "domestic law because the men are uncomfortable with it." While Arsht was making up her mind, a vacancy opened in juvenile court. Influential women like Mrs. E. Paul DuPont, who respected Arsht's community dedication, recommended her for the position, but she was not selected.

"In retrospect, I'm glad I wasn't appointed," Arsht says, "because it gave me a ten-year time span to grow." She accepted an unpaid position as a master in juvenile court, which allowed her to hear all cases assigned to her unless either party objected. "For nine years I went in five days a week and was not paid, but I learned a tremendous amount because I heard all the cases that the judges did."

That experience prepared Arsht for her appointment as judge when the new statewide family court was instituted in 1972. "I brought to the court the obvious difference of being female," Arsht says simply. "Maybe I was even tougher on some women, if I felt there was a need for her to shift gears . . . that a particular woman ought to be independent and not just vegetate. A woman couldn't complain to me that it took all day to get the house in order because I'd say, 'Look, I know how long it takes to iron a shirt. . . . But I was also tough on the men and would say, 'What the hell do *you* do?'"

I brought to the court the obvious difference of being female.

From her years of volunteering in community organizations, Arsht knew firsthand the "difficulties people face. I learned way back about the fear of a child who has to testify against a parent and the need for representation for children against the parent. . . . I was willing to try things."

Cookies in Chambers

When she presided over custody cases, Judge Arsht discarded her robe to greet children in the waiting room and invited them to sit behind the bench and pound her gavel. Toys, games, and cookies were always available in her chambers. "Children became more relaxed with me because I wasn't overwhelming and didn't look threatening. I wasn't a big man in a black robe."

"Originally, a lot of lawyers in family court were men, and they were aggressive and defeated the needs of the child," Arsht says. She still keeps a note she wrote to herself about a lawyer in a case: "'The lawyer and his client won. The child lost.' We had been very correct in applying the rules. . . . Gradually, we got more women lawyers, and they were super. They were as businesslike as anyone would want, and they brought a humanity and understanding. I enjoyed the court more when the women lawyers increased."

A Breath of Fresh Air

Now that Judge Arsht is retired from the bench, she feels "like a teenager. I wear the wildest clothes and say anything I please. I never could do that before. I wore my basic black robe and behaved myself . . . I had to be more under control. I had less freedom as a judge. I was off all boards that were seeking funds. My long-term support of Planned Parenthood had to stop publicly, and I couldn't be involved in any political things. I couldn't even go to the annual Jefferson-Jackson Day Democratic fund raiser."

"The Sanctity of Their Sex"

Less than one hundred years before Roxanna Arsht went on the bench, the Wisconsin Supreme Court denied Lavinia Goodelle's application to practice law on the basis that "Woman is modeled for gentler and better things." Chief Justice C. J. Ryan wrote that courts of justice deal "with all that is . . . criminal, coarse and brutal, repulsive and obscene in human life. It would be revolting to all female sense of innocence and the sanctity of their sex, shocking to man's reverence for womanhood and faith in woman" for women to practice law.

One Judge's R.S.V.P

At age 33 in 1984, Deborah Agosti was elected to the Second Judicial District Court, Reno, Nevada, where she is now chief judge.

She used the authority of her position to go to bat for women lawyers by responding in an unusual way to a routine invitation to attend the 1993 Christmas dinner of the twenty-eight member Reno chapter of the American Board of Trial Advocates (ABOTA).

Judge Agosti turned ABOTA upside down by writing, in part: ". . . I would like to confirm our attendance at this time. However, I need clarification on one point. . . . You enclosed for my perusal the names of the members of the Reno Chapter. I couldn't help but notice that the membership is exclusively male. . . . Since I cannot believe that there are no women in Washoe County who meet [the] stated qualifications, it crossed my mind that perhaps the bylaws of the organization prohibit the membership of women. If this is the case, I simply cannot attend. I would consider it unethical under the rules to participate even in the social functions of a male-only professional organization."

Agosti never intended for her stand to become a public issue, especially after being assured by the president of ABOTA that women would be admitted to membership the following spring. But then, learning through the grapevine that a woman had in fact been turned down, she sent another letter to the members, charging that ABOTA "has engaged in a policy of de facto discrimination on the basis of gender." She sent copies to many women lawyers and other political officials.

Lawyers gain referrals by being members of organizations like ABOTA, Agosti notes. "If women are systematically excluded from their share of the pie, it is unjust. I wrote that letter because I was the only person who could speak out about this discrimination, and if I didn't say anything, nothing would change. When you're in an elected position, you don't rationally set out to gratuitously irritate the people that can vote you in or out of office, or can run against you, or not contribute to your campaign. But those issues are small and petty compared to what was going on. It wasn't the earth-shattering issue of Western civilization, but it was big to me."

I was the only person who could speak out about this discrimination, and if I didn't say anything, nothing would change.

"All I ever wanted to be was a good judge," she says. "I cared a lot about women's issues, but when you're a judge, you're not always in a position to say and do things about issues that are of personal concern to you. . . . I didn't start out to be a leader. I never really thought about myself as a local feminist leader. But I would be hard-pressed to get anyone in the public to see me in any other way now. I don't want to sound like Joan of Arc or imply that I was fearless. I was scared. But I felt that there was something more important than my being scared."

Only Girls Are Judges

Although her working-class parents were encouraging, Agosti claims that the first woman attorney she ever met was herself.

As a child in Toledo, Ohio, Agosti decided to be a lawyer while watching the *Perry Mason* television series and "figuring out that his job was a lot more exciting than Della Street's." Although her working-class parents were encouraging, Agosti claims that the first woman attorney she ever met was herself. But not so for her five-year-old son, who says he wants no part of being a judge "because only girls are."

Acknowledging Everyone's Experience

Carolyn Engel Temin is a judge in the Court of Common Pleas of Philadelphia County. Perched prominently on her desk is a crystal paperweight inscribed with the words of Justice Oliver Wendell Holmes: "The life of the law has not been logic; it has been experience." When she was a criminal attorney new to the bar in 1964, she noticed that the sentencing laws of Pennsylvania required that convicted women were to be sentenced to the maximum allowed by law, while men could be sentenced to anything up to the maximum sentence.

"Does that sound a little discriminatory?" Timen asks. "Well, nobody bothered with it before I came along, because no one was interested. Women see things that relate to women that men don't see."

So, as a young lawyer, Temin challenged the constitutionality of the law and won. Subsequently, she served on the original board for New Directions for Women, an alternative program to incarceration and a halfway house for women offenders. Once she became a judge, she left the board because women she had sentenced were being sent to the New Directions facility; if they violated the rules of the program and were brought back in front of her, the staff for New Directions would be testifying against them. It was an untenable position for Temin, who had to avoid the appearance of giving greater credibility to her former employees than to the offender.

Judicial Restraint

"It's ironic that very often judges can't participate in the things where they really need us, because of the conflict of interest," Timen contends. When members of the judiciary want to influence social policy, they have to deal with a complexity of nuances. They may be as adamant as any legislator or policy wonk, but judicial restraint curtails their expression of political convictions or policy preferences. Judges are therefore highly circumspect when interpreting their role as public leaders.

The model code of judicial conduct was adopted by the American Bar Association (ABA) in 1972 and revised in 1990. While codes of judicial ethics may vary slightly from state to state, they agree that judges must always appear and, in effect, be nonbiased.

"[But] judges don't have to completely shut up about their causes," says Attorney Cynthia Gray, director of the American Judicature Society's Center for Judicial Conduct Organizations. "They can't make a statement on how they would rule on cases, but they can advocate changes in the legal system."

They can't make a statement on how they would rule on cases, but they can advocate changes in the legal system.

Judge Temin has been able to continue her commitment to women's prison reform by chairing a committee for the National Association of Women Judges, which is writing a curriculum on sentencing women offenders. Trying to combat the stereotype that the generic prisoner is "he," she also heads a national task force that is drafting a policy statement on women offenders for the National Committee on Crime and Delinquency.

Her leadership is helping to break the cycle in which a woman is arrested and booked by male police officers, defended by male lawyers, sentenced by a male judge for breaking laws made by male legislators, and then consigned to a prison where the male superintendent thinks it is noblesse oblige to stock maxipads for all the female inmates.

A Champion for Inmates

When compared with the numbers of male prisoners, so few women are in prison that little attention is given to their specific needs. Programs are designed to support men. "Women have two strikes against them," Temin asserts. "Women in general are less employable than men, but if you are also an ex con, it's even harder. Yet there is little concern for training women in prison for jobs they could get on the outside and making contacts for them."

Of great concern to Judge Temin is that "zero attention" is given to the fact that many women inmates are mothers. If they are pregnant when they go to prison, "they often give birth under terrible conditions," she says. Most heartrending are her stories of women being unattended or even shackled during labor. Some women's prisons entirely lack gynecological services, a situation that is improving, according to Temin, now that more women are becoming superintendents in the correctional system; until recently, all superintendents for women's prisons were men.

Another problem Judge Temin notes is that drug-addicted pregnant women are frequently sentenced to prison by well-meaning judges who regard incarceration as a way of keeping them healthy. In fact, Timen points out, going "cold turkey" will cause a miscarriage. "Often the last people into a drug program are pregnant women, who probably need it most." She wants to focus attention on this group, not only for judges, but for people involved in the court system at all levels.

It is a troubling paradox, she says, that when they were free, male prisoners were seldom the primary caregivers for their children; when they were jailed, generally mothers, wives, or other significant others were available to nurture the children in their absence. "But if they're lucky," Timen says with irony, "the women are leaving their children with the same people who abused *them* growing up, and who are partly responsible for the situation that they are in."

Women are also penalized more often for their technical violations of parole than men are for their infractions. "If a man is supporting a family and all that he has done is violate a rule, nobody is going to put him in jail," Timen notes. "But if a woman is caretaking a family, that's not given the same weight."

Timen is concerned that by not paying attention to what happens to the children of women who are put in jail, we are creating a whole new generation of criminals. "We have to make sure that these children have proper care and nurturing and keep bonds with their parents, or else they will repeat the history of their parents."

We have to make sure that these children have proper care and nurturing and keep bonds with their parents, or else they will repeat the history of their parents.

Getting In There

Patricia M. Wald, Circuit Judge, United States Court of Appeals for the District of Columbia Circuit, believes that women judges are necessary for maintaining the perception that the judicial system is fair. "Women are not monolithic and have many different experiences, but just because you *are* a woman, at least, in our time, you are much more likely to have suffered slights or discrimination or at least obstacles and to recognize them when they are happening to others," Wald says.

Courts are intended to mediate the disputes that other agencies of society do not mediate "and to work toward this very ephemeral thing called justice. In a country that has a diverse population, over half of which are women, it is almost incredible to suggest that we shouldn't have a strong representation on those dispute-resolving bodies."

Judge Wald, who has been on the shortlist for an appointment to the U.S. Supreme Court, graduated from Yale Law School in

1951, when only 3 percent of attorneys in United States were women. She grew up in a working-class family in a Connecticut mill town and would not have been able to attend college without securing scholarships. A course in Constitutional law at Connecticut College, taught by the legendary Marjorie Dilley, fascinated her with its Socratic method and case study approach. "It awakened my interest in going to law school," she says. "Plus I used to work during the summers in the factories, where my relatives also were, and I got very interested in the labor movement. In one period of my career, I was interested in labor law."

Wald did not have a preconceived plan. She practiced law for two years before she married, and then had five children within seven years. "But my husband was very supportive, long before it was fashionable. So when I went back part-time after ten years, he took care of the children then and on weekends when I was in the library."

During the sixties, Wald wrote policy material on poverty when Robert F. Kennedy and Nicholas Katzenbach were U.S. attorneys general. "Even though I was not earning a great deal of money," she says, "I was able to get in there and do something. I liked public service and did public interest law and developed some name recognition. Now I look at a particular instance and can say, 'Well, I did pave the way on that.' I brought a lot of cases which established the legal principles for children, for the mentally ill."

The law thrives when attorneys are creative and vigilant in the cases they bring to judges, she says. "We [judges] can't go out in the streets and say, 'Well, that's an interesting case. Let's try that one.' But lawyers can choose and even target their cases to challenge existing law or press for social change."

Her career owes much to historical opportunity, she says modestly. When the women's movement was at its peak in the 1970s and networks of women were pressing President Carter to appoint women, her experience and credentials made her a prime candidate to join the administration. "I kind of hit the age," she offers, "where people were beginning to put women on boards and courts and commissions, and I had the qualifications. I had interviews with the attorney general and went to the Justice Department.

From there I went on to the court. I was the first woman to be chief judge of this court."

A Circle Widens

When women are in positions of leadership or power, "people act differently toward other women who are in the same orbit," Wald believes. She was conscious of setting a certain tone when she joined the circuit court and then became chief judge. "I hoped that women counsel might feel more comfortable, and that their law firms, by seeing me on the panel, might think it would be a good idea to have more women at the counsel table as well. So an atmosphere is created in which more women are likely to be brought into the circle."

Wald notes that women employees in lesser positions in the legal system also receive greater respect when a woman is at the head of the court. "These are very subtle things," she suggests, "but when there's a woman at the top, people are a little bit more reticent [sic] to stay with the feelings of the status quo or accept the superiority of the traditional old boys' network. Now it doesn't always work that way because some women—my daughters tell me a lot about this—don't care and are happy to be *the woman,* the token, and not help anybody else get up there because they like being the queen bee. But I don't think that's the norm."

These are very subtle things, but when there's a woman at the top, people are a little bit more reticent to stay with the feelings of the status quo or accept the superiority of the traditional old boys' network.

Nineties Pioneers

The list of women "firsts" in the law continues into the present. For example, now sitting on the Superior Court of Pennsylvania are Phyllis Beck and Kate Ford Elliott, the first women in the court's one-hundred-year history.

Regardless of how the rules of judicial ethics may curb their expression when they are off the bench, women judges continue to

A nyone in this position had better see and accept herself as a leader.

break new ground in the courts. "Anyone in this position had better see and accept herself as a leader," Elliott says, "because every day I am cognizant of the authority that goes with this job, of the law. The heart of the matter is that by expanding the law in regard to women's life experiences, perspectives, and needs, women in the judiciary are agents of change.

Relaxing in her Pittsburgh office, Elliott points to her credenza, covered with family photographs, and hands me pictures of her mother and mother-in-law: "women ahead of their time, who still inspire me." Her mother, Loretto O'Toole Ford, had seven children when her husband died, but she was able to create opportunities for herself in television and advertising during the fifties because she had graduated from Carnegie-Mellon with a degree in home economics. From her mother's example, Elliott learned the practical value of becoming credentialed. She graduated in education and worked as a reading specialist in the Pittsburgh public schools. Then her mother-in-law, Mary O'Loughlin Elliott, a gutsy attorney who opened a private law practice in the dark days of 1929, persuaded her to start night law classes at Duquesne University. "We have to keep imitating those women who were at the front lines in the twenties and thirties," Elliott says, "in order to empower women who come after us. We still need to provide examples so that women can become anything they want to be, and make sure that the doors stay open."

Consequently, Elliott is dedicated to bringing the authority of her experience as a woman to the Superior Court of Pennsylvania. "When we hear cases and go back to vote, we have all heard the same facts, and the same laws apply. But when we sit around the table and talk about the issues based on life experiences, mine are very different," she says. She is 45, married, and the mother of a young son, and whether the court is dealing with children, criminal matters, contract, or consumer issues, she is certain that she brings a unique perspective to the discussion. "And I generally get a positive response. [In many cases] if I hadn't been there, they probably wouldn't have thought of it."

Explaining the Law

One particularly interesting quality Elliott points to is that women judges, in general, take more time than men to explain their reasons for making decisions. For example, if the superior court was deciding a rare case of child abuse

. . . women judges, in general, take more time than men to explain their reasons for making decisions.

in a Pennsylvania county outside of a metropolitan area, Elliott says she would write a formal opinion in order to place the issue within a historical and cultural context for those who might lack perspective on the phenomenon as a social issue. Anyone reading her opinion would then have an appreciation of the *problem* as well as the *law*.

"I would put as much reason and common sense into the opinion as possible," she emphasizes, "because it's probably one of the most important cases to come through that county in years; whereas in Philadelphia, regrettably and unfortunately, a case of child abuse would not be high profile. But you have a responsibility to the people of the state when they have a case which they think is very important. The judiciary can't just say 'This is the law and here's our decision.' The judiciary has an obligation to explain why they have done what they have done. That way the law is enhanced for all of us," she asserts.

Yes, a judge can become fairly jaded after a while because of the tremendous volume of such cases in the court, she says. "Yet it's also important not to lose the perspective that [child abuse cases] are some of the most important cases we handle," she notes. "So my approach to support, divorce, and custody matters is a little different, because I like to take the time to really explain a situation."

Dysfunctional Pronouns

The law has such a long history of masculine orientation that generalizations in written decisions have traditionally been expressed with male pronouns. Numbers of women in the judiciary try to influence the courts to use gender-neutral language that cuts through stereotypes and promotes fairness. In 1990, when she was writing her first formal opinion for the Pennsylvania Superior Court, Elliott's general statements used only feminine pronouns.

"When I circulated the decision among my colleagues, you can't imagine the flurry of activity on the telephone," she laughs. One judge was so troubled by the language that he intimated that he simply might have to concur in the result without joining the decision. The opinion was finally unanimous, however, and sent to the Supreme Court. The all-male Pennsylvania Supreme Court filed an opinion affirming the decision, but every time Elliott's passages were quoted, each feminine pronoun was followed by [sic], as if her choice was an embarrassing grammatical error, or at least one with which the state supreme court did not wish to associate itself. Now Elliott avoids using any pronouns in her opinions and is strictly gender-neutral.

Terry and Pat Divorce

Mary Kay Bickett, the executive director for the Texas Center for the Judiciary and former academic director of the National Judicial College in Reno, Nevada, teaches continuing education courses to judges. Bickett's hardest challenge, she says, is to persuade male judges that their choice of words powerfully conveys their attitudes toward other persons, particularly in the forms of address they use. "Every judge knows that you're not supposed to call a female lawyer sweetie, but the subtle way that they call one of the counselors Mr. Smith and the woman attorney Mary Kay is biased and demeaning. The hardest lesson to get across is intent versus impact."

Even when they are giving speeches off the bench, a number of otherwise respected male judges often refer to the spouses in the audience as "wives" though many female judges are there with husbands. "They'll say, 'Well, I didn't intend to do that. Everybody knows that when I say *he* that I also mean *she*,'" Bickett reports. "Explaining to them that the impact of their language is very alienating is difficult."

To convince such male judges of their biases, Bickett uses exercises that she designs to involve and engage rather than to confront or embarrass. "If you tell judges, 'Today we're going to teach you about gender bias in the courts,' they cross legs and arms and don't want to hear it," she explains. She creates scenarios where husbands and wives with names like Terry and Pat divide their assets in a divorce settlement. After the case is discussed, she identifies their gender and then reverses it. "We can't beat judges over their heads with studies that show gender bias in the courtroom, but through these activities, they see there's something to it," she says.

If you tell judges, 'Today we're going to teach you about gender bias in the courts,' they cross legs and arms and don't want to hear it.

Be Yourself!

Bickett's experience in planning conferences, courses, and seminars for judges, along with developing basic training curricula for new judges, has convinced her that female judges still have a hard time being taken seriously by many of their male colleagues. "Women have to be aware then of overcompensating and becoming brittle and hard and all the stereotypes that are assigned to successful women," Bickett cautions. "Judges who are women should use all those good instincts of compassion and caring that enter into the decision-making process and not push them to the back." She notes that sometimes female judges become unhappy "because they are suppressing what is theirs and what served them well all of their lives in making decisions. Women need to be themselves because they add something that men can benefit from, and it makes the legal system more inclusive."

One judge I spoke with affirmed this when she said, off the record, that from her experience a "remarkable difference" exists between the perspectives that men and women bring to the bench. "Male judges are more driven by ego, but women judges are more conciliatory and they look for common ground. It's easy to fall into an ego trap because you're constantly flattered and told how

Male judges are more driven by ego, but women judges are more conciliatory and they look for common ground.

terrific and wonderful you are," she advises, "so you have to keep your head straight about it. A critical part of this job . . . is to reconcile and compromise and try to appreciate all sides of an issue in order to resolve a problem in a just and fair way. Women do that very well. They don't see things in black and white the way men tend to."

A wise old man and a wise old woman reach the same conclusion.

The paradox that men and women judges reach the same decision in different ways was acknowledged by Ruth Bader Ginsburg at her inauguration as associate justice of the United States Supreme Court. In her acceptance speech, she quoted Minnesota Supreme Court Justice Jeanne Coyne, who was asked if women judges decide cases "differently by virtue of being women? Justice Coyne replied that, in her experience, 'A wise old man and a wise old woman reach the same conclusion.'"

"I agree," Ginsburg added, "but I also have no doubt that. . .a system of justice will be richer for diversity of background and experience. It will be the poorer, in terms of appreciating what is at stake and the impact of its judgments, if all of its members are cast from the same mold."

Lawyers as Social Visionaries

At her daughter's graduation from the New York University School of Law, Judith S. Kaye, chief judge of the State of New York, gave the 1991 Commencement Address. She told the practitioners-to-be that judges count on them to keep the law just and responsive to people's real lives.

"Courts and judges—necessarily somewhat removed and isolated from everyday affairs, necessarily somewhat passive and reactive to issues put before them by litigants—look to and depend upon the sensitivity, creativity, and dedication of lawyers to enlighten them with new insights into old principles. As the world changes and values evolve, courts look to the Bar to deepen their understanding of the context and ramifications of legal issues, to help keep the law attuned to the needs of modern society, and to lead in the progress of the law. As is evident in the example of women during the hundred years since 1891, the law can perpetuate ideas in need of reform, but the vigilance of lawyers who perceive wrongdoing and press for relief can assure that the law also is an instrument of justice. . . . Lawyers [can continue] to advance this nation toward its dream of equality for women and the multitudes for whom that promise also remains unfulfilled. . . . "

. . . the law can perpetuate ideas in need of reform, but the vigilance of lawyers who perceive wrongdoing and press for relief can assure that the law also is an instrument of justice.

Trailblazers

Between 1980 and 1995, according to ABA statistics, the number of women lawyers increased by 15 percent. Women now comprise 23 percent of all lawyers and nearly 50 percent of all law students. Within the next ten years, many more women will be on the bench.

It was a very different world for the now-distinguished group of young women lawyers who gravitated to Washington in the late 1960s. As children, they first learned to express themselves on public issues from parents with liberal political convictions. They did not arrive in the nation's capital specifically to advance the rights of women: At that time the issues that they would educate a generation about had scarcely been articulated.

But as they practiced with private firms or government agencies, these attorneys came into daily contact with the fact that women as a class were legally denied rights that men took for granted. They began to volunteer their services pro bono (without pay) to represent women, primarily on domestic matters and in addressing problems of credit and employment discrimination. Their work placed them at the cutting edge of representing women's rights in the courts, and they became the shapers of the strategies that would transform public policy. These Washington lawyers refer to the seventies as halcyon days, because, despite the intensity of their struggle, within a short time they were able to see the dramatic gains of their hard work. They seized the opportunities for making their careers happen, and they were catalysts for bringing women's rights issues to national prominence.

Among them were Nancy Duff Campbell, Marcia D. Greenberger, Judith L. Lichtman, and Brooksley Born. And among their many accomplishments, their efforts created the Women's Legal Defense Fund and the National Women's Law Center, both of which have evolved into the capital's most successful lobbying organizations for advancing and securing women's legal rights.

A License for Activism

A basic tenet of my mother and father was that we're put on this earth to leave it better than we found it.

Judith L. Lichtman became executive director of the Women's Legal Defense Fund (WLDF) in 1974 and president in 1988. She credits her instincts for public policy to "roots and family values. Family values in the good sense of those words," she quickly adds, "not the way they're tossed about today. A basic tenet of my mother and father was that we're put on this earth to leave it better than we found it. Whatever our life choices would be, it was understood that we would pursue that goal."

The daughter of union organizers, she never had the urge to rebel against the principles she absorbed at the dinner table. She remembers discussing, for example, the significance of Jackie Robinson's breaking the racial barriers in "Brooklyn Dodger Land," where she grew up. Lichtman knew she wanted to work in the field of public policy, and she was headed for a graduate degree in American political theory. "Law school was a very scary, gutsy thing for me, but Shirley Abramson, a lawyer who now sits on the Wisconsin Supreme Court, talked me into it. She said a degree in political theory wouldn't be active enough for me." At the University of Wisconsin Law School, Lichtman was one of two women in her freshman class of 150 students.

She went to law school determined to work in the area of civil rights and civil liberties, so she never experienced the crisis of conscience that some law students confront about whether to go into corporate practice or public interest law. "I knew from the very beginning what I wanted to do with that law degree. What I say

I knew from the very beginning what I wanted to do with that law degree.

to students is that I viewed [it] and still view it today as a license for activism."

The Civil Rights Act of 1964 was implemented in the spring of 1965 when she graduated. "It created jobs for me that were made in heaven," she recalls. Her first position was with the Department of Health, Education, and Welfare to implement Title Six of the Civil Rights Act. She traveled throughout the South, advising school superintendents of their new obligations in racially deseg-regating the schools. She also worked at the Urban Coalition and acted as the legal advisor to the Commonwealth of Puerto Rico.

Outside of office time, Lichtman and a coterie of young attor-neys of like mind continued to volunteer their services to represent women. They organized to take telephone calls from women in need of legal advice and selected cases to represent. In 1971, this informal collective of feminist lawyers then formed the WLDF to work in both the courts and Congress to expand opportunities for women. Since then, Lichtman has devoted her professional career to WLDF. During the 1970s, the fund's focus shifted from concentrat-ing on direct litigation to advancing and changing public policy.

The WLDF was key to passage of the Pregnancy Discrimina-tion Act of 1978, the Civil Rights Restoration Act of 1988, and the Civil Rights Act of 1991. In 1985, it developed the federal Family and Medical Leave Act, enacted into law in February 1993—the first piece of legislation signed by President Clinton. "It took eight long years of many staff members working together to bring about the passage," Lichtman says.

Asked to describe her own strengths as a leader, she mentions "being a damn good advocate; I'm good at marshalling arguments and making a persuasive case. And I have known for a long time that by dint of my arguments, I can either affect policy or the way that people think about public policy. In my context, a leader is a person who can make a difference . . . change public policy in

A leader has to make hard calls but leave people whole in doing so.

order to make the world a better place. A leader has to make hard calls but leave people whole in doing so."

Lichtman is convinced that having a law degree is the best way for a young woman to get into public policy. "Part of my message is that lawyers have a disproportionate amount of power in the public policy process, more power than probably we should, but we have it as lawyers. We're the people who say 'Wait a second, maybe we can say it this way.' If you want to be a plumber, you have to get a license," Lichtman observes. "Law school is a very good training ground, better than just getting experience. It's also a way of building self-esteem and self-confidence for the kind of leadership that you need in the public policy arena. Law school is just invaluable."

O ver time, it's much more likely that the culture of law firms and corporations will change than that women will.

Judith L. Lichtman's lifelong commitment to social justice for girls and women has earned her many awards. She has been named by *Washington Magazine* as one of the city's one hundred most important women, and *The Ladies Home Journal* has listed her as one of America's one hundred most important women. Assessing the future of women attorneys in the private sector, she is optimistic that large law firms will begin to catch up with gender equity. "It's been only fifteen to twenty years since women have been graduating from law school in great numbers," she says, "and that isn't very long for cultures to change. Over time, it's much more likely that the culture of law firms and corporations will change than that women will."

Choice and Destiny

Marcia D. Greenberger, founder and copresident of the National Women's Law Center (NWLC) was also drawn to Washington in the late sixties. Her clearest childhood memories are of her parents, particularly her schoolteacher father, engaging her in conversations about how government programs and policies affected their personal lives. Her delight in polemics was further encouraged at the Philadelphia High School for Girls. "We had fewer resources than our male high school counterpart and nothing like the scholar's program. We did not have the same strength in science and math or the number of library books or teachers with advanced degrees. Still, the environment was very reaffirming for validating achievement on the part of young women."

This early self-confidence gained from home and school served Greenberger throughout college and law school at the University of Pennsylvania, for she had not one female professor throughout her education. Even though she was an honor's major in history, her advisor counseled her not to apply for graduate school "because I would only drop out and marry before completing a Ph.D."

"I was upset, but not outraged," Greenberger recalls. "In the end I decided to go to law school. The Vietnam War was heating up, and when I went to take the LSAT [Law School Aptitude Test] with three friends, young men started yelling that we were taking spots away from guys who needed graduate deferments."

As a law student, Greenberger was "called on for all the rape cases, in the stereotypical way that young women were." And they were not singled out for discussing these cases as a nod to their sensitized understanding of the issue, she remembers, but purely in order to make them feel uncomfortable. When she graduated and interviewed with one Washington law firm, she was told that the "city wasn't safe and they didn't want the responsibility of having women lawyers going home late at night. So I could understand certainly why women lawyers were not hired," she observes sardonically.

Greenberger practiced tax law with the Washington firm of Caplin and Drysdale from 1969 to 1972. Then, because she had gone to law school with the intention of working in public policy, she responded to an ad for a research position at the Center for Law and Social Policy (CLASP). The project was to determine whether enough need existed to hire a full-time attorney in the area of women's legal rights.

Greenberger says she loves to tell the story: "The reason they were even looking for someone to employ was because the secretaries in the office demanded that this all-male public interest group look at women's rights issues along with all the other things they were doing. So it was actually women who were in the support staff who were responsible for my job, and who, in fact, interviewed me."

The need was determined, and Greenberger was hired by CLASP as their attorney on women's rights. "There were other job possibilities," she clarifies, "but I explicitly chose women's rights because I cared about the issues then as I do now. The whole notion of women's rights was just in its infancy. In law school, there was no such label, so I certainly did not have the level of expertise to define what they all were. I remember tremendous debates about whether sexual harassment was sexual discrimination."

So it was that the NWLC, which Greenberger founded in 1981, grew and developed out of the original Women's Rights Project of CLASP, which she had launched in 1972. For more than twenty years, the center has litigated groundbreaking cases and filed briefs in landmark Supreme Court decisions; advocated before state and federal policymakers to shape legislation and policies affecting women's lives; and educated the public about issues central to women.

In contrast with traditional law firms, where attorneys are in competition with each other and work in relative isolation, the NWLC is focused on one issue—the advancement and protection of women's rights. This central mission requires attorneys to collaborate with each other and to see their role as litigators in combination with policy strategists.

An Early Maverick

"The notion of teamwork and bringing people together in consensus is paramount," says Nancy Duff Campbell, NYLC's copresident with Marcia Greenberger. "But the danger is that you can be too consensus-oriented and end up being wishy-washy and never reach consensus. So you have to articulate as strongly as possible your own vision about an issue in a way that enables others to push for it too, even, if possible, in different ways."

But the danger is that you can be too consensus-oriented and end up being wishy-washy and never reach consensus.

Campbell and Greenberger have worked together from the early days of the Women's Rights Project at CLASP. Like Greenberger, Campbell grew up in a family with a strong sense of social justice, but in a conservative community in Indianapolis. Republican Party affiliation was so much the order of the day that, spotting her high-school history teacher at a rally for John F. Kennedy, she was shocked that somebody she knew was actually a Democrat. "I was always the kid who sort of left the room during the school prayer and wondered if I were weird," Campbell says.

For a grade-school essay contest, she wrote that she wanted to be a lawyer in order "'to better the rights of people.' I included racial minorities, and my teacher was shocked that a twelve-year-old in the fifties would be aware of that. But again, I saw in my community that it was lawyers who were fighting for these kinds of things. I was too young to have watched the fall of Joe McCarthy, but something must have impressed me about lawyers standing for Constitutional rights."

As a student at Barnard College, Campbell was convinced that she wanted to be a lawyer, and she was surrounded by people who "thought the same way." Phoebe Morrison, a judge who taught government and politics "had the foresight to see the role that women could play both as lawyers and social change agents, and she was always encouraging us," Campbell recalls.

How she would use her law degree was never a question for Campbell. "I was lucky that legal services programs were just starting. I came to Washington at the right time to find a job in the area I liked and wanted to stay in. I would be the last person to say that a young woman today should think first about dedicating herself to a professional career in women's rights. What's so exciting is that women have many ways of becoming leaders in all careers, and then can be a leader for women in that field and outside of it."

At the same time, Campbell is constantly aware of the urgent agenda that remains to be completed for women and children, and she hopes that her generation of committed women has given enough attention to replacing themselves.

Passing the Torch

I'm not certain that young women realize how far we've gone in women's rights in a short period of time.

This is why Brooksley Born, chair of the board of the Women's Law Center, accepts invitations to speak at law schools about the need for public service. "I'm not certain," she says, "that young women realize how far we've gone in women's rights in a short period of time, and how much more needs to be done—how vigilant one must be to protect what's been achieved!"

Her mother's best friend from college, an attorney with the California Attorney General's Office and later the director of the Port of San Francisco, helped Born to see that it was "okay to be a woman lawyer." Born was graduated from Stanford Law School in 1964, one of only four women in a class of 165. She was first in the class and president of the law review.

After a one-year clerkship on the U.S. Court of Appeals for the District of Columbia circuit, she joined the firm of Arnold & Porter, whose record of pro bono work attracted her. Washington was also a good place for women lawyers in the sixties, because the federal government, unlike the private sector, was hiring relatively large numbers of women. Born's first public interest was prisoners' rights and the rights of the mentally ill. But the more she juggled child care and career, the more strongly she became drawn to women's issues; she believed, too, that she owed something to younger women lawyers and to women in general.

Born's commitment deepened when she and Marna Tucker designed "Women and the Law," a course they taught at Catholic University and Georgetown. "By reading the cases on sex discrimination," Born recalls, "I realized from a lawyer's point of view how very, very few rights women had under the law and how discriminated against they were by the law at that time."

This understanding propelled her to begin speaking to groups throughout Washington on the topic of women's rights and the need for the ERA. At the same time, she was participating in the collective effort to start the WLDF and the NWLC.

"Now I'm getting to a stage in my life where I welcome younger people coming along to take up the cudgels," Born says. "I don't want to say there's a limited amount that any one generation can contribute, but I worry that so many of us are of the same age. We started when we were in our twenties and early thirties, and have continued

. . . but maybe we didn't do as good a job as we could have bringing along the younger generation and putting them in positions of responsibility.

on, but maybe we didn't do as good a job as we could have bringing along the younger generation and putting them in positions of responsibility. My age group looked for what had to be done and created the setting in which we could do the jobs."

Generational Differences

Caithlin Donnell, a Denver attorney who is over 50, offers another perspective on women lawyers of her age. "I really don't think my generation thought our responsibility was to change the law or mold it in a way better for women. I was a minority voice on that issue. Women were just trying to make it and get ahead. They were more concerned about networking and acquiring political power to be elevated as judges." Donnell was the driving force that started the Colorado Women's Bar Association (CWBA) in 1978, despite the opposition of some peers who thought *women's* was too confrontational a word to have in the title. The CWBA was a "place where women [attorneys] could feel comfortable and not so isolated," Donnell says. "They could get together to talk about their perspectives and not feel so marginal."

After law school, Donnell's first job was as an assistant deputy district attorney in Denver; she went on to work as an assistant United States Attorney, then as Acting U.S. Attorney. When she left that position, she joined a small firm and then moved on with an associate to create a women's law firm in Denver.

From her firsthand experience, she characterizes the partnership in a traditional law firm as a "complex dynamic where partners

It was [perceived as] threatening when I received flowers or awards. are really competitors; nowhere in your professional life are you without competition. You come back from a trial and just want to be comfortable and chat, but success is met with ambivalent messages. It was [perceived as] threatening when I received flowers or awards." Donnell started her own firm partly so that its partners could enjoy a more relaxed environment and "let their hair down and celebrate each other's successes."

After years of practicing as a tough litigator, she decided to turn her energies elsewhere. "The cost of winning is so extraordinary," she says, "that now I want time to be more reflective about the state of the legal profession and not go into battle every day." What she calls the "current lack of civility" in the practice of law is also distressing to her. "Everybody is scrambling now. Partners are firing lawyers that they have worked with forever. The legal profession is just not as attractive to me as it once was."

The Money Gap

Donnell was key to a study undertaken in 1993 that located revealing differences in the average annual incomes of male and female Colorado attorneys. Analyzing the data, she concluded that for women the "glass ceiling occurs at the very beginning. There's a gap in the compensation between men and women the first year out of law school, and that's before they have even had an opportunity to build up a client base. And we haven't yet faced that issue in the profession."

While law firms seem to offer opportunities to young female attorneys, women generally are not able to build a strong client base as quickly as men. Donnell wants to pursue more qualitative studies by "getting inside law firms to see how we stratify the profession based on gender, and to see how and why decisions are made, and by whom." The odds of being successful at this are daunting. Asked how she would describe herself as a leader, Caithlin Donnell says, "I never considered myself a leader when I was the Acting U.S. Attorney, but I always do when I'm moving against the status quo, and if others are interested in following."

Partnership Track

One lawyer who has benefited from Donnell's efforts to elevate women in the legal profession is Kathleen Ann Odel, a partner with Sherman & Howard LLC, a Denver law firm. At the age of 37 in 1995, Odel was given an award designated for a Denver attorney under the age of 40 who combines professional excellence "with creative civic, cultural, educational, and charitable leadership. . . ." While senior women attorneys had been among the only females in their law school, she says that her generation of students "may have been arrogant," and felt cushioned against gender discrimination because their law school classes had almost male/female parity. "We didn't hit problems until we realized how hard it was to make partner," she explains.

She found it singularly uninspiring when, as a new associate, she was invited to lunch by women who had been practicing law for a number of years. "They wanted to pass on their knowledge, which . . . amounted to 'Watch your backside or you'll be screwed.'"

They wanted to pass on their knowledge, which . . . amounted to 'Watch your backside or you'll be screwed.'

Odel thinks it is surprising that younger women attorneys are often criticized for self-interest. Only three of the twenty attorneys who comprise the present board of directors of the CWBA are older than forty years, she notes. This fact is especially significant to her because the major work of the CWBA is to "provide legal services to women and to the underrepresented." The organization raises funds for Safehouse, a shelter for battered women, educates lawyers about restraining orders for abusive spouses, and offers classes for women on divorce process.

Odel says she is the "happiest lawyer in America. I wouldn't feel like a complete human being if I couldn't be involved in community service and pro bono work. I can't imagine a man or a woman wanting to devote every waking moment to the law to the detriment of their life as a whole."

But the reality is that associates in large firms do not generally have the latitude to pursue the kind of civic activities they prefer.

In general, law firms perceive community service as a luxury unless it helps the bottom line and enhances the firm's image. Their first priority is usually to gain some solid footing on a partnership track. An attorney's competency, productivity, and professionalism are typically measured by billable hours and rainmaking, that is, by the business she brings into the firm. In general, law firms perceive community service as a luxury unless it helps the bottom line and enhances the firm's image.

Odel is optimistic that women are making positive changes in the culture of law firms by inventing new rules about community service and creating fresh ways of being rainmakers. "It's slowly hitting home," she observes, "that playing golf on Friday afternoons is not the only way of bringing in clients. And a woman's way is to focus on the community and her professional development. Holding out a carrot and a stick, when the carrot is the almighty dollar, is not enough anymore," she says.

Striking a note somewhere between pride and humor, Odel says she has seen subtle changes in law firm culture in the fifteen years she has been with Sherman & Howard. "It's a joke that my women colleagues laugh about, but we all know that women practice law completely different from men. It's kinder and gentler, not as much screaming and yelling . . . not as much posturing . . . not so much a do-or-die situation, but rather how do we get out of this with the least injury to everyone. That's a bonus that women bring to the legal profession."

She describes a telling scenario: "It used to be if men won a hearing or even the simplest motion, they would do laps around the office and stop in doorways. But women could win a case and you'd never know about it. So some of us got together and pointed this out. And now women are more self-promoting, and men do it less. It's more even now."

Entrepreneurial Lawyers

Impatient with the slow pace of change, many women have left traditional law firms to embark on other enterprises. Holiday Walsh left a law firm where the chief partner walked around the office wearing a cowboy hat with a snake wrapped around the crown. But her decision was not motivated, she clarifies, by a desire for civilities; she started a law firm in San Francisco with two friends, a woman and a man, because she wanted to be more independent and make her own choices. She was determined to formulate her own policies and bring together hardworking people with similar philosophies. "In fact," Walsh says, "my self-image has evolved to practicing attorney/small business owner."

Shortly after Allswang, Smith, & Walsh opened their door, Holiday Walsh noted that other women in the Bay area were leaving larger firms to start their own businesses as sole practitioners or in groups. Some were pursuing areas of the law that historically, Walsh says, had been dominated by male practitioners, such as business and commercial litigation. She has learned that when women are pioneers in areas not traditional to them, networking is always vital; she describes how she decided to approach Karen D. Kadushin, then president of the San Francisco Bar Association, and propose the creation of a subcommittee on Women Owned Law Firms (WOLF).

Kadushin welcomed her proposal, and the first project of the new committee was to compile the WOLF Directory, a listing of more than two hundred women-owned firms within seven counties of the San Francisco area. As a result, an important network is developing in San Francisco. Women attorneys are taking advantage of their growing numbers by making referrals to each other, and their activity is changing the traditional structure and attitudes of the profession.

The Joy of Trout Fishing

Karen Kadushin was enthusiastic about Walsh's proposal for WOLF because she, too, had once practiced in her own law firm. "When the idea came up, I said yes and it was established by fiat," Kadushin confirms. "As a leader in an organization you need to take advantage of your ability to focus the efforts of an organization. I don't shirk from using the word power. It's there and it's exciting to have, and

Power is having the ability to change people's minds and actions, and that's very positive.

the potential for using it to make a difference is something that I want to exercise as long as I am able. Power is having the ability to change people's minds and actions, and that's very positive."

Karen Kadushin started classes at Golden Gate Law School at age 29 in 1974. She had worked in theater production and says by that time she knew herself very well. "I was creative but had had people telling me what to do for a long time. I knew I wanted to be in a profession that had longevity, intellectual challenge, and would allow me control over my environment."

After graduation, Kadushin went trout fishing instead of concentrating on getting job interviews. One day she received an urgent phone call from an attorney in private practice. "I was in jeans and had salmon eggs smeared all over me, and said I at least needed time to change clothes. But she said to come as I was because she didn't have time to waste." Within a short time, Kadushin was a partner with Gloria Richmond in Richmond & Kadushin. When they split, she maintained her own independent practice for five years before opening Kadushin Fancher Wickland.

I was in jeans and had salmon eggs smeared all over me, and said I at least needed time to change clothes. But she said to come as I was because she didn't have time to waste.

"It was always critical for me to be my own boss," she says. "I would never put myself in the position of starting up the law firm ladder and in seven years hoping to make partner. I started my own firm because I was clear about who I am, and that I would never be able to tolerate people telling me who my secretary was or who my clients would be. I live to the perimeters of my physical environment. I don't live internally; I live externally, so people I'm around affect me tremendously."

Rainmaking Advice

Whether they work in firms or on their own, women attorneys still are considered to be less effective rainmakers than men, but that image is changing. "It's not that young women can't make rain," Kadushin says, "but that women make rain differently and have to focus on where business is for them. Men relate more easily to men. If women connect with women, they bring business into the firm. The connections that women make are different. They talk about family and personal interests. So women have to be creative and find a way that feels right for them."

A woman is being severely limited, Kadushin believes, if the law firm she works for does not permit her the latitude to focus on the civic projects or leisure-time activities that she cares most about. "You are the best person to star in your own life, and you can't get ahead by imitating someone else. All the activities I have liked have made business for me because they make me look competent. If you have to be involved in activities you don't like, then you don't look successful and they won't make business for you."

You are the best person to star in your own life, and you can't get ahead by imitating someone else.

Kadushin says she developed her family law practice by being very active in the San Francisco Bar Association. Beginning in 1979, she served on a variety of its committees and was appointed to a seat on the association's board of directors; she became its president in 1993. "I made myself known by doing well in highly visible jobs, so then other attorneys learned what I did and sent me clients. It was all very deliberate on my part."

Kadushin gave up her lucrative practice in 1995 and became Dean of the Monterey College of Law. She was ready for "something less confrontational," but wanted to use the skills she had acquired. "It's a tremendous strain to run a family law office. I was tired of taking things apart and wanted to put things together. I wanted to do something that was more congruent with my personality traits. Now I feel as if I've died and gone to heaven."

She likes being in leadership positions, she says, because she can make a difference. Kadushin believes it is crucial for women to *act* on behalf of women and encourage them to develop their own goals. A top priority for her as dean is to attract more nonwhite students in order to reflect the diversity of the community. "As dean I can say, I want more effort in recruiting in nonwhite communities. I want to visit nonwhite schools and talk in assemblies. And when nonwhite students come on campus, I want more attention paid to their financial planning so we can see what we need to do to bring them in here. That's using leadership and power, and it's easy enough to do."

Women are culturalized to please, but that makes us good negotiators because we get to the hidden agenda.

"Women bring an extraordinary panoply of skills and talents to the law that are underdeveloped in men by virtue of how we were raised," Kadushin believes. "Women are culturalized to please, but that makes us good negotiators because we get to the hidden agenda. Men are not too reliant on the perception of others." As for the future, she notes that across the country, criminal and civil courts continue to be backed up with cases; she predicts that the skills of keen negotiators will therefore be increasingly valued, because a mediation process is far faster and cheaper than going to trial.

2100 Billable Hours

Leaving a large law firm in Los Angeles in 1984 to become an "entrepreneurial businesswoman in the practice of law" was also a logical choice for Marcia C. Todhunter. "The trend was just beginning that if the law firm wasn't your life, you were questioned whether you were sufficiently committed to be a partner," Todhunter asserts. "I was interested in having a substantial other part of life, and it became clear that I wasn't going to be able to explore other areas and be successful in a large law firm. I saw the writing on the wall."

Todhunter's major community interest was juvenile delinquency, not the most promising field for potential rainmaking. "No way was I going to bring in big corporate and banking clients by doing that kind of work," she laughs. "I wasn't interested in giving my free time to do things that were determined by others as a way to bring in money. Other lawyers do that, but I really wanted to ful-

fill an avocation, and my passion was juvenile delinquency."
Although she was single at the time, Todhunter wanted a family
life and could not imagine arranging it around 2100 billable hours.
(This was the direction she chose, but the point must be made that
thousands of women lawyers thrive on doing it.)

When she first went out on her own, Todhunter worked in San
Francisco for a nonprofit foundation on juvenile delinquency and
spent two days a week in her private practice, where she specialized in bankruptcy law. Her practice grew, and she married and
had children, but she eventually felt isolated as a sole practitioner.
Her daily experiences differed from those of women in law firms
and from the men in private practice who had offices in her suite,
and she wanted to talk with other entrepreneurial business women
in the practice of law. With a bit of research, in 1992 she identified
one thousand women lawyers in the San Francisco Bar Association
who were sole practitioners and invited them to a luncheon meeting. Expecting perhaps thirty to respond, she was thrilled when
150 women attended. Since then, the Women's Lawyers Network
has been meeting every month and, among their projects, has published a network directory.

Sole Practitioners and Trade-Offs

Sole practitioners have very particular issues to discuss, and one of
the most important is rainmaking. "If you are not getting the clients,
no one is bringing them to you," Todhunter says. Collecting delin-
quent fees is also a special problem for sole practitioners with no business apparatus to insulate them, for when sizable clients fail to pay,
the firm is far more vulnerable than a larger enterprise with a broader
client base and a number of attorneys. Similarly, in large law firms,
such other crucial nonlegal work as hiring personnel and keeping
track of malpractice insurance are decisions made and implemented
by management committees. And when needed, professional guidance on a specific legal problem may be only an office away.

These trade-offs are minor to Todhunter when compared with
the qualities she treasures about her work. Practicing in her own
law office in San Mateo, she makes lifestyle choices without concern about how she will be judged. She drives an eight-year-old

car, but does not have to suffer "client development" dinners. "Instead of spending my extra time doing volunteer work that is not of interest to me, I'm president of the PTA and room mom for my two children," she explains. "Neither one of those would be possible if I were expected to bring in business and bill 2100 hours. Working for a large law firm, I wouldn't be able to do motherhood the way I want to do it. I'd be talking about nannies and help."

Practicing Law Inside the Corporation

Women who work in corporate law departments are also influencing the habits of the legal profession. In a 1995 study for the *National Law Journal*, Ann Davis concluded that in the past twenty-five years women "who felt undervalued or found the [law firm] culture inhospitable have flocked to in-house legal departments." One of these women is M. Caroline Turner, vice president and general counsel, Coors Brewing Company, who was a partner in a Denver law firm specializing in securities law and corporate transactions when she left in 1986 to join Coors.

I knew I'd miss the juice of closing a big deal and the intellectual stimulation, but my life was short on human values.

"I was making a difference in what I was doing at the firm, but I was a single mother, and time pressures made it impossible to carry out my responsibilities to my family and have a life. I knew I'd miss the juice of closing a big deal and the intellectual stimulation, but my life was short on human values," Turner says. "I was neglecting the children and not taking care of my health. I couldn't see a driving reason to keep doing what I was doing."

The office of general counsel did not exist at Coors when Turner was hired as its director of legal affairs. It was a position that was below officer rank, so when she left the law firm she was giving up a beautifully furnished corner office with a view for a middle-level job, a much lower salary, and a room with barely a window. But her first perk was in knowing that her colleagues valued and cared about her counsel in a way that had been missing in the law firm.

"At first, the problems were not as sophisticated and didn't require a lot of brainpower, yet I had a sense of making a difference for the internal client that was fulfilling. But it took me a long time to show them what needed to be done. I took a company that did not know how to use lawyers and built a highly functioning, fully functioning legal department. I help frame business decisions and help support where the company wants to go, and I watch its hindside."

Fifteen years ago, going in-house was considered a second-class route for attorneys, Turner recalls. Today in-house counsel is a coveted, challenging position. "In-house lawyers are business people who bring legal training to their decisions," Turner says, "whereas outside lawyers in private practice are legal experts first. We don't have legal problems; we have business problems with legal aspects to them. It's a different perspective today that makes this work so rewarding. It's much different from having a narrow specialty; it's more humbling and richer."

According to the ABA, "In 1995, 528 female general counsels were members of the American Corporate Counsel Association, up from 444 in the prior year. . . . Despite the many advantages of the corporate law environment, female corporate counsels continue to face inequities in both promotion and pay."

Despite the many advantages of the corporate law environment, female corporate counsels continue to face inequities in both promotion and pay.

Turner points out that her title is *vice president and general counsel*, not *executive vice president*. "But I value what I have accomplished because of my leadership. I knighted myself; no one knighted me. Value comes from inside more than outside, so I'm not making executive vice president a priority goal to fight for."

Weighing Corporate Advantages

Helen C. Pudlin weighed her decision in 1989 before she left a partnership with Ballard, Spahr, Andrews, & Ingersoll, a prestigious Philadelphia law firm, to become general counsel for Provident National Bank, which she had served as outside counsel. She

To be afforded the opportunity to be general counsel is a terrific experience.

wondered if she would miss the diversity of private practice and the excitement of being a trial attorney. Now as vice president and general counsel of PNC Bank Corp. she says, "I don't miss being a litigator at all. It's dynamic and interesting to work with multiple constituencies and to be a part of a very vibrant business. To be afforded the opportunity to be general counsel is a terrific experience."

With a panoramic view of Pittsburgh's rivers and hills behind her, Pudlin talks about the differences between outside and in-house corporate counsel and why she likes her present position. As outside counsel, "you are given a specific question or project and asked to come back with a response, and then someone takes it from there," Pudlin says: "You give advice and don't know what happens to it. For a person who likes being a generalist and a counselor in the broadest sense and wants to have a broader context, then the place to find that now is in a corporate or institutional legal department as opposed to a law firm."

From her experience with both law firms and corporations, Pudlin understands the level of frustration women often experience in law firms as opposed to corporate law departments. "It's not difficult, assuming you have a level of competence, to become a partner in a law firm," she contends, "because lawyers are judged on their analytical ability and communication skills. But to cross the line into a leadership position in a law firm more often than not requires a tremendous amount of business generation." As a result, she says, very competent women who made partner easily and were accustomed to being highly successful academically may no longer see a correlation between how competent they are and the success they achieve in moving up the ladder.

"Women reach a wall and are frustrated by not being able to run a department or to get the top level of compensation," Pudlin says. Consequently, many transfer to the corporate world because they can be in leadership positions and flourish as very influential lawyers. And without having the pressure of rainmaking since the business they serve is the corporation, they can devote their talent to what they are most valuable at: applying their expertise as lawyers.

A Delicate Line

Not only are in-house lawyers spared the hours required for rain-making activities, but attorneys generally encounter a collegial atmosphere within corporate legal departments because its members are focused on working together for a common client. "In a law firm the competition never stops," Pudlin says. "Where business generation is very important, lawyers become proprietary about their clients because they want to be perceived as indispensable." The lawyers who are often most successful in corporate legal departments enjoy working with interdisciplinary teams, a mode that Pudlin notes is particularly gratifying to many women.

She cautions that women in corporations still have to be aware that they walk a more "delicate line than men" in monitoring their management style. "Women are perceived as being too assertive when they are very assertive, and if they are not assertive, as not being tough enough," she advises. "So I try to be an observer of myself. Getting right to the right line is much more an issue for women than for men. Men don't have to deal with issues of toughness versus assertiveness. I don't think they think about it all that much."

> *Women are perceived as being too assertive when they are very assertive, and if they are not assertive, as not being tough enough.*

Corporate Lawyers Are Players

Only eight years after she graduated from New York University School of Law, Teveia Rose Barnes made a conscious decision to leave a New York law firm for the world of corporate counsel. She often worked around the clock, and it was not unusual for her husband to bring a new set of underwear in a paper bag to her at the office. She went in-house with the Bank of America National Trust and Savings Association, where she is now associate general counsel and senior vice president. She is one of six who report directly to the firm's general counsel and is responsible for managing fifty attorneys. "I still have to work all-nighters," she says, "but not as many nor as frequently."

Barnes thrives on knowing the client and feeling the "closeness of being a member of the business team. So I'm more involved with the business transactions, but also with policy development and strategic planning. I'm a player in that I'm a part of a team that puts that together." In the past, lawyers were called upon to answer "discrete questions," Barnes says, "but now we come in earlier in the planning stages, and so we make a difference." She likes having a sense of the "big picture and really being a part of the business."

Corporate attorneys have another asset. By having the authority to hire outside counsel, they have the opportunity to give business to women attorneys and to withdraw it from firms that do not sufficiently promote women.

For example, Teveia Barnes was on the task force that designed the diversity initiative for Bank of America. She is particularly sensitive to diversity issues regarding women and minorities. "More and more corporations are learning that diversity in business is critical as we go to workforce 2000," she says. Barnes stresses that a diverse workforce is crucial if businesses are to come up with new products and new services to meet a multitude of customers' requirements.

For this reason, corporations are learning that it is in their best interest if their own vendors, including lawyers and accountants, are also diverse. "If we are going into a corporation that sells washing machines and therefore has product liability, we are not going to risk going before a diverse jury with an all-white legal team," Barnes explains. "Or if we are developing a product that we want to sell globally, I want a law firm that has a diverse team of lawyers who will help me to develop a better product. If a law firm hasn't put together a diverse team, I don't have time for them to get it together. I may call on them once in a while as a backup, but they are not going to be my primary providers working on big deals."

Conserving Clout

"Within my organization there are so many levels above me that I wouldn't want anyone to think that you 'make it' where I am. I'm only halfway there," Barnes says. But no matter what her position is within the corporate structure, she volunteers, she would "still say the same things, to the extent that anyone would listen. I haven't really changed my position; we all have to state our conscience no matter where we are in the food chain, but as I've moved up

I'm more comfortable taking risks. . . . I don't fight every battle because I want to be around to fight the next really big one.

the corporate ladder, I'm more comfortable taking risks. . . . I don't fight every battle because I want to be around to fight the next really big one."

The Qualities That Count

"To be a good advocate, you have to work within the confines of your own personality as opposed to trying to be something that you are not," says Jean Kneale, a Miami attorney with Hicks, Anderson, Blum, P.A. When she started practicing law eleven years ago, she discovered quickly that she had a better rapport with clients, colleagues, and judges when she acted according to her own temperament rather than assuming a stance of being confrontational and aggressive. Nonetheless, certain qualities are important to cultivate, according to Mary C. Cranston, a highly visible antitrust attorney and a partner with Pillsbury Madison & Sutro LLP, a San Francisco firm with offices in other U.S. cities, plus Tokyo and Hong Kong. "Real discrimination, subtle and otherwise, is out there, which makes it tougher for women than for men," Cranston says. "But a woman is able to make it if she has a proactive attitude, high energy, and a strong sense of being responsible for making a difference in her life wherever she is." She remarks that it can become a self-fulfilling prophecy if a woman thinks that others in the law firm are trying to block her or will not help; as in so many situations, assuming the good will of colleagues will often elicit it.

"You have to start from inside yourself, and think about what really attracts you about your career, and then take steps in that direction by seeing yourself doing those things," Cranston asserts. Describing her early work, she says she knew she had to create her own model of a woman as lead lawyer in important antitrust cases, for when she began she had never seen a woman in such a role. She kept visualizing herself as a smart, effective antitrust litigator so that she would have "an image, a goal to move toward."

Bias toward women is a factor in law firms. That's there and not in your control. But what is in your control is your own reaction to it.

"Bias toward women is a factor in law firms. That's there and not in your control. But what is in your control," she elaborates, "is your own reaction to it. You have to see yourself doing what you need to do, and then bias becomes a nonoperating principle for you."

Cranston was commission liaison representing large law firms for the 1995 ABA Report on the Status of Women. She, too, is optimistic that women will increasingly flourish within the next ten years in the legal profession because their sheer numbers are increasing so quickly.

If the 1990s counterpart of ten-year-old Stephanie Domitrovich were to drop in on a courtroom trial today, it's entirely likely that the judge who notes her presence will be a woman.

Chapter Four

Women in Journalism:
"Hire This Girl"

The words and voices of women in print and broadcast journalism are part of our daily lives. They are often inseparable from our homespun rituals: Sunday brunch with Cokie Roberts; early evening traffic jams with Nina Totenberg; coffee on the run with Ellen Goodman and the *Boston Globe,* or Gwen Ifill talking politics on *Today.* All are pioneers in their fields, and while they acknowledge that their work and their visibility make them role models and opinion makers, all are vividly aware that their prominence does not give them the power to influence the major policy decisions of their employers. It is a further paradox that to get where they are, many of these journalists had to resist being idealized and "protected" by their employers as too innocent and pure to cover hard news.

No Alternative to Courage

Nina Totenberg, legal affairs correspondent for National Public Radio (NPR), makes a distinction between her highly visible—and highly audible—image and her modest perception of her work. In answer to my question, "Do you consider yourself to be a leader?" the first response was the familiar Totenberg laugh and then: "No, not really. I'm not in a management position. I may be a role model to some people, but I'm not really a leader because I'm not affiliated with any cause, particularly. In fact, I scrupulously avoid it, other than things involving reporters' rights and things of that sort.

I'm not identified with any political party. I'm a registered independent. So my job is not a leadership job. It's an information job." As a role model, Totenberg inspires many young women to emulate her pioneering investigative reporting and her persistence in the face of pressure to stay away from conflict and controversy.

Totenberg started out writing fashion and recipes for the women's page of the *Record American* in Boston. To gain experience, she worked a double shift at night, covering the crime beat and school committees. Only one woman at the paper wrote hard news, and she was a beacon for Totenberg. "I didn't know her at all because she wasn't even in the same room, but she was what I aspired to be—somebody who didn't have to do recipes and fashions."

The year was 1965, the beginning of the sexual revolution, and contraceptives were still illegal in some states. Totenberg wanted to write on an issue that would have a life outside of the women's pages, so she did the groundwork for an extended story on the real—as opposed to the annunciated—policies regarding birth control in Massachusetts. What was it really like to have contraceptive counseling on New England college campuses? First, she made appointments at various college clinics by saying that she was worried about becoming pregnant. Then she unveiled her plan in a memo to the paper's managing editor.

"His name was Eddie Holland, and he was a very nice man," Totenberg remembers. "He said, 'Nina, are you a virgin?' And I said yes. Then he said, 'I can't let you do this. Have you ever had an internal examination?' I said no. He said again, 'I can't let you do this.' And that was the end of the discussion."

Totenberg knew better at the time than to try to force the issue: Despite her creativity and her daring, her status, her gender, and her presumed innocence were too daunting for her boss's courtly sensibility. Thirty years later, in October 1991, Totenberg commanded the status and the expertise to force one of the decade's biggest stories into the spotlight of international attention. As legal affairs correspondent for NPR, she revealed that the Senate Judiciary Committee had set aside allegations regarding sexual harassment against Judge Clarence Thomas made by Professor Anita Hill at the time of his confirmation hearings for the United States Supreme Court.

"People commend me for my courage, and I very much appreciate it, but I really don't think I had any alternative," Totenberg says. "It's like being in a room with somebody who's trying to kill you, and you know that they're not going to let you out alive. You have

People commend me for my courage, and I very much appreciate it, but I really don't think I had any alternative.

only one thing to do, and that's to try to get out! This was really no different. I was a reporter, and this was a big story. I did everything I knew to check it out. The woman was a credible witness. I had corroborating evidence, to some extent. I couldn't bury the story, not if I'm a decent reporter. . . . So I did the story, and then I get attacked for it, and so what do I do? I have to stand up for myself and for my story, and then I get subpoenaed. No reporter worth his or her salt is going to give away their sources. There really weren't any alternatives! It was very scary. It was very intimidating, but it was really part of my job not to let myself be intimidated."

Between You and You

Ellen Goodman, Pulitzer Prize–winning syndicated columnist, stirs up a good deal of public dialogue with her writing. Asked if she considers herself a leader, she says: "I consider myself to be a writer and an observer, and my own definition of leadership is more active than contemplative. If you put up a board of little pictures and you had three congresswomen, the head of a social activist group, a supreme court justice, and two journalists and said, 'Which are the leaders?' the journalist wouldn't pop up on my screen first."

Goodman says Ronald Reagan may have reclassified ketchup as a condiment in school lunches—it had been classified as a vegetable—because of pressure from many journalists, but that she alone cannot affect a public policy vote on Tuesday by whatever she has written on Monday. "Now certainly there are some journalists who go back and forth between running for office and being columnists, but it's something I have grave doubts about," she observes dryly.

*W*riting is just plain thinking and that's why I don't think of it as leading.

Goodman describes writing as a solitary, internal, and reflective experience, which makes it much different from politicking. "The process of writing is not the process of *leading* so much as it is the process of thinking things through," she ponders. "Journalism is less isolating than writing fiction or poetry, but when you are actually working something out, you put the bell jar over your own head and it's between you and you. Writing is just plain thinking and that's why I don't think of it as leading."

Shifting to a more playful tone, she adds: "But when you tell people what you think, you want to be very sure you don't open the paper the next day and say, 'What asshole wrote that?' and that you don't still think it six weeks later!"

Revisiting Issues

Goodman says she hopes to make a difference by inspiring readers to "turn an issue around and look at it from another viewpoint." She considers it "a wimp-out" to not tell them what she thinks, and she often revisits the questions in her columns, each time, she hopes, from a deeper perspective.

Over the past few years, the subject of biomedical ethics has been the focus of more than twenty of her columns. "Those are hard questions for me and everybody. You're trying to figure out for yourself as well as others what we should do about physician-assisted suicide. That's no day at the beach. Each time I probe a little differently. Most people don't have time in their own life to talk to twelve bioethicists, so they're interested in some guidance through some very, very thorny stuff. And you cannot end by just saying 'This situation bears watching.' But I'm not hitting people over the head with what I think. I'm trying to carry them through a thought process to where I am. Even if they don't agree with me then, they have some respect for how I got there."

Expanding News

Goodman was hired as a researcher at *Newsweek* just prior to the passage of the Civil Rights Act of 1964, when it was still legal to discriminate against women. All the magazine's writers were men, and all the researchers were women. "That's just the way it was," she shrugs. "We were conscious of what we would now call sex discrimination, but we didn't have a name for it; it was just the way things were."

> *We were conscious of what we would now call sex discrimination, but we didn't have a name for it; it was just the way things were.*

Her second job was at the *Detroit Free Press*, at a time when city rooms across the country were opening up to women. "Without forming a monolith," she says that women "brought into public dialogue a whole lot of issues that were falsely excluded and considered to be unimportant. Abortion wasn't on the editorial page and the front pages then. But as society changed and women were part of that change, the issues that were always around them moved into visibility, and so did their bylines; so did they. It all happened together."

While this new freedom was exhilarating, she notes, it also created new problems—which still exist—for journalists who are women. The tension is in balancing their individual opinions while writing and talking about the traditional subjects of gender: "We represent the whole range of opinions and points of view. We're pro-life, pro-choice, conservative, and liberal. A definitive *woman's voice* is impossible to define. We cannot be lined up, no matter how some people might like to do that," she points out.

"Women have brought originality, range, and flexibility to print and broadcast journalism: a certain set of concerns having to do with relationships, connections, and community. But we also have a whole set of journalistic values that are gender neutral, and which we're likely to be criticized for—all the reasons that make journalists unpopular." Goodman is firmly convinced that women in journalism, whatever their differences, share a legacy that claims all of life is worth writing about.

A Family of Leaders

Cokie Roberts, anchor of the ABC news program *This Week* and an analyst for NPR in Washington, says the main reason she has thought of herself as a pioneer "has to do as much as anything with the juggling act. It's not just achieving something that's public. It's having done it while raising a family and keeping a marriage."

For her the first priority of reporters and commentators is to dispense information. "There's always a hesitancy on our parts to see ourselves as players rather than observers," she says.

There's always a hesitancy on our parts to see ourselves as players rather than observers.

Roberts measures herself against the achievements of her mother Lindy Boggs, ambassador to the Vatican and retired member of the U.S. Congress, and her sister Barbara, now deceased, once mayor of Princeton. Contrasting political leadership with news commentary, she observes: "A leader has a firm set of beliefs and is able to articulate them and try to convince people to follow her. She also knows when to moderate them to get something done but knows beyond which point she will not be pushed," she says. "I think that certainly not me alone, but I and others like me, who were considered sort of congressional experts talking about the refusal of Congress to debate the Persian Gulf War, made a difference in getting Congress to do it. But I can't point to something the way my mother or my sister could, and say I made that women's shelter happen, or I got that red light up there that stopped children from getting killed on that corner, or I got 2,000 veterans their benefits today."

She agrees that certain issues of social conscience or public morality are more likely to engage women journalists than men. Women care about children's health and education, human rights, poverty, and employment. Without apology or self-righteousness, she says, "I think all of the things we always say that women bring are true—a sense of compassion and concern about other people. One of the reasons I'm always on a soapbox about a diverse newsroom is that women are more interested in issues that concern families and children. We just are. On an off day when no news is breaking, we are much more likely to do a story about how older women in housing projects have taken over the day care of the children so that the younger women can go to work. A man is just never going to think that up."

"Our great strength is our long view of the world," she says. "What men do is get up every day fresh and fight the next game, war, whatever. And that is their great strength. They do it very well, and our great strength is to say, 'Hold on a minute. How is this effective in the long term? What does this mean for the greater community? What does this mean for the people who are old and who we are caring for? The people who are being born who we are caring for?'

Our great strength is to say, 'Hold on a minute. How is this effective in the long term? . . . '

"I always think about living in Greece for four years and going to a little museum in Marathon that has artifacts from about seven thousand years ago. And you look in those cases and see needles, buttons, mirrors, frying pans, jewelry, containers for make up; and then there are altars, bows, and arrows. So the men have nothing to identify with unless they are priests or warriors. But women can open these cases even today and use any of those things. Now that is the continuum, and I worried horribly that we might lose it. But I really have great faith in young women. When my sister died, my daughter, who was a student at Princeton at the time, was there taking care of her every day, as were a couple of other kids. I think they have 'got it.'"

As women continue to gain authority in the media, many use their clout on behalf of younger women because they remember how few women were there for them. Roberts remembers when women were told that their voices were not authoritative enough for radio. Overt discrimination has changed, not only legally, she says, but "in the hearts and minds of those who hire at entry level." But it is still necessary, she says, "to continue to fight for younger women. As you get older and achieve power within your institution, then it's up to you to have the conversation with the male bosses and say, 'Come on, why isn't she moving up? Why did you promote him over her?'"

The continual need to ask this question impels her to offer a poignant insight about her contemporaries in journalism: "Individual women came before us, but we are the first women to come as an entire generation and break down one set of barriers after

. . . we are the first women to come as an entire generation and break down one set of barriers after another, and clearly we are going to have to do that until we die.

another, and clearly we are going to have to do that until we die."

Forging Reality

In 1978, when Susan Anderson, who was working as the first woman reporter and anchor at WBBM-TV, Chicago, was pregnant, producers and cameramen had lengthy discussions about how to camouflage her figure. "I felt we should just let the pregnancy [visibly] move along, which is finally what we did," Anderson says, "and viewers reacted very positively."

When she began, Anderson was the lone women at the station; there were no female producers, editors or technicians. In fact, a news editor told her that women could not be producers because the "pressure would get to them in the producer's booth. . .and when women anchor, the news sounds like gossip." Anderson remembers many nights when she cried about how lonely and humiliated she felt. She made her way, she says, by "developing as thick a skin as possible." As more women joined the station, the success of their lobbying campaign for tampon dispensers in the women's bathroom was considered a paramount achievement. And it was.

Setting a Standard

Mentoring younger colleagues is an honorable and gratifying tradition, and it can take many forms. Rita Braver, former Chief White House Correspondent for *CBS News,* is proud of being tough on young reporters and interns. One day, an elected public official demanded that the young reporter who was assisting Braver on a story turn off the camera and tape during an interview. Intimidated, the young woman complied. Observing the scene, Braver was irate. She took the reporter aside and said, "'Look, you shouldn't work here if you don't understand that you don't ask a public official's permission to ask him a question regarding his public work. And you don't turn off the camera because he tells you to!' She wasn't doing her job, and if I hadn't said, 'Wrong move,' she wasn't going to learn the difference. The press is supposed to be independent of the government."

From an early age, Braver knew she wanted to be a reporter because she enjoyed being an observer. "The ability to see both sides of the story is really what drives me and a lot of journalists," she says.

As a student reporter at the University of Wisconsin during the Vietnam War, she covered campus events that supported and opposed the war. "I felt I was really lucky," she says, "because I was reporting and didn't have to take a side. I could simply describe what was happening and think about it. Journalists are just life's observers." Journalists with integrity, she says, do not believe "we're right, or we're morally right," but know "it's not our job to take a stand or offer a vision." She warns that self-expression can equal self-indulgence; for her, the power of the journalist is a truth seeker whose findings offer a view on what is happening in society.

> *Journalists are just life's observers.*

"Hire This Girl"

Braver got her start when she went looking for work at the CBS television affiliate in New Orleans and found that she had entered its FM radio station by mistake. A friendly woman at the desk told her she was at the wrong place and advised her not to enter the television station by the front door because "they'll just take your résumé and you'll never hear from them again." The motherly receptionist pointed her toward the back door, where, she said, she would have a better chance of getting one of the news staff to introduce her to the boss.

Grateful for the tip, Braver took the route suggested, and the first person she met inside the station turned out to be the sportscaster who had covered the University of Wisconsin, her alma mater, at the Rose Bowl. He introduced her to the boss by saying, "Here, hire this girl. She knows everything about radio and television." In truth, it was Braver's first look inside a television studio.

If you still want the job, it's yours. We think that a man won't take it for what we're going to pay.

The only job open was for a "copy boy," a position the station director had never considered giving to a "girl." She left without much hope of hearing from him again, but after a few weeks, just when she was considering substitute teaching, he called: "If you still want the job, it's yours. We think that a man won't take it for what we're going to pay."

Up Through the Ranks

Only one woman reporter was in the newsroom at the time, and she went out of her way to be encouraging to Braver. But "attempts were made to pit us against each other," Braver recalls. "The scene was like the old Mary Tyler Moore shows—guys would ask me to read copy on their story, and the next minute they wanted me to giftwrap an anniversary present for their wife."

Braver has spent her career with CBS, moving from behind the scenes to the editorial desk and then to producer of the CBS evening news and morning news, before going before the camera herself. She has covered major cases on the Supreme Court and presidential summits, and she is most proud of her work at bringing women's health issues to public understanding.

As law correspondent for *CBS News*, she began to follow stories about the aftermath of breast implants, hardly a conventional focus for a traditional television reporter covering the law. When she developed a feature about the subject, she received hundreds of calls from women who said, "'I saw your story—and I thought I was the only one.' By the time I actually got the story on the air, there had been quite a bit of print media on it. But television has a personal relationship, and I think women felt comfortable talking to me. And perhaps I asked questions that a man wouldn't have."

The Authenticity of Experience

When NBC correspondent Gwen Ifill covered the Housing and Urban Development Department as a young reporter for *The Washington Post*, she brought an invaluable dimension to the subject: She had lived in public housing. "People could not demonize public housing residents when talking to me because I could say, 'Hey, I was there.' I am a black woman and a child of immigrants, raised in a certain way, but everybody brings their own veil of experience, and that's what's good about having a diverse population in journalism. You need to have someone who recognizes what is important to people who are not like you."

I am a black woman and a child of immigrants, raised in a certain way, but everybody brings their own veil of experience, and that's what's good about having a diverse population in journalism.

It was the traumatic events of the sixties that first caused Ifill to think about having a career in journalism. The importance of "getting it right" hit home when she found her father crying on the living-room sofa on the afternoon of President Kennedy's assassination. She had seen on the early morning television news that the president was in Dallas, so when a third-grade classmate had told her that somebody had broken into the White House and killed JFK, she knew he was wrong.

"The essential message was true, but I learned the importance of accuracy and remembered it partly because of seeing how stricken my father was. And everything else that followed all seemed to tumble together—JFK, Martin Luther King, RFK—we watched all of them through the view of journalists."

As a child, Ifill liked to write, and she enjoyed family discussions about politics. Her minister father appreciated the value of television to record and convey historical events, and he made sure that the children watched them. From this exposure, she developed an "early, almost naive faith that news was always the true and honest story." As a youngster, she says, she even believed that the front-page picture in the Christmas Eve edition of the Buffalo newspaper was really Santa Claus leaving the North Pole.

Reminiscing about her childhood, Ifill recalls being aware that the faces on television were generally white males, but she had no idea what newspaper writers looked like. "I remember being struck, even then, by the women who were breaking barriers. I was riveted by a black woman named Melba Tolliver, who had a big Afro, and did news break-ins. I knew early, at some level, that I liked the anonymity of newsprint, and I'm still having trouble with the lack of anonymity on television."

You Could Do It

Ifill's parents never placed boundaries on her world. "As immigrants from Barbados and Panama, they were in the way of many immigrants, who saw only possibilities in America," she says. "They saw the limitations because we were black, clearly, but they also figured if you applied yourself, you could do it. . . . So I thought okay, I'll be a newspaper reporter, and it never crossed my mind that there would be any kind of blocks along the way that would stop me from doing what I wanted to do."

This attitude was further fostered at Simmons College, where Professor Alden Poole, "a crusty newspaperman," encouraged her toward journalism. Taking advantage of internships, Ifill soon learned that she preferred newspapers to television. She began her career at the *Boston Herald American* and then went on to the *Baltimore Evening Sun,* where she covered city and state politics. From there she moved to *The Washington Post* for seven years and then to *The New York Times* as a White House correspondent covering Congress and reporting on the 1992 Clinton campaign. Steeped in this deep and wide print experience, she made the transition to broadcast journalism and joined *NBC News* as a national correspondent, based in its Washington bureau. Now she is a frequent panelist on *Meet the Press* and *Washington Week in Review,* and a political analyst on *Today.*

Centered

Ifill is measured and decidedly low-key when she comments on cultural perceptions about gender and race. Women have "interesting challenges," she says, "when they're on a set with three or four men. It's a little harder to get heard, but you have to. You have to have a centered sense of yourself and your own accomplishments, because if you do not have it, nobody else will." If women stand their ground too harshly, they risk being called a "bitch," she notes. "So you have to find a way of being effective. . . . If I suspect someone is ducking my question on *Meet the Press*, haranguing them doesn't help because it changes the focus from them to me."

Male interviewers are more tolerated when they press guests than women are, she observes, "but that's just the way it is. In broadcast journalism especially, a woman has to develop a voice which isn't so harsh that it distracts from what you're trying to do, but isn't so soft that you look like you're batting your eyelashes all the time, and that's pretty hard."

Ifill refers to a colleague who always felt that she had to "smile politely to take the edge off" after asking questions of certain guests on shows like *Face the Nation* or *Meet the Press*. "I don't know a woman who doesn't do that," she offers. "I hate when people say to me, 'Smile,' but you do if it basically gets you there and doesn't cost you anything. . . . It's a constant balancing act. But when do we stop doing this? When do we stop taking the edge off?"

Before appearing on television roundtables, Ifill prepares well, but she also trusts her experience and intuition. "If three white male journalists are interviewing two white male politicians, it just won't occur to anybody to ask certain questions. I'm proud I'm in the position to be able to ask the unasked questions."

Being Responsible

Ifill enjoys the freedom of television roundtables because the expectation is that reporters will say "This is what *really* happened, not this is what *I* think. I do not know if anybody really cares what I think," she adds.

Like Ellen Goodman and Rita Braver, Ifill asserts that "part of being a journalist is not to be the person standing out, but being part of the mob, observing. I'm a reporter first and foremost, so I do not get up on television and say 'This is what the administration should be doing.' I provide analysis about what my reporting reveals: why something happened or how something happened. But I separate myself out from people who say 'You should think this way.' So my

So my definition of a reporter or journalist is first of all to be responsible.

definition of a reporter or journalist is first of all to be responsible, to report really hard and pay very close attention and get what you say right. That's what I do every day."

A High Calling

Ifill says that reporters and journalism get a bad rap by people who confuse true journalism with pseudo journalism. All journalists end up "getting tarred with a negative brush," she explains, "when our highest calling and responsibility is to get it right and present the news as it actually occurs. And that's really hard to do. But it's really easy to do badly, and a lot of people do it badly." She bristles at the widespread use of the word "media" because it blurs the distinctions between genuine journalists and tabloid writers or popular talk-show personalities.

No Freak Stuff

Only months before Marie Torre died of lung cancer in January 1997, I had the privilege of talking at length with this legendary newspaper columnist and television anchor. Among her other accomplishments, Torre was host of one of the first television call-in shows in the country: *Contact*, aired from KDKA-TV in Pittsburgh during the 1960s, focused on social, political, and economic issues. "None of this freak stuff you see today," Torre huffed. "It's really distasteful to me. I do not care what they paid me, I couldn't do shows like you see now. And that's the kind of conscience I'd like to see more of in this business, but you don't find it."

First Amendment Protector

It was the first time in U.S. history that a federal judge ordered a reporter to identify a source, and the first time that a reporter went to jail for refusing to do so.

The risks of exercising conscience were realized for Marie Torre. She served a ten-day jail sentence in 1959 because she refused to reveal a confidential source of information for one of her daily columns in the New York *Herald Tribune*. It was the first time in U.S. history that a federal judge ordered a reporter to identify a source, and the first time that a reporter went to jail for refusing to do so. In 1959 only twelve states had *shield laws* that gave journalists the privilege of protecting their sources; there are twenty-eight today, an improvement, but hardly a comforting fact for reporters. Torre's resistance still remains an inspiration. "I was doing what I had to do and would not have considered otherwise," she said. Indeed, Nina Totenberg calls Torre her "hero." Totenberg told me that at age 14, she followed the case very closely and remembered reading that Torre had painted her cell a shade of pink.

When I told Marie Torre what Totenberg had said, she chuckled appreciatively, then observed that the pink jail cell was "pure apocrypha." But the story conveys how the 1950s culture perceived a female journalist who acted to affirm her convictions.

Torre's ordeal began with a routine bit of information. As a syndicated daily columnist, writing television news, reviews, and commentary, she received a tip saying all was not well between Judy Garland and CBS regarding an upcoming special. She phoned a CBS executive who was a friend. He told her that Garland would not make up her mind about various proposals they had suggested and then said, "We just think she doesn't want to work." He speculated to Torre that the reason was that "she thinks she's terribly fat."

Torre phoned Sid Luft, Garland's husband, who said they were "still talking" with CBS about the program and did not specify any particular problems. Torre used the item in her column the next day, and Luft phoned her to say that he was angry, "not with me but with CBS for doing Judy a disservice; that the network hadn't offered her as many options for a format as I had been told." In her next column, Torre recounted Luft's explanation, and no one at CBS refuted or denied what she had reported. She thought the matter was behind her.

But within two months, Judy Garland filed suit against CBS for libel and breach of contract for $1.39 million. Never anticipating that she could be involved in a lawsuit between Judy Garland and CBS, she was astounded when, on the morning that she gave birth to her son Adam, she received a phone call in the hospital from Luke Carroll, her city editor at the *Herald Tribune*. He told her that she was to be questioned by Garland's lawyers, who wanted to establish the identity of the CBS executive.

Torre met with Garland's attorney and refused to reveal the name of her source. Within a short time, her deposition was scheduled; when she refused again, she subsequently was ordered to appear in court.

Defending Principle

Torre described how she stood before Judge Sylvester J. Ryan in the federal courthouse in Foley Square and testified: "If I give the name of the CBS source, nobody in the business will trust me or talk to me again." Reliving her outrage at the demand, she said to me: "I would have lost my lifeline for news and the respect of my peers. I just couldn't do that." But the judge was unrelenting. He ordered her to comply and said that if she refused she would be held in criminal contempt and sent to jail—again and again—until she decided otherwise.

Her attorney encouraged her to call her source and tell him that she had to give his name, but Torre held fast. "I just couldn't do that," she repeated. "He didn't come to me with the information. I had asked him. . . . So what was I going to say? 'Because you gave me what I wanted, I'll reveal your name!'"

"Whenever this issue came up in the past," she explained, "publishers tended to say to their reporters, 'Look, we don't want to put up with the expense of this. Give them what they want.' But thank God, I was very firm in my conviction, and I really felt that if I had to leave my job, I was prepared to do so."

Torre's own employer behaved in an exemplary fashion. Ogden R. Reid, the editor and publisher of the *Tribune,* assured her that the paper would back her all the way to the United States Supreme Court. "'I don't know what you've decided,' he said, 'but if you choose to remain silent, I want you to know that I feel a very important privilege is involved here for journalism.' That was music to my ears," Torre said, "because I couldn't afford to take it to the Supreme Court, and secondly, I realized that I didn't have to quit my job. It was the most wonderful moment," she said.

After she reappeared before Judge Ryan, her attorney, Mathias F. Correa, appealed the case to the U.S. Court of Appeals. Judge

Ryan sentenced her to ten days in jail and released her on her own recognizance pending the appeal. During the year she waited for the court's decision, Torre's daughter Roma—today a television anchor in New York City—was born. The case attracted an enormous amount of press coverage; when the decision came down, the court had unanimously upheld Judge Ryan's decision on the basis that while it was a curtailment of press freedom to require a reporter to reveal a source of information, the individual's right to fair trial was a more "precious freedom."

The decision ricocheted in editorials across the United States. The United States Supreme Court decided not to review the case, with Justice William O. Douglas dissenting. With no further recourse, Torre returned to Judge Ryan's courtroom. He ordered the marshall to lead her away immediately and relented only when her lawyer said that she had to make arrangements for her two young children. Five days later, she was incarcerated in the Hudson County Jail in Jersey City.

No Other Choice

The night before Torre's surrender, the distinguished Boston attorney Joseph N. Welch, respected as the special counsel for the Army in the national hearings that ended the career of Senator Joseph McCarthy, phoned Torre and said that in having refused to reveal her source, "You're going above and beyond the call of duty." She told him that she was deeply troubled that after she served her sentence the judge might order her to return to jail. Welch's response was hardly reassuring: "It's a certainty they'll send you back. You'll spend the rest of your life in and out of jail."

Torre served her ten-day sentence and was released, but the threat of her being jailed again was still constant. The CBS executive never revealed himself. CBS countersued, and two years later, Garland and CBS cancelled their suits and signed a new contract. Only at this point were Torre's fears about a life time sentence finally eliminated.

"When I went to jail, people said to me, 'Boy that was a courageous thing to do,'" Torre said. "And I remember saying to them, 'No, the easier thing for me was *to go* to jail' because if I did talk and did not have to go to jail, I would have been ashamed of myself for the rest of my life."

She knew her decision would have a profound effect on her children: "They were very young, but all I could think of was when they grow up, they're going to say 'Mommy was a snitch.' Living with some sort of betrayal would have been far more difficult than spending ten days in jail. The kids could not be proud of you for it."

She knew her decision would have a profound effect on her children.

Torre was happy that I had asked for her story. "Every now and again," she remarked, "when similar issues come up, my history is reviewed. Had I been a male, I think I would have had more attention from the news fraternity. I think because of being female that I didn't get quite the support that I should have gotten from my journalistic brethren. I have always felt very strongly about that. The fact is that I am the first reporter to have gone to jail for refusing to reveal a source. Some also downplayed it because it involved a show-business personality. Well, you can't pick your cases. . . . It would be nice if you could pick your test case, but it was the first time that the issue had come before the court in quite that fashion."

In jail, Torre was sustained by others who appreciated her decision. Some were unlikely supporters: The sheriff of Hudson County, where she was incarcerated, had once been a newspaper reporter and the head of the local press club; he had helped to pass a state shield law protecting news sources, and if Torre had identified her source, he had feared that New Jersey's statute would have been jeopardized.

Clergy from many denominations as well as many nuns believed that if a reporter could be forced to talk, their own immunity to being coerced to reveal confidential information was threatened. Torre received mail from people all over the world, much of it from people who did not necessarily understand the guarantees of the First Amendment, but who respected her integrity.

New Vistas

In 1962, Torre left the *Tribune* to join KDKA-TV in Pittsburgh as a coanchor and general assignment reporter covering hard news, an unusual beat for women at the time. *Contact,* the daily one-hour talk and call-in show, was soon added to her schedule. She left Pittsburgh in 1977 and returned to New York, where she worked in television news as a producer, writer, and on-air reporter for WABC and WCBS. Two of her documentaries won Emmy Awards. For the last four years of her life, she continued to produce, write, and conduct interviews for a weekly radio series called *Newsmakers* at WILM Newsradio in Wilmington, Delaware. Always the complete professional, Torre presented her last big program in August 1996; the subject was cancer. She then returned to Pittsburgh, which she considered to be home. When she died a few months later, her obituary was carried throughout the world.

A Voice for the Powerless

Barbara Reynolds, senior columnist for *USA Today,* is a veteran journalist who also takes special pride in setting standards for thinking independently. She is committed to being a "voice for the powerless" because her own struggles remain so fresh. As a child who simply wanted to be heard at the dinner table, she remembers her grandfather announcing that women's ideas did not count and that life would be easier if she learned that lesson while she was young. She grew up in Columbus, Ohio. "Within my immediate society, the opinions of women were not valued, and in the larger society, no one cared about what blacks thought," she says.

Reynolds entered Ohio State University intending to become a pharmacist, but from an early age she had always enjoyed writing, and seeing the name "Barbara Reynolds" on a book jacket in the college library made her wish that person were herself. Inspired, she enrolled in a journalism *He replied: "Negro women cannot be journalists."* course. She loved it so much that she approached the professor and asked him for information about becoming a newspaper writer. He replied: "Negro women cannot be journalists."

In response, Reynolds immediately changed her major from chemistry to journalism. "That would have been my second dream killed," she says. Earlier, she had been turned down for the marching band, even though she was a fine trumpet player and violinist.

"I gave up music, so when I was also encouraged to give up journalism, I figured they couldn't take everything away from me. . . . I just wondered, what does gender have to do with my ability? And now they are going to tell me my race disqualifies me from being a writer. Something inside of me just took a stand."

Being Invisible

Reynolds's first job was with her hometown newspaper, *The Columbus Call & Post*, which served the black community. Later, when she joined metropolitan newspapers, she was usually the only African American on the staff. "My loneliness was not from being a woman, but from being the only black person in a newsroom and being on segregated assignments, in segregated reporting," she says. She felt "totally demoralized and antagonized"—in the Washington Bureau of the *Chicago Tribune*, for example, covering the federal agencies and the urban policies of the Carter White House. "I was even told at times, 'Wouldn't it be nice if we had a woman in the bureau?' and I would be the only woman sitting there. . . . So my story is not of the loneliness of being a woman in journalism; it's the story of being a woman in journalism and not being considered a woman or a person."

An Outsider's Insider

As it would turn out, race and gender would also matter a great deal in the difference Reynolds has been able to make. She knows how it feels to have no one care about what you think, but she does not dwell on negatives. "When you end up on the editorial board and a columnist for the nation's number one newspaper, you know that God really loves you, because I could have given up. I could have walked away." If she is exhausted from speaking engagements, television commentary, and writing, she reminds herself that all these activities were once closed to her. "I didn't grow up seeing people do the kinds of things I do. And I always say 'Thank you, Lord' for changing America so that I would have a role, and keep me strong so that I will always be a sister for those people who need a friend.'"

To give voice to the powerless, Reynolds says she has to be "an insider who really has the mind of an outsider, [yet not the kind] who wants to go to Georgetown cocktail parties and court the powers that be. My views are in season and out of season and not to be changed because of what's popular or who's in power."

Reynolds is deeply loyal to *USA Today,* but she will "always be ill at ease" with the media in general, she says. She observes that women in the field are expected to act by ultrahigh behavioral standards that tend to keep them from advancement.

Reynolds says that women make an important difference in how the news is approached. They bring heart to the issues by not allowing themselves to be limited by facts and figures. "If more women were writing about whatever policies we have, we wouldn't be droning on about a balanced budget," she observes. "We would be concentrating on what's in the budget for children and how can we help them to be able to go to school without being shot. Women would not have created a situation where we're all beating up on welfare mothers. Women are just more sympathetic about how economic circumstances affect the situations people are in."

> *They bring heart to the issues by not allowing themselves to be limited by facts and figures.*

Only when more women are in management positions will so-called "women's issues" like children without health insurance and pay inequities based on gender consistently land on the front pages of the nation's newspapers, she emphasizes. She is known to be outspoken about her own convictions, she says, but she stresses that it is editors and publishers, not writers, who make key policy decisions.

Making the Connections

Liz Walker, the popular coanchor of *Eyewitness News* at Boston's WBZ-TV, is also a community activist against domestic violence. For her, women "stress the humanity of it all."

Walker is very specific: "Every night we report on people being killed or killing themselves, or mothers killing their babies, and there's nothing that really makes life sound very good after you do that for a while. So the special stories you do or the community involvement—that's what gives you the energy to keep doing the news. Little things keep you going, like the kids and the people who say, 'I got out of a bad situation, and thank you for putting that number on the air.'"

Walker carefully distinguishes between her role as a social activist in Boston and her position at WBZ-TV. Being news anchor gives her the visibility to become involved in solving community problems close to her heart. "The community makes you a leader, and that's good because I want to give something back," she says. She sits on a variety of civic boards and committees. "But if there's anything I'm proud of, it's the fact that I've gone to [speak at] probably every public school in Boston. I have kids tell me I spoke to their fourth-grade class about goal setting and success, particularly inner-city children. It's because they know my face that I'm able to do that."

U ltimately, I think that's the next frontier: having more women in decision-making positions to decide the stories that are going to be told.

Walker, too, stresses that name recognition, visibility, and even celebrity do not bestow the clout to make policy in broadcast journalism. An anchor may be out front, she says, but as far as editorial decisions go, "management and producers have more power about what goes into content. Their position is much more powerful than those who present the news." Nonetheless, she often has opportunities to contribute to decisions about stories, she notes. For example, through her efforts, WBZ-TV launched "Stop the Violence," one of the first antiviolence campaigns initiated by a television station. "Ultimately, I think that's the next frontier: having more women in decision-making positions to decide the stories that are going to be told."

On the Way Up

Liz Walker grew up in Little Rock, and she has always thought about her next step because she was part of the first generation to benefit from the civil rights movement. "I was the first black to go to a particular junior high school. That's what was happening down south in the mid-to-late sixties and early seventies. So to me there were all kinds of possibilities—I could do anything because that was the message I was getting from people like Martin Luther King, that it was up to me to break down barriers."

When she graduated from Olivet College in Michigan, Walker returned to Little Rock and applied for a job on the *Arkansas Gazette,* which she did not get. "But television stations were being pressured to hire minorities because of affirmative action, and that's how I got my first job."

She had no one to gauge herself by in broadcast journalism, she says: Women reporters did not yet exist in local television markets, and Barbara Walters was the lone female on network news. "But I felt strongly that I was part of the first group of women who were going to change things," Walker says. "It was a sense of doing something more than just reporting the news. It was a sense of mission. It was part of being part of the whole women's movement and also a part of the fruits of the civil rights movement."

Holding Up a Mirror

Linda MacLennon is a big-city anchor who also was inspired by the women's movement to do more than report the news. She had been at the cutting edge in bringing previously veiled major issues to public dialogue.

Before health reporters existed at WBBM-TV, Chicago, MacLennon, an anchor/reporter since 1984, did a revolutionary series on women and cancer—cervical, ovarian, breast, lung, and colon. She based the segments on interviews with women who were going through treatment, and she was recognized for her work with a local Emmy Award. "I felt fortunate to be able to meet these women and then reveal to the whole city what they were going through. It gave a lot of women hope and insight and made some others sit up and take notice of themselves."

MacLennon also did a pioneering series called *The Sanity Track.* She interviewed men in their mid-thirties to early forties who were leaving the corporate fast track in order to rearrange the priorities in their lives. "It's the old holding up the mirror to society that I enjoy," she says.

It's the old holding up the mirror to society that I enjoy.

The Power of Celebrity

From many such small beginnings, women in broadcasting have created a vital and inspiring legacy. MacLennon worries that this continuing history of fortitude and devotion to the issues will be compromised for the power of celebrity. She agrees with Liz Walker that anchors can lend clout to community campaigns, but the risk of celebrity is often an inflated ego. Broadcast journalists need to monitor themselves against self-importance, she observes.

"You forget that you didn't start out here. We are paid so well that you lose touch with the way most of your viewers live. Most of them do not live in half-million-dollar homes and do not have nannies for their kids and don't have the luxury of going to a job where every day they get paid to learn and meet people that, in their wildest dreams, they would never meet. It's so important for us not to lose sight of that, and to stay in touch with the problems of the people who we're addressing every night."

Do Not Brag

Linda MacLennon's mother first lectured her against bragging when she overheard her bubbling with friends about skipping third grade. Such memories from her Scottish working-class background help to keep MacLennon's own ego in check. She recalls that when she went to London years ago to cover the wedding of Prince Andrew and Sarah Ferguson, she returned to her hotel after an interview with Margaret Thatcher at 10 Downing Street and found herself sobbing: She was thinking about her father, who worked so hard and had little time for enjoyment. "I kept wondering, my goodness, where I come from, how am I so lucky to get to do these incredible things?"

It was not luck, of course, but MacLennon's own talent and hard work that account for her success. But the memories keep her work fresh, she says.

The Figures Speak

Since 1977, the National Federation of Press Women (NFPW) has surveyed the number of women in top publishing and editing positions on U.S. daily newspapers. According to the most recent statistics, the growth rate has been an average of one percent a year since the survey began. At that rate, women will reach parity in 2036, a prediction made by NFPW researcher Lois Lauer Wolfe.

Women hold 25.5 percent of directing editorships on the smallest U.S. newspapers, those with under 10,000 circulation. On those with a circulation of 100,001 to 250,000, the figure is 21 percent, and only 22.8 percent of the editors are women at newspapers with over 250,000 circulation. The six woman editors of those over 250,000 circulation are Wanda Lloyd and Marcia Bullard, *USA Today;* Carol Stogsdill, the *Los Angeles Times;* Mary Jo Meisner, the *Milwaukee Journal;* Sandra Mims Rowe, the *Oregonian;* and Jennie Buckner, the *Charlotte* (North Carolina) *Observer.* The National Association of Editors, founded in 1922, has had only two woman presidents: Kay Fanning, former editor of the *Christian Science Monitor,* who served in 1988, and Sandra Mims Rowe, editor of the *Oregonian,* who served in 1997.

A Landmark Decision

As editor of the *Des Moines Register,* Geneva Overholser made a landmark decision in 1989 when she printed the name of a rape victim and retained the direct language of the reporter's description of the rape. Until then, rape cases were given minimal attention, and readers were prevented from understanding the psychological damage that women endure when they are raped. The policy of the *Register* was to not print the names of rape victims, but Overholser has "wish[ed] it could be otherwise."

> *Geneva Overholser made a landmark decision in 1989 when she printed the name of a rape victim and retained the direct language of the reporter's description of the rape.*

When "One Woman's Story," a five-part series on the rape, was published, it swept aside the cold statistics and anonymity that had cloaked rape cases and illuminated the subject as an issue for the first time in the national press. The rape victim, Nancy Ziegenmeyer, a wife and mother from Grinnell, Iowa, did not want to remain faceless and nameless, but she did not immediately reveal her identity. She says she garnered the courage to come forward after reading a column by Overholser. The column detailed the consequences of being raped and urged women who had been raped to speak out about their experiences.

"This is just not modesty," Overholser assured me, "but the credit really goes to Nancy Ziegenmeyer and the reporter, Jane Schorer, who did a brilliant job. The coincidence was that I had written an op-ed piece for *The New York Times* on the effects of rape, which I didn't even intend to put into my own newspaper. But I did, and Nancy's husband saw it and gave it to her." Within a few weeks, Ziegenmeyer called Overholser with her story.

In her op-ed piece, Overholser had observed that she understood "why newspapers tend not to use rape victims' names. No crime is more horribly invasive, more brutally intimate. In no crime does the victim risk being blamed, and in so insidious a way. She asked for it, she wanted it. . . . This stigma, this enormously unfair onus, brought most newspaper editors years ago to conclude that they shouldn't worsen the plight of rape victims by naming them in the newspaper. . . . Editors do not hesitate to name the victim of a murder attempt. Does not our very delicacy in dealing with rape victims subscribe to the idea that rape is a crime of sex rather than the crime of brutal violence that it really is?" After the Ziegenmeyer case, Overholser continued to have reporters ask a rape victim's consent before printing the name.

Breaking the Silence

The role of a newspaper is to "create change and stir ferment," Overholser says, and she believes that "One Woman's Story" is an exemplary case of having done so. The account included Ziegenmeyer's picture, her graphic description of the assault, and details of how the rape had damaged the intimacy of her love life with her husband. The series provided the paper's 335,495 readers with a human context for understanding rape as a total assault, putting to rest the hateful impression that it is the expression of a sexual aberration rather than a serious crime of violence.

Some feminists argued that printing Ziegenmeyer's story exploited her, and Overholser strongly disagrees. "On the contrary," she counters. "I proved I could be both an editor and a feminist. The story was good journalism, good for women, and the timing was right. We need to talk about the private side of issues as well as the public, because relationships are really important to people."

> *We need to talk about the private side of issues as well as the public, because relationships are really important to people.*

Overholser left the *Register* in 1996 and become Ombudsman for the *Washington Post*. Now she is syndicated columnist for the *Washington Post* Writers Group. Women are better at writing about relationships than men are, she observes. "I don't mean that women should be writing about relationships and men about Somalia. Both men and women can write about a full range of topics, but if you make sure that your reporting and editorial staffs are a good mix, then the newspaper will better reflect the full, rich array of human experience. It's important to have women and people of color and different ideologies and socioeconomic backgrounds in the newsroom," she notes, "because news judgment is a product of our experience." As a famous example, she refers to Nan Robertson, the reporter on *The New York Times* who first brought toxic shock syndrome to the nation's attention because she herself had suffered from it.

A Pulitzer Future

Katherine (Kay) Woodruff Fanning was editor and later publisher of the *Anchorage Daily News* for fifteen years, before she left in 1983 to become editor of *The Christian Science Monitor*. A graduate of Smith College, where she had the benefit of a number of writing courses, Fanning did not have a career when she divorced Marshall Field, Jr. Shortly thereafter, she left Chicago with her three young children to live in Alaska. There she married Lawrence Fanning, a former editor of the *Chicago Sun-Times* and the *Chicago Daily News;* they bought the tiny *Anchorage Daily News,* a morning newspaper that was being dwarfed by the entrenched afternoon newspaper, the *Anchorage Times*. The Fannings ran the *Daily News* together for four years. When her husband died suddenly in 1971, she became its sole editorial director and manager.

"Alaska was a benign environment for women," Fanning says, "because there were many women editors and publishers, and still are, of small newspapers out in the boondocks." But the *Anchorage Daily News* had drastic financial problems, and the "business community probably thought only a woman would be crazy enough to stay," she laughs. The real reason for the financial crisis was that the larger afternoon paper "marched lockstep with the business community, and we took editorial positions that they didn't like. During the building of the [$8 billion Trans-Alaska oil] pipeline, we were pro-environment. And we were cheerleaders and supporters for the Native-American population, the Eskimos, and the Aleuts. These were not popular stands, and so we had a hard time with advertising."

In 1976, the newspaper won a Pulitzer Prize gold medal for public service for an investigative series on the power of the Alaska Teamsters Union during the building of the pipeline. The project, conceived and directed by Kay Fanning, brought Alaska its first Pulitzer.

Even after leading the newspaper to a Pulitzer, Fanning still had to struggle to prevent it from folding. She sold 80 percent to McClatchy Newspapers and retained 20 percent and a contract to manage the paper with editorial independence. Within three years, the weekday circulation of the *Daily News* grew from 12,000 to 50,000, surpassing the *Times.* The consequence of this was that in less than four years, the staff of twelve expanded to sixty and then to three hundred.

A Changing Culture

Fanning felt forced to revise her management style. She had been accustomed to having close staff relationships, but as the number increased, she became less collegial and more hierarchical. It was a mistake, she says. Later, in an essay published in *New Guardians of the Press,* edited by Judith G. Clabes, she would write: "If there is a single virtue that . . . is vital to women editors, it is flexibility, even humility. Perhaps because we're trying to make it as women, we think we must know it all."

Perhaps because we're trying to make it as women, we think we must know it all.

Having become sensitive to the disadvantages of having all the decision making reside only in the top editor, Fanning was therefore "astounded" and "uncomfortable" with the power given to her when she became editor *of The Christian Science Monitor* in 1983. Her first priority was to revamp the paper's stolid hierarchical structure so that more editors and staff participated in everyday decisions.

Global Content

In her new position, Fanning was also able to expand her interest in marginalized social groups to include coverage of minorities around the globe. She sent two women reporters and a photographer throughout the developing world for a major series on women and another story on children forced into prostitution, hard labor, and military service. The paper also ran an investigative series on worldwide hunger.

Kay Fanning doubled the number of *Christian Monitor* bureaus around the world. In 1988, she and two other *Monitor* editors resigned, citing major philosophical and practical differences with the publisher. The same year, Fanning became the first woman to serve as president of the American Society of Newspaper Editors(ASNE)—a position that a member attains after four years of moving up a ladder from treasurer and secretary through vice president. "In those four years, I realized what a male-oriented culture the ASNE was, so I brought some changes, but had to move carefully," Fanning says. For the annual ASNE conference in 1988, she arranged a panel on the topic "Where Are the Women in the Masthead?" "That was a very controversial thing to do at that time," she observes. "It was considered groundbreaking."

Fanning has taught ethics and journalism at Boston University for several years, and she continues to speak at institutes and seminars on the topic of journalistic values. Her main message is that journalists have a tremendous responsibility because of the enormous impact they have on people's lives. "A newspaper is the nerve center of a community, and everything going on in the community passes through that newspaper. The

A newspaper is the nerve center of a community, and everything going on in the community passes through that newspaper.

journalist therefore has an opportunity to make a tremendous impact on the thought structure of the community," she says.

Leadership by Osmosis

Sandra Mims Rowe became the editor of the *Oregonian* in 1993, the largest newspaper in the Northwest, with a daily circulation of 360,000 and Sunday circulation of 450,000. Rowe says she grew up working on newspapers and writing copy for radio. After she graduated from East Carolina University, she joined the *Virginia Pilot* and *The Ledger-Star*. She remained there for twenty-two years, working up from reporter to become executive editor in 1984. The newspaper won the Pulitzer Prize for general news reporting in 1985.

Rowe claims that she was motivated more by fear than ambition and observes that she did not envision a career path until after she was a reporter. "I was never ambitious in wanting the next job and was scared at every step. I have always doubted my talent. But I was naturally curious and always there and willing to take on assignments, so I was given jobs earlier than might have been wise," she says. "I never said my goal was to run a newspaper, but I did internally verbalize that I wanted to make a difference."

She learned how to be an editor "by osmosis," she says, watching in the newsroom how others behaved. "If someone was screaming or making a decision about a story, I could immediately judge if the decision was good and why, or how it could have been more effective. I never set a goal saying 'I want his job,' but I was naturally curious and tended to absorb things about leadership styles. I began to see how individual behavior influences individual effectiveness and organizational effectiveness."

Slow to Change

Rowe completely remodeled the organizational structure of the newsroom when she became the *Oregonian*'s editor. In some departments, she faced seven layers of management between her and the staff reporter. "Newsrooms are the slowest organizations to change. They are traditionally hierarchical," she says. "Intuitively, I knew if an editor is talking only to four top editors, something's wrong." Intentionally using a feminine image, she says she did "some dusting and cleaning," flattening the organizational chart and introducing a more open system of communication.

Had she been appointed editor ten years earlier, Rowe says she would not have been prepared to undertake these changes. "I'm a thief," she smiles. "I tend to gather string." She read studies on how successful businesses and corporations "get information and ideas to the table" and adapted team-based management to restructuring the paper.

I'm a thief, I tend to gather string.

Leadership Is Breaking Rules

Being a leader goes with the job description of a newspaper editor, Rowe agrees. But how one exercises leadership depends upon "internal perception," she says. "If I didn't see myself as a leader, I would do this job differently and see it as more task-oriented. There are very important tasks that an editor has, and I could parse the job to carry out those tasks and simply manage. But leadership is setting vision and occasionally breaking through rules rather than enforcing them."

An effective editor has a sense of responsibility for creating the "best working environment for the staff and making sure the charges are clear so that reporters and photographers can do their work," she says. The staff's primary responsibility is to the reader, she emphasizes; as editor, her own duty is to make sure that obligation is always foremost. In the rare situation where her responsibility toward the reader is in conflict with her responsibility toward an employee, she says she decides in the best interest of the reader.

Front Page Equals People

At one time, Rowe asserts, she was "blind" in her news judgment, but came to recognize that if "women and people of color and various ethnic groups are represented at the table, the front page will come closer to matching what people consider to be news. Imagine that!" she adds and wonders aloud why it took her so long to make such a breakthrough. "It's not that [a diverse group makes] any less bad decisions than a bunch of white men, but too many pieces are

Too many pieces are missing from the prism by not being inclusive.

missing from the prism by not being inclusive." Women have made a tremendous difference in the news by asking new questions and "going against the grain of traditional thinking," she notes.

Making Good Decisions Fast

One of the reasons Sue Bunda enjoys her job as executive producer of *CNN and Co.* is that each day she counters the cultural stereotype that favors men as experts on political and social issues, she says. The premise of *CNN and Co.*, hosted by Mary Tillotson, is to hear from women on topics where audiences have typically listened to men. "A woman can bring whatever a man can bring," says the thirty-year-old Bunda, "but women offer a different perspective at times."

Bunda also works as the network's supervising producer one day a week, assuming responsibility for all of CNN's programming between 7:00 A.M. and 4:00 P.M. "Basically that means I'm accountable for the direction of the network during that shift and have broad editorial supervision," she says. Her work includes booking guests, overseeing the assignment desk, and making sure breaking stories are well-covered and that producers have what they need.

The anchors at CNN have less involvement with specific programs than anchors on other major networks do, she says, but they have more airtime. CNN anchors also have a strong presence in the newsroom and interact with the writers, copy editors, and producers who put the shows together. They have to exercise responsible judgment when stories are breaking on the air, and viewers count on them for information, she says.

Showing Up for Life

Women who are open to possibility are often the first to be tapped for important and interesting positions. Instead of focusing on specific goals and the strategies for reaching them, their actions are inspired by an affirming, joyful attitude toward life. Gail Evans is vice president of National Booking at CNN and executive producer in the network's Atlanta headquarters. "I don't do goals," she says. "My philosophy is show up for life and you can never tell what's going to happen. And I say that laughingly, except most people don't show up, and most people do

I don't do goals, My philosophy is show up for life and you can never tell what's going to happen.

not arrive on any given day in their own lives fully present and attentive to what's happening. They just sort of arrive in some kind of semi-resignation, or they do not live in possibilities; they live in problems."

Evens began her career in the early sixties, serving on several congressional staffs. During the Carter administration, she was on staff at the White House in the Office of the Special Counsel to the President. Later she lived in Moscow with her husband, Bob Evans, who was then Moscow bureau chief for *CBS News*. When she returned to Atlanta, Evans explains: "I took nine years off from my career, which really was politics, to do motherhood. I drove to baseball games, football games, basketball games, and led the life of a politically active suburban housewife. I was on every volunteer committee in the city."

Eventually, she started a small firm, Global Research Services, which investigated the landscape for companies that were exploring the possibilities of expanding overseas. Global Research Services gained a "minor reputation" when Evans stopped a very large construction company from doing a project in Iran about a year before the Ayatollah came to power. She was enjoying her success in business and did not respond enthusiastically when Atlanta-based CNN asked her to be an editorial producer of a two-hour talk show on politics and world affairs: "I said, well, I have this nice small company and it works just right for me. I'm not a television person, I'm a *content* person. But CNN wanted a content person and said they had other people who do the television part. So that was attractive to me, and the rest is history."

Leaders Do Vision

Commenting on who commands power in the broadcasting industry, Evans says ". . . the Ninas and the Cokies and the rest are role models in that they show women what's possible in a very public kind of way, but their power is very personal. When they're hot, they have a lot of power because [employers] want to keep them, but they are not in on the day-after-day decision-making process of 'How many women are on the air? Are we making sure that as many strong women are speaking their minds on the air as we do men? Are women diverse on the air? Not just white women, but are they black, Hispanic, and Asian?'"

Evans continues: "Newscasters don't sit in the meeting that decides which anchor is hired and aren't able to say, 'I don't care how pretty she is, she doesn't stand for the kind of intellect women should have who are in that position.' But management has that power."

Leaders move the people who work for them to operate at the highest level that they can.

Without missing a beat, Evans acknowledges herself as a leader—and a leader more than a manager. Her explanation fits any career. "Managers do organization. Leaders do vision. Leaders move the people who work for them to operate at the highest level that they can, and actually are able to translate their vision to the people around them." Using a visual image to make her point, she elaborates: "Leadership is really a discussion about boxes. Managers have to be able to move the boxes around so that they are in the right order. They don't have to have a vision about how the boxes are supposed to look. But leaders have to know where the boxes are going."

Evans's work at CNN involves the development of new programs. Her staff of twenty-five is responsible for all the live interviews CNN does in any place in the world on any of its networks. As a member of the small management team on the executive committee of the network, she participates in the critical day-to-day decisions at its heart.

Where the Buck Stops

Evans says she builds trust with the people she works with by being "straight" with them. She does not want to know "who got it right, or when things go wrong, I don't want to blame anybody. When it works, the praise goes to everybody, and when it doesn't work, the blame goes to everybody. Everybody who works for me is equal except for me. I'm always the first to take the heat if something is wrong, and I'm pretty good about making sure other people give the credit to everybody else when it works. I'm clear that the buck stops here."

Only recently has she felt free to admit how much she values her intuition, Evans says. "I was a better man than a lot of men on my way up the ladder, and then all of a sudden one day I got so secure that it was okay to be a woman again! . . . I bring a gut instinct, an intuitive risk-taking mentality to the table. I don't have to have facts to open my mouth. I am actually willing to go with my gut. I think that's feminine."

I bring a gut instinct, an intuitive risk-taking mentality to the table.

It is also feminine, she thinks, that her primary identity has never been tied to her job. In the same breath, she says that walking away from being a top CNN executive would be "tough. It's actually a harder identity to let go of than 'She works at the White House,'" she observes.

"Senior vice president is such a powerful identity that I actually check and recheck with myself to make sure I can let it go tomorrow," she adds. "When we get attached to anything in this world, we have to do things to survive, and survival is actually the most stifling place to me, because then you can't have any vision," she cautions. Her position as a television executive is the best job she has ever had, Evans says. It carries a number of risks and responsibilities, but she thrives on shaping the broader picture at CNN and on making the big decisions that develop it.

Chapter Five

Women and Business: Negotiating the Culture

Women establish their own businesses outside of the traditional corporate milieu because they "want to create their own way to balance what they think is important, their families, and work," says Linda Tarr-Whalen, president and executive director of the Center for Policy Alternatives in Washington, D.C. "They are not going to try to change the rules, but rather write their own rules so that work doesn't have to be on one side and family on another. They want to live by rules that women think make sense."

The stories that follow focus on women within and outside corporate life. What they have in common is the spirit and creativity they have brought to their careers.

"They Wanted Me to Succeed"

Ruth Fertel, the founder and chief executive of Ruth's Chris Steak House, turned a sixty-seat restaurant in New Orleans into an $80 million business with a chain of forty-four restaurants throughout the United States, as well as in Mexico, Puerto Rico, and Taiwan. When her marriage of ten years ended in divorce, Fertel returned to the workforce as a lab technician at Tulane Medical School. Four years later, in 1965, she realized that her salary was inadequate for sending her two teenage sons to college. These were days before women were encouraged to do self-inventories of their talents, and Fertel simply scoured the Sunday ads for business opportunities. "My only goal was to make money and live a little better than I had been. There were bars for sale, but I just wasn't into liquor. There were also service stations, and I didn't think I could do that. To tell you the truth, I was really, really lucky that I saw a little ad that said 'Steak house for sale,' and I said 'I can do that.'"

Stakes Are High

I just never thought that I might fail. But it took a lot of hard work and long hours.

Against her lawyer's advice, Fertel mortgaged her home to buy Chris Steak House. Even though she had no previous restaurant experience and had never prepared quantities of steaks, she says she knew she would succeed. "Failure just was never a word in my vocabulary. I just never thought that I might fail. But it took a lot of hard work and long hours."

Undaunted by the conventions of her new enterprise, Fertel taught herself to butcher meat by hand. "One of the rules of butchering at the time was never to use an electric saw. But all of the meat was in short loins which had the bone, and so I had to use a hand saw for porterhouse or T-bones. After two weeks of that, I said no way and bought an electric saw, which made it easier for me."

She learned to cook from Chris's staff. With heartfelt enthusiasm, she says, "Thank God for them because they did carry me for the first couple of months while I was learning everything. But I cooked every Monday from 11:30 A.M. to 11:30 P.M., and we were still open for lunch and dinner. So I learned by doing."

For the first six months, Fertel worked sixteen hours a day. Soon she had more than doubled her $4,800 lab technician salary. Her restaurant was particularly popular with men. "They loved the quality of my food, but they rooted for me because they saw me butchering and cooking, and doing the books, and mixing drinks and seating people, and they wanted me to succeed."

Franchising Her Talent

In 1977, Fertel reluctantly granted the first franchise for a locally owned Ruth's Chris Steak House. When I asked her whether she considers herself to be a leader in business, her reply was: "Well, I think that the industry considers me to be a leader. Personally, I'm just doing my thing, and I guess I just don't think about it."

Describing her daily operation, Fertel conveys a style that's based on brainstorming with her corporate staff of eleven. "I don't say, 'Do it this way or do it that way.' I get everyone's input, and if it makes sense, we go forward. I try to hire people who I feel are more knowledgeable than I, and I try to keep an open mind about new ideas, and it just seems to work." Instead of reporting to regional management, the company's restaurant managers throughout the country have direct access to its corporate officers in New Orleans.

Fertel says she learned her ethics from her parents, who instilled her with a strong sense of honesty. "Following the Golden Rule is really my leadership philosophy with my employees, vendors, and customers. By operating that way, I find that 99 percent of the time people are honest. You treat people the way you *Following the Golden Rule is really my leadership philosophy with my employees, vendors, and customers.* want to be treated, and of course, in the hospitality industry, boy, that is rule number one. And you never try to cheat anyone. I'm most proud of my excellent credit. From the beginning, I have always paid the bills by the end of the month, and I still insist on that. My reputation is in an excellent credit record and wonderful steaks."

Survival Skills

Clare L. Rothman, president of the California Forum, started into the world of sports and entertainment as a bookkeeper at The Spectrum in Philadelphia. Her goal, after a divorce with two children to care for, was survival. Ironically, that was also the aim of The Spectrum. Within a short time, she became business manager and helped move the huge arena out of bankruptcy. Then she accepted a new job at Wild Kingdom in Florida as vice president in charge of finance. Wild Kingdom folded, but Rothman has a healthy outlook on experiencing failure: "Failures are important because you learn from them. . . . I look at my life as a tapestry, and if I hadn't had the failures and problems, my picture today wouldn't be the same; I wouldn't be in the same spot."

After Wild Kingdom, she became manager of the newly opened Cleveland Coliseum in 1973, where she stayed until joining the

California Forum as its general manager two years later. She is responsible for the arena's smooth operation, which includes negotiating with unions, rock stars, and boxing promoters, and overseeing all that is required to get the Lakers on the boards for a sold-out game.

I think we can trip ourselves up by always looking and expecting the worst.

Rothman claims her secret is being a "sponge. I always said that I want to learn everything there is to be done, but I always conveyed that I don't want your job. . . . I was never a threat to anyone. If you hunger for the next person's place, they can smell it, and it's a disaster. I don't automatically think that people are out to get me or to do harm to me, or that more people are wanting to hurt me rather than help me. Now, I'm not a Pollyanna; I recognize the cricks and crannies in people's characters, but I think we can trip ourselves up by always looking and expecting the worst."

Under New Management

"You would think I'm some jock that always played sports," she says, "but I didn't." When she arrived at the Forum, Rothman offered the staff a new deal. She intended to run her business like a team, not a puppet show. "I'm not Gepetto pulling the strings," she told them. "I want to know about the parking lot from the people running it. I want to know about operations from the people who run operations. Every victory we have we're going to share equally, and every failure will be mine only." This style of leadership felt natural and productive to her, but the staff needed time to trust it. "They were always used to covering their own ass, not being concerned if the guy down the hall tripped. But the new way just became magic," she says.

Don't Get Bloody

Part of Rothman's magic is that she trusts her intuition. She counts on its being right 80 to 90 percent of the time, while she gives her logic only a 50 percent chance. "You can't run a big business only on intuition, but you listen to your inner self and then proceed logically and either prove or disprove your theory."

Rothman hopes that her twenty-plus years in sports management will encourage other women to work in nontraditional fields, and not simply for the sake of breaking down barriers. "Go for it if you have the talent and education to bring something unique which will cause it to work well. But if you end up in a situation where the ceiling is glass or steel, don't get bloody. Don't fight it. Get out and try something else because if you have a whole wall of people that are determined to keep you down and that you have to change, then why waste that energy?"

Collaborate

Susan Davis is the inventive president and founder of Capital Missions Company. Based in St. Charles, Illinois, the company creates networks for members who want to invest in socially responsible companies, especially women-led businesses. Her vision is to recruit and develop a wide base of these investors so that the global economy will become accountable for improving the environment, conserving energy, sustaining agriculture, and, among other commitments, developing educational opportunities.

"I just made up a career that didn't exist," she says, "which was to use for-profit businesses to solve social problems. I have had a thirty-five-year-career in this industry that now has a name: Corporate Social Responsibility, or if you're talking about companies that are just starting out, Social Ventures."

"There's nothing more exhilarating—no money, no power—than knowing deep in your heart you are making the best difference you could possibly make," she says. "Once you start taking risks around your values, you get so much psychic energy because you believe in your life. . . . No matter how much social ostracism and criticism I had to endure, it was always worth it to me."

Davis looks for investors who want to invest in keeping with their values, but who also expect market and social dividends. She organized the Investors' Circle, a group of key venture capitalists who share a common commitment to directing the flow of capital to socially responsible companies while increasing their own profits. Their individual interests include protecting the environment, supporting women's economic developments, and generally encouraging corporate and institutional responsibility.

Susan Davis's ideal was to find a career that would integrate her personal and social values with her daily work. In her senior year at Brown University, she had met the son of an African chief and learned how he had suffered while trying to serve his people. Inspired by him, she decided at the age of 21 that she wanted to live her own life as close as possible to her values, whatever the cost. Throughout her life, her own entrepreneurial father has been an example to her of how business could be accountable and humane. She opted to use the principles of business as a positive social force for empowering others.

Women need to believe that they have a right to live a life that is the most inspiring to them.

Proud of the changes she has created in the venture capital industry, Davis affirms her early decision as a path to pleasure and authenticity as well as social responsibility. "Women need to believe that they have a right to live a life that is the most inspiring to them, which is a life befitting their values. Until women take that risk, they are not going to have the lives that they deserve and that they need, and that we need them to have."

Women, in general, are still reluctant to bring attention to themselves in a public, male-oriented world, she says. Among themselves, they are comfortable speaking a separate language and shorthand that is "collaborative, inclusive, and participatory . . . but we don't bring that voice forward in mixed company," she notes. "We listen, and sometimes we'll say a little bit, but we don't intrude; we don't interrupt. We don't assert our values. Until women speak with their women's voice in mixed company . . . we will not be telling the truth. . . . We will not be playing the role that we must play in leadership on the planet."

Insurance Assurance

As president of Management Compensation Group, Inc., in Atlanta, Barbara Balser is in a business realm that has long been run by men and serves mostly men. Starting out, she says, the hardest adjustment she had to make was in showing sincere interest in her client without implying a romantic or intimate relationship. ". . . I'm a good package. I think I look good and speak well, and these two things attract people. But I have learned to deal deftly with whatever preconceptions people might have."

Balser says she arrives for meetings with staff or clients on time, well-prepared, and "ready to play. I see myself as having a decidedly feminine style, but it's not what one would have thought of in my youth," says the fifty-something Balser. "I'm not fluttery and unsure or, in a more contemporary vernacular, a ball breaker. I stand

I stand up for myself without being sharp-tongued and venomous.

up for myself without being sharp-tongued and venomous. I think growing up in the South has something to do with it. So while I may be strong, I'm refined with it."

Everybody in Balser's family owned businesses, including her mother, who leased an accessory department in a chain of upscale ladies' stores. At an early age, Balser helped out there by posting accounts and waiting on customers. She married in the middle of her senior year at Boston University and moved to Atlanta to become "the ideal of what I thought a married, suburban, well-to-do Jewish housewife was. I played tennis, mah-jongg, bridge, had babies, drove car pools, had immaculate toilet bowls, and worked in the community."

The marriage ended in divorce when Balser's three children were very young. Eager to move on with her life, she accepted a position in public relations for a small bank. She loved it until she had to work on the Friday of her first Thanksgiving when her children were on school holiday. The situation spurred her to research other possibilities for earning a decent salary. She was disappointed to find that at the time, the highest-paid female banking officer in Georgia earned about $17 thousand; Balser wanted to aim for $30 thousand so she would be able to maintain a housekeeper. "I just couldn't accept day care because my three-year-old daughter was in shock anyhow: Daddy disappeared and then Mommy disappeared [to go to work] and a few days later the house disappeared."

Still working at the bank, Balser explored the alternatives. She was tempted to launch herself in the retail business, but the prospect of working seven days a week until nine every night was unacceptable. "That is what you have to expect will happen if you own your own store, because you can't assume that your help is always going to show up." A friend offered her an opportunity in the development office of a national foundation located in New York, but when she factored in the cost of living and the potential consequences of uprooting her family, the higher salary did not compensate for the steep price. Balser suspected that the only way for her to earn serious money was to get an advanced degree in business or law, but the timing was not right for her.

Weighing Advice

About then, a young man who came into the bank to sell advertising space suggested that Barbara Balser meet a friend of his in the insurance business. She postponed the conversation, protesting that she knew nothing about insurance, but her young mentor noted that neither had she known anything about banking. For further advice, she consulted some old friends established in the life insurance and property and casualty business.

"Most men of 45 or 50 thought it was ridiculous for me to think about working so hard and that someone would come along to take care of me. Frankly I had had enough taking care of for a lifetime," she says, "so I stopped going to older men for advice and listened to younger men." One suggested that she talk with Massachusetts Mutual. She did, and she was hired as an agent. Two years later, she married the man who had steered her there. "Anyhow, that's how I originally got into this business," she explains. She bought into Management Compensation Group, Inc., and now is president.

But I am most proud that my children and I have all grown up together.

"I must have done a few things right," she says. "But I am most proud that my children and I have all grown up together. We emerged on the other side of the struggle. That's the greatest reward."

Balser enjoys her work completely. "There are just not enough days to do all of the things I would like to do," she says, "but I wouldn't be happy any other way. I wouldn't be married again unless I were married to someone I was in business with. It would never last."

Peripheral Vision

Her leadership style of building consensus is the result of having played "very traditional feminine roles" in her early years, Balser says. At the urging of her mother, she learned to observe and listen in order to be gracious and responsive. "I don't know if I would have had the same strengths if I had gone right into business after college. I think I bring a certain sensitivity to my relationships. . . . I really see things that are going on in meetings that others who are with me don't notice. They don't see that somebody didn't get a chance to finish a sentence, or that three people still had questions that nobody answered. All those unspoken, interactive kinds of things that go on often escape my male counterparts."

Years ago her male colleagues would look askance when she made character judgments that they did not think were evident. "Now they listen when I say someone's a snake in the grass," she says. "I do pick up. I can really smell a bad person." She accounts for the difference by observing that when she was growing up, little boys were encouraged to be physically strong and "king of the mountain," while little girls had to develop a sixth sense to know when they were in danger.

Now they listen when I say someone's a snake in the grass.

Balser values her intuition as integral to her success in a business so heavily populated with men. "They think of me as one of their own," she says. "I'm enjoying watching [this new generation of] men-children grow up and appreciate the fact that a woman doesn't have to look or act like a man in order to be as smart and capable."

Choice, Not Luck

Like Clare Rothman, Linda LoRé, President and CEO of Giorgio, Beverly Hills, also calls herself a "sponge" for wanting to learn as much as possible about any job she has ever had. In 1987, LoRé joined Giorgio as the fragrance firm's vice president of planning and development and became president and CEO in 1991. LoRé, too, learned to turn a liability into an asset at a very early age. The oldest of eight children, she shared a bedroom with four sisters, while the boys had another. Playing family games and sports was economical entertainment, but Linda was not athletic. She was tired of always being the last one chosen for the team, so she took a new approach: She organized the games and appointed herself as manager. "I was the coach; the inspirer; I helped with the strategy."

Extending her metaphor, LoRé says, "Too many women sit back and wait for things to change and come to them, instead of looking for creative solutions. You can't let fate take you. People have told me all my life that I'm lucky, but it's because I know how to use opportunities."

LoRé seized her first opportunity when she was a teenage Christmas temp at J. W. Robinson's, a premiere California department store. Her sales were so high that she was asked to stay on full-time. "But I just thought I was doing what I was supposed to do," she observes. Because she could not afford university tuition, she continued working at Robinson's while she took classes at a local community college. She was soon on a winning streak at Robinson's, and she faced the choice of staying there or postponing her undergraduate degree. She opted for Robinson's and has never second-guessed her decision.

Concentrate

"I did it the hard way," LoRé says, "but for me that was the right way because on a smaller scale I did every job there is to do in a corporation. . . . I didn't ever think I would be in this spot, but I never thought I wouldn't be, either. All of my goals my entire life have always been to be the best at what I do, and the next step will take care of itself. If you focus on the next step, you're not paying enough attention to what you're doing. . . . Then you look at others in a spirit of competition, trying to beat them, instead of competing with yourself, trying to be the best you can."

If you focus on the next step, you're not paying enough attention to what you're doing. . . .

Her personal philosophy, which she also stresses at Giorgio, is that "energy follows focus," meaning that a positive focus produces positive results and a negative one produces negative outcomes. "And if you fragment your focus, you're going to be chasing your tail," LoRé warns. "You need to decide what things mean the most, prioritize, concentrate on doing them well, and go."

Pleasurable Hurdles

Once a woman chooses to enter the corporate system, her first commitment should be to work hard, learn, and seek opportunities to grow and advance, LoRé advises. While she does not dismiss the reality of the glass ceiling, she agrees with Clare Rothman that women often undermine their own progress by being angry toward men. "And that is not where we should put our energy. We need to understand that men have been in the game longer than we have, and try to work with them instead of against them. What you give, you get back. If you think you know it all, trust me, you're going to lose. There's no doubt that many men are threatened by the entrance of women into the top levels, but trying to prove that women are better than men, or vice versa, gets you nowhere. All efforts are thwarted. Nobody wins and everybody's angry."

Without minimizing the obstacles women often face in business, LoRé encourages them to assess a situation realistically. If you encounter barriers at each step of the way, perhaps you are on the wrong path, she says, and should find another place to work. "But if the work is challenging, has hurdles you enjoy, and things happen for you—you're probably in the right place."

. . . if the work is challenging, has hurdles you enjoy, and things happen for you—you're probably in the right place.

Even successful women sometimes trip by focusing on what they do not have, rather than what they have accomplished, LoRé says. She recalls a female vice president who complained that everyone was moving up except herself, despite the reality that she loved what she was doing and was valued for her performance. "She felt that it was expected that she should be doing this, that, and the other thing, instead of accepting the fact that she was performing very well, liked what she did, and wasn't at all failing anyone else's expectations." Had this executive continued to be so negative, LoRé believes she would have fulfilled her own dire prophecy.

CEO Training

LoRé's practical advice is the result of her own hard-won experience. She did not sail into middle management straight from a college campus. She advanced in the old-fashioned way, similar to the young men of an earlier generation: She pulled herself up through increasingly important jobs—in sales, merchandising, operations, human resources, and finance. In 1980, she became business manager of the cosmetics division of the entire Robinson chain. Within a four-year period, she introduced more than thirty different perfume labels and increased the division's annual sales from $1 million to $27 million.

Her earliest association with Giorgio came about when she was trying to pursue its products for Robinson's. Like many other women, she was attracted to Giorgio's scent strips in major magazines but found that the perfume was available only at the company's Rodeo Drive boutique. For a year, she tried to get an appointment with Fred Hyman, founder of Giorgio, to convince him to sell the perfume at Robinson's. Her persistence paid off: During the 1980s, Robinson's was the biggest single seller of Giorgio fragrances, with a peak year of $13 million.

LoRé credits every position she had at Robinsons's for helping her to become a successful CEO at age 41. She says she values the mentorship of two hard-driving presidents, Michael Gould, head of Robinsons's, and Fred Hyman, founder of Giorgio, but her "sponge" qualities have formed her own perceptions of how a corporation should run.

You Can't Do It Alone

"I don't think there is anything you can really do alone and be truly successful and happy at it. . . . I really believe that the sum of the parts equals the total. Everyone has a purpose, and whether that purpose has lived out its usefulness or not, one has to look at all the aspects. . . . In a turnaround as well as in the development of a new product line, it takes a total team effort. . . . We spend more waking hours in our jobs than anything else we do, so people should feel they're making a contribution and are more than just a product on a shelf." For LoRé, it is critically important for a company to have that kind of a conscience.

To create an organizational climate where everyone is valued, LoRé surrounds herself with the most highly skilled people and the best possible resources. But she also knows every single aspect of the business, from strategic planning to budget planning to marketing. She says her job is to ask the right questions and inspire the team. "A good leader is always on," she asserts. "You never know when a good idea is going to hit you. It could be in the middle of the night or while you're in the shower."

She is convinced that business leaders lose their effectiveness when they become territorial. Consequently, she tries always to be open, not only to her own ideas, but those of others. "It doesn't matter where a good idea comes from as long as the good idea is used," she says. "And it doesn't matter who gets credit for it because ultimately the whole team will. If you have a motivated, enthusiastic, and inspired team with good skills, then watch out!"

It doesn't matter where a good idea comes from as long as the good idea is used.

During her interview for the position of president and CEO at Giorgio, she was asked why she was the right person for the job, and her reply was secure and forthright. "I get results," she responded. "I'm action-oriented." LoRé recalls that she once turned down a big promotion at Robinson's because she felt she was not ready for it, though her supervisors and peers had urged her to take it on. "I knew intuitively in my gut and my soul that it was the right decision, even though everybody else thought I was crazy," she remembers, "particularly when I then stayed on with the same company!"

Premature Promotions

The wisdom of LoRé's choice offers a refreshing lesson for those who assume that the only way to advance is to move upward, instead of coasting for a while, honing their skills, learning operations, and enriching their networks. In some cases, victory might be illusory. For example, one young woman who asked to speak anonymously won a prestigious position at the home office of a major corporation immediately after completing her MBA. Bright, competent, and articulate, she moved into the office of executive vice president at the age of 35. But her speedy ascent had serious consequences for her future at the company.

Indeed, as we talked, she confided that she had been fired and was in the process of negotiating her termination package. She attributed her change in fortune to having cracked the glass ceiling prematurely. The company "wanted a female in a very high-level position and they looked around and thought they could take a risk with me. I obviously didn't have the depth of experience someone coming up through the normal ranks would. What I've learned," she said, "is that power doesn't come with the position; it comes with credibility and competence. . . . Someone else who is brought along a little more gradually and has time to build connections with other people in the hierarchy wouldn't be spending the time I did trying to get myself in. It's really not the position in itself that gives you power."

She tried to be as positive as possible about her situation and said that despite the outcome, her trailblazing would continue to benefit women behind her. She believes that she has successfully changed the company's stereotype that a woman executive in a male world automatically has a chip on her shoulder. "If I had acted like one of the boys, I would have been accused of being bitchy. But I did change some of the rules and tried to relate in a more human way to employees."

Prior to her promotion to executive vice president, this young executive was responsible for administrative layoffs in her division. Facing the decision about which jobs were vital and which must be jettisoned, she sat down with every person whose position was to be eliminated. "It's very painful to look someone in the eye and see their life fall apart . . . [but] my people really appreciated the fact that I walked the course with them. I sat with those I was laying off and also the ones that remained behind. I hugged people and put my arms around them. . . . I basically was a mom for that period of time. But I felt that is what I needed to do. I was able to steer my group through a very difficult phase because it was obvious that I cared about what happened to them."

I was able to steer my group through a very difficult phase because it was obvious that I cared about what happened to them.

Some executives would see her sensitive approach to downsizing as proof that women bring heart, sensitivity, and intuition to the leadership of corporate America. Other female executives are reserved in detailing how women may be influencing big business: They say that women should be in corporate executive positions as a matter of equity, and that the bottom line—money—is gender neutral.

Spreading the Talent

Another executive vice president who wants to remain unnamed affirms that corporate women generally look out for the best interests of their employees. For example, this anonymous vice president was worried that staff in her financial department were vulnerable to downsizing because they were highly individualistic in carrying out their jobs. To protect them, she restructured them into a team. They cross-trained and learned to do each other's work. This process allowed them to gain new knowledge and guarded them from becoming too specialized, less flexible, and thus disposable.

Her plan had advantages for everyone, she says, but her male staff had trouble adapting to it "because there was a lot of ego involved: 'I'm not going to show you mine' kind of thing.'" From her experience, women are much more willing to be multidimensional in business, she adds. This characteristic, she conjectures, is a domestic legacy, for women have traditionally had children hanging around while they cook dinner, talk on the telephone, and execute other household and social pursuits. Even

Even though women have earned little credit for their domestic dexterity, it transfers well to business.

though women have earned little credit for their domestic dexterity, she says, it transfers well to business, where the trend is to be able to switch tasks and work on different teams in order to reach a goal or solve a problem. "If you can't be that, you're not going to do a lot of good for the company," this young corporate officer observes. Her team finally did jell, she reports, and the members continue to learn from each other. She is gratified for having put into place "something good for the company and also for these people."

Interlude: The First Bullets

As president (1994 to 1995) of the National Association of Women Business Owners, Patty De Dominic is known across the country as an outspoken advocate for women in business. She is founder and CEO of PDQ Personnel Services, Inc., the largest woman-owned personnel service in the greater Los Angeles area, and one of the most successful in the country, with a multimillion-dollar annual revenue.

De Dominic says she recognized herself as a leader from early childhood. "Even in play, I was motivating others. My parents tell lots of stories about my being an instigator. Sometimes I think that people think women suffer from the white knight syndrome and that we always want to find somebody to come along and do it better."

I personally prefer being number two to a strong leader, but quite a while back I ran out of strong leaders to be number two to.

Later in our conversation, she said: "You asked me earlier if I felt I was a leader and I do, but it's not by choice. It's more by process of elimination. I personally prefer being number two to a strong leader, but quite a while back I ran out of strong leaders to be number two to. But I really enjoy working on teams and building consensus. I understand the power of being able to accomplish something, or helping, or changing laws, or making a difference in general public awareness through the collaboration of business groups, professional organizations, and business owners."

Players From Everywhere

As corporations grow in size, it is becoming increasingly difficult for a single individual to know everything that must be understood in order to make major decisions. Team efforts will therefore be the most productive method for conducting business in the future, according to Roberta W. (Bobbi) Gutman, vice president and director for human resource diversity, worldwide, at Motorola, Inc. "That's the way the world is going now," Gutman says, "and that's a trait that women have. Women are potential stars because it's almost an instinct for them to work effectively in groups. The team sinks or swims on the team's efforts."

To solve a problem, teams will not necessarily be related to hierarchical levels, but rather to functional competence, Gutman notes. The strongest leaders, she says, are those who can make the lowest person on the payroll feel as if the organization cannot be run without him or her. "That's a leader," she says, "because you never know who you're going to need on a team to solve a business problem. Most people are much more myopic than that and assume that leadership has to do with those who are at high levels. Wrong answer!"

The strongest leaders, are those who can make the lowest person on the payroll feel as if the organization cannot be run without him or her.

The Best Minds: Not an Add-On

Gutman has had an interesting career at Motorola, the immense telecommunications and electronic manufacturer located in Schaumburg, Illinois. "I'm a relationship person and I get fueled by the fires in corporate America," she says. "I'm not happy without having fires and many, many people to bounce things off. . . . But some people aren't like that." She makes a point of noting her appreciation that her talents for innovative leadership have been fostered at Motorola.

She was handpicked by the corporation's former CEO George Fisher to manage its diversity initiative. Before Fisher became president, Gutman had left Motorola in 1986 because she saw few women and people of color moving into management positions. Fisher recruited her back to help him change that situation: The new goal was to attract and retain the best minds to Motorola, regardless of gender or race, on all management levels and in numbers more representative of national percentages. The responsibility for setting this campaign in motion went beyond the department of human resources. Line executives and senior managers throughout Motorola's giant system became accountable for measuring their progress in achieving these aims. The implementation of this quantitative process took three years, and Gutman was the catalyst for making it happen and seeing it through.

For her, diversity is a business asset that supplies a competitive advantage in a global marketplace, "It's not something that is simply nice to do, or an add-on," she says. "The idea is not to exclude white males, but if we have only white males in management positions in a global arena, we will not be competitive with other countries that are using the best of their talents."

In 1994, Motorola won the Labor Department's highest tribute, the Secretary's Opportunity 2000 Award, for its diversity achievements. The company also won an award from Catalyst, the national nonprofit organization dedicated to advancing women in business and promoting their recruitment for corporate boards, for "demonstrating a commitment to the leadership development of female employees."

Gutman now spends 25 percent of her time giving speeches and consulting with companies on using the talents of a variety of people that will help U. S. businesses succeed throughout the world. She has reaped the same kind of satisfaction that entrepreneurs experience when their businesses grow and prosper.

Men in Drag

Gutman is disappointed by women who arrive in senior management and "keep doing it the male way" instead of "turning around and saying 'Now let me show you through my modeling how decisions really should be made'. . . . I beat on all my women friends who are executives and say, 'I know you had to act that way to get where you are, but if we believe the way we like to work is the way it should be done, let's start carrying out that behavior.' But it's scary for some people."

To work effectively on a team, she explains, a leader needs to know when to take charge and when to blend into the group, respecting that every person, regardless of level, has an important contribution to make. A self-confident leader is able to bring out the best in each team member. But a leader who lacks self-confidence will not relinquish control even temporarily to another person, out of fear that she will no longer be perceived as being in charge. "So dealing with what each person brings to the party can be very threatening and dangerous," she says. "Yet women are more open and do this far better than men."

> *Dealing with what each person brings to the party can be very threatening and dangerous.*

Women at all levels of management need to act on the conviction that they "bring a very different vantage point, and they shouldn't sit on it or trip and swallow it," Gutman asserts. "They need to make sure they are heard and stop projecting that they are grateful to be there, but rather, 'Gee I'm glad you were smart enough to bring me in.'"

The Hidden Legacy

Gutman developed her strength as a child of African-American parents who "did not allow hiding behind differences," she says. Her mother, whom she calls a "powerhouse," inspired her to excellence by stressing that "people who are successful are those who look at their barriers as challenges they have to overcome. And the people who are not successful look at challenges and barriers as the reason that they never were."

> *People who are successful are those who look at their barriers as challenges they have to overcome.*

Her mother quietly insisted that her children be the best at whatever they decided to do. "I came to the party believing that I bring something very different and just as valuable as the other people in the room," Gutman says. "To feel happy or privileged to be in the company of white men was not something I had in my bag of tricks; whereas I have noted otherwise with many white women."

When women business executives discuss how they practice leadership, they often uncover, as Roberta Gutman did, the hidden legacy of their mothers. They see affinities between their mother's nurturing style and their own way of leading. On the other hand, conventional wisdom and most research affirm that women who advance in corporate careers are more likely to be their "father's daughters." Women in corporate leadership do not necessarily reverse this perception, but they do see new connections between how they operate in business and how their mothers ran a household and maintained a family.

Mother Oils Wheels

Bridget Macaskill, president and CEO of OppenheimerFunds, Inc. a leading mutual fund company in New York, says that she, too, is aware of this identification between her mother and herself. She praises her mother for possessing "very human qualities. She was a wonderful consensus builder . . . a peacekeeper. I don't mean there was a lot of strife, but she was the smoother and oiled all the wheels. She made everything happen and everything work and kept everybody smiling. I admire her enormously for quietly doing that. Somewhat unobtrusively, she kind of kept things going."

From her father, a career officer in the English army who "believed in doing things right," Macaskill says she learned the value of organization and discipline. She was one of five children in a "regimented household where we were told to be ready to go somewhere at a certain time, and we were there." She credits her father's influence for her ability to bring order and structure to business situations, but does not intend to characterize herself as a leader in the style of a "general. I use that expression," she says, "because that is the leadership role I was closest to growing up, but I don't fit that old style. The days of the typical hierarchy, when the boss knows more than all the employees, are gone."

Macaskill's first job was in England as the personal assistant to the marketing director of St. Ivel, Ltd., a major United Kingdom food company "completely dominated by men," she says. Advancing through the ranks, she was offered the position of director of marketing operations, which carried with it a seat on the board. But a few days after accepting the job, she was told that new directors had to serve for six months before they could expect a board appointment. "That's very interesting," Macaskill responded. "When did that rule get invented? The production director went straight on to the board, and he got his job last month."

The officer who delivered this news promised Macaskill that she would be invited to every board meeting as a guest. She says she had two choices: "I could either resign in a fit of pique and say I will not tolerate this discrimination. Or I could say, 'All right, I'll call their bluff and I'll sit it out, and in six months they'll have to *D*on't get so focused on the obstacles relating to your gender that you are distracted from your ability to get the job done.* put me on the board.' And that's exactly what happened! I learned something important from that and it's advice I give to a lot of women: Don't get so focused on the obstacles relating to your gender that you are distracted from your ability to get the job done, because inevitably you jeopardize yourself. Find ways past the obstacles, rather than focus on here's a whole bunch of men who are trying to stop me."

Fortune and *Vanity Fair* have named her one of the most powerful women in U.S. business.

Consensus and Its Downside

Macaskill says she tries to create an organizational culture that is friendly, pleasant, and enjoyable for people to work in, because then they produce the best results. She believes in fostering team spirit by building consensus, delegating responsibility, and letting people make decisions. She makes it a point to listen very hard when employees comment on her ideas. "It may be that they can convince me in five minutes flat that it's a really stupid idea, or it won't work, or maybe there's a germ that we can develop. . . . So then it goes into a process of discussions."

But Macaskill knows that team leadership has its perils. On one hand, the process creates a positive environment where everyone has been consulted and believes her opinion is valued. Meetings are often enjoyable because conflict may be minimal. But the risk is a proliferation of paralyzing meetings where nothing moves forward until every person is convinced about every single detail. "If all decisions have to be unanimous, that is death! If you say that no decisions are going to be made unless everybody agrees, then the result is very mediocre decisions or low-risk options," Macaskill warns. "It's difficult to find a path through this, because I do believe people work better when they have input and are part of the process, but there is real risk when management delegates the decision-making role to groups and nothing gets achieved."

Women are particularly well-suited for team management because they are "practical, pragmatic, and less bound up in the politics of a situation."

Macaskill notes that women are particularly well-suited for team management because they are "practical, pragmatic, and less bound up in the politics of a situation. They are sometimes willing to just get on and do stuff and not worry too much about who gets credit for it."

Redesigning Silos

If, as Roberta Gutman says, "women are potential stars, because it's almost an instinct for them to work effectively in groups," then the current collaborative modes open more possibilities for women than ever before. According to Sandra Woods, vice president and chief environmental, health, and safety officer at Coors Brewing Company, the best way for women to promote themselves within this expanded organizational system is to accept challenges enthusiastically and not have a limited view of what they can do. "They need to build a really broad base within the corporation," Woods advises. "Business today is saying 'Get out of your silos. See the way you interconnect.'" She says that it's possible to gain experience in all aspects of the corporation—marketing, sales, operations—by remaining open to cross-training and working with cross-functional teams. When a woman diversifies her work experience, she places herself in a better situation to be promoted from within or to change career paths.

On the Move

Named by *Business Week* as one of the Top 50 Women in Business, Woods reinvented her own career every few years. She has either changed from the public sector to the private or added a new focus, as she has done at Coors.

Before she joined Coors in 1979, Woods worked with the federal government in the Department of Housing and Urban Development. She is part of the baby-boom generation that benefited from the Civil Rights Act of 1964. After college and a master's degree in public administration, she chose government as a "more hospitable environment for giving women opportunities than the private sector. . . . I had a promotion [within] a year and was on a fast track. I got a lot of management experience because I never said no to any assignments and learned how to do them. Part of my history is that I've taken risks. . . . I didn't ever protect myself or go into an area that I thought was limiting. I was always trying to grow and did a lot of cross-training between agencies."

These rapid promotions also advanced Woods in subtle ways. When she first assumed a new position, she says, she often had to depend on others who had far greater technical skill than she. As a result, early in her career she learned and appreciated the practical advantages of team management. Her *A successful leader in business or government has to be constantly learning and open to her own ideas and those of others.* first lesson: "A successful leader in business or government has to be constantly learning and open to her own ideas and those of others."

The bridge for Woods into the corporate world was the "President's White House Exchange," a competitive program designed to give fifty people from government and business an opportunity to trade sectors for a year. Her placement with Coors was a definite career test, for she was acutely aware of breaking ground for women in a traditionally male industry.

From 1980 to 1993, she was responsible for planning, acquisition, development, management, and issuing permits for the company's real estate and water resources program. During her years at Coors, she has never held a job that had previously existed. Her assignments have always been to "plow new territory." Consequently, she learned early on that if she were going to gain people's support and participation for bringing about change, she had to see the connections and cross-functions throughout the organization. "I didn't have to start with *what was* or *what existed,* but if I wasn't going to get lost or never be seen, I also had to build collegial teams drawn from all parts of the company. That style worked very well for me."

At Coors, Woods became known as a problem solver, addressing challenging issues in real estate, land use, and the environment. "But I didn't always have a lot of security in some of those positions," she says, "because they were not the tidy black boxes on the organization chart; sometimes they had dotted lines rather than straight lines, and when you're in those dotted-line boxes, causing new activity, you have to build a collegial team and find support throughout the organization or you get lost and you're never seen."

So long before it became fashionable, Woods initiated team management strategies for dealing with issues that were new to the Coors system. "If you have just one person as the champion, that is a pretty small effort for building support for any change or concept," she observes. She never felt at ease with "hierarchical or authoritative leadership because it's based on sort of military traditions—'I am the general and you are the private' mentality—and I had never served in the military. I'm much better when I'm building consensus and gaining support of others," she says.

New Seat, Old Hand

The media called Washington lawyer Mary Schapiro "top dog," "top cop," and "new cop" when she became in 1997 the first president of the National Association of Securities Dealers Regulation

(NASDR). She is in charge of making rules for the nation's 500,000 brokers, 5,400 securities firms, and the National Association of Securities Dealers Automated Quotient System (Nasdaq). So how does Mary Schapiro, age 43, operate in this command-and-control position?

Soft-spoken and low-key, Schapiro says: "I guess if I have a style, it's to create a very collegial atmosphere. It might even be too collegial because so many views are solicited before we make decisions. I surround myself with the smartest people I possibly can and put all of us to work solving the hardest problems. And we're better off doing that, rather than having one person lionized or one person, including myself, making all the decisions." Typically, she even asks staff their thoughts on questions outside their special fields. She finds that "insightful comments often come from someone who hasn't been involved with the problem before."

Insightful comments often come from someone who hasn't been involved with the problem before.

Schapiro hopes her reputation for being tough stems from her strong belief in what NASDR does. "Effective, balanced regulation is one of the great strengths of the capital markets in this country. It's one of the major reasons our markets are so successful as compared to others around the world," Schapiro says. "Investors have tremendous confidence in the quality of the markets here, and regulations have played a role in that. Everybody working with me knows that I believe this to the core of my being. So someone not sharing this view will be uncomfortable here."

"That's not to say we want to have an 'us versus them' view of the industry. But at the end of the day, what we do at NASDR has to be right for investors," Schapiro says. "I believe in our mission of protecting investors in a way that doesn't impede the markets from operating. We deal with the practice and problems out there that need to be dealt with."

Public Service/Private Sector

Few women are at the highest levels of the financial services industry. Schapiro is disarming about her success and says: "If it were not for rising up through government, I'm not sure I would be in this position. Government is much more of a meritocracy than business is right now. I'm convinced," she adds, "that it's much harder for women coming through the industry side to be promoted."

But Schapiro is a natural fit for NASDR. Before taking the helm, she was chair of the Commodity Futures Trading Commission (CFTC), and spent six years on the Securities Exchange Commission, including a term as acting chair. The values she brought to NASDR, she says she learned in government. "What we do," she explains, "is public service for the private sector, and I'm absolutely committed to our mission of insuring the integrity of the markets for the investing public."

*B*ut when people are really confronted with regulations, it's often not a good experience for them.

When she is not in the room, Schapiro doubts all people are speaking nicely about her. Her suspicions are tied to being a *regulator* in a competitive business rather than a woman in a macho field. "Regulators say you can't do things and punish you when you've done something you shouldn't have. In the abstract, everybody loves regulations because they do add credibility and quality to the markets. But when people are really confronted with regulations, it's often not a good experience for them," Schapiro admits. "So I'm sure things are said—and often in the context of my being a woman —but I don't dwell on it."

Inadvertently, she turned a sexist remark to her advantage. A newspaper reporter called Schapiro, then chair of the CFTC, to tell her that a securities executive was blustering that he would not allow a 5'2" blonde to push him around.

"I'm 5'6," Schapiro countered. "My first reaction was to correct my size! But that bullying comment was one of the best things that ever happened to me because it became a rallying cry and sparked a lot of camaraderie."

Dividends

Schapiro learned the value of camaraderie and team spirit on the playing fields of Franklin & Marshall College in Lancaster, Pennsylvania. "Nothing in my life was more important for laying the foundation of my career than playing lacrosse and field hockey," she says. "I love being a part of a team and sharing a common goal. I wasn't a great athlete," she quickly clarifies, "but I loved competition and knew it wasn't the only thing in life. I studied hard and wanted my parents to be proud of me. And that desire to please doesn't necessarily go away just because you're not in school anymore," she elaborates. "I want people to know I'm working hard and contributing."

Mary Schapiro says she "obsessed" for two decades about advancing in her career, "but my husband was the same way about his, so that was right for both of us." Now Schapiro is concerned about balance. Two preschool daughters and family pets put things into perspective for her.

An Interlude About Office Mothering

"I bottomed out. I was tired of being mother: mother to my husband, my children, my employees," says Christine Toretti, president of S. W. Jack Drilling Co., of Indiana, Pa., one of the largest independently owned gas drilling firms in the country. Toretti relates that she confided these feelings to a small session at a meeting of the Young Presidents' Organization (YPO), an association for presidents of multi-million-dollar businesses who are under the age of 50. She was the only woman in a group of fifteen men. The gist of their response was: "You've gained some weight lately, Christine. Try exercising more. Get a private trainer. My wife got one and feels better."

The gist of their response was: "You've gained some weight lately, Christine. Try exercising more.

The meeting's facilitator, apparently satisfied that the advice was sage, said "Next. . . ."

Toretti left the meeting feeling misunderstood, exasperated, and determined. She scoured the membership directory of the YPO, looking for a woman within driving distance. Three days later, she and Carole Bitter, president of Friedman's Super Markets in Butler, Pennsylvania, met at a restaurant in a small town halfway between them and talked nonstop about how women, even in big business, are expected to be selfless, pleasing, and useful, taking care of others without asserting leadership.

When employees had regaled Toretti with their financial and marital problems, she says she had felt complimented for being approachable. "I felt an obligation to take care of the world," she recalls, "and then was guilty that I couldn't." In their first meeting, she discovered that Carole Bitter, ten years older than she, had once dealt with the same problems. Toretti learned from her how "to let go of the apron strings and encourage employees to be independent and solve their own problems. By helping them to grow, I also helped myself."

Army Surplus

As Bridget Macaskill and Sandra Woods describe the shift away from traditional management styles, their use of words such as "general," "military," and "army," demonstrates how the idea of leadership has long been equated with a rigid chain of command ruled over by "captains" of industry. This style of leadership is still ingrained in corporate life, and women who also value collaborative efforts often successfully employ power relationships to attain their goals.

Before she became founder and president of the Education Communications Consortia, Inc. (ECCI), a multimillion-dollar telecommunications business in Charleston, West Virginia, Sherry Manning says she had a pragmatic lesson in leadership strategy that she will never forget. What she learned is that command-style leadership is not necessarily inconsistent with maintaining a humane business relationship.

Manning was president of Colorado Women's College from 1978 to 1982 and presided over more than academic and fund-raising responsibilities. For example, she depended upon the plant superintendent, a sixty-two-year-old retired Army sergeant, to keep all the mechanical systems going, including a patched boiler that he regularly resuscitated. She had often expressed her appreciation for his skill and was surprised when he nervously walked into her office one morning and offered his resignation.

"Why?" she asked.

"I never worked for a woman," he said. "I want you to know my daughter works as a nurse, but I can't work for a woman who is younger than my daughter."

"You've spent thirty years in the military," Manning prodded. "Was that a good experience?"

He said he loved the military because its clear lines of authority made it easy for him to know what he was supposed to do.

Manning responded: "If your commanding officer asked you to do something, what would you do?"

"Oh my God, I'd salute, say 'Yes sir,' and move as fast as I could," he answered.

"Okay then, this is real simple," Manning remembers saying. "I want you to consider me your commanding officer. When you look at me, don't see your daughter, but your commanding officer. I want you to stand and salute and say 'Yes ma'am' or 'Yes sir' and you're out of here."

From then on, the retired ex-sergeant said "Yes sir" to Manning, and they both enjoyed the verbal irony. "All I did was help to make him comfortable because he had operated under traditional authority structures his whole life."

Today, Manning says, a good leader "meets people where they are . . . by being empathetic and understanding and allowing them, in this case, to call me *sir*."

At Colorado Women's College, Manning reinforced this style by visiting the furnace room crew every Monday morning. As the men stood, Manning addressed them by their last names: "Jones, how's the boiler?"

"We simulated a kind of male bonding," she recalls. "They didn't want collaboration or somebody who *cared* about them."

> *We simulated a kind of male bonding. They didn't want collaboration or somebody who cared about them.*

Adapt, Adapt

Applying that lesson to corporate life, Manning maintains that women do not behave one way and men another, but that people in communities learn certain communication patterns with which they are at ease. "The corporate one is not quite military," she clarifies, "but it is quite male, and so to be successful in the corporate world you have to be effective in that style of communication."

This means that women have to be more adaptable in the workplace than men, Manning says firmly. "Women can stick by their guns if they want to make a change in the long run, but look at the numbers. If there is one Linda LoRé and fifty Charlie Revsons, how much difference can one person make?"

"You Babble Too Much"

The expectation that women are naturally collaborative in business can also limit their ability to get things done, Manning observes. For example, a man who has an "s.o.b. reputation can say to an employee, 'Would you consider flying to San Diego for the weekend because I'd like you to be there Monday morning for a seminar?' and the person says 'Yes sir' and is on the next plane. If I say the very same words," Manning explains, "I have to listen to a lot of talk. That happens to me every day of my life, and I think it happens to most women because we look softer than a tough man, and people treat us differently."

She enacts the hypothetical dialogue that would follow her request: "Well Sherry, I would really love to fly to San Diego on Saturday, but I can't because I was going to take my mother-in-law for brunch on Sunday. You know she lost her husband a few weeks ago, and she's really been looking forward to this. We already have reservations at Cafe Le Boheme, and you know how hard they are to get. So if you don't mind, I'd rather fly out on Monday about nine-thirty. That way I can miss the morning traffic but be there for the one-thirty session."

And how does Manning respond?

"I listen to him or her and then start at the beginning and say in a very measured way how important this seminar is and how much we care about the person's career advancement. It's a question of the corporation investing in him or her, and maybe we could call the restaurant and get a reservation for when he gets back. In fact, instead of brunch, why don't we pay for a dinner for a big evening so that you can go to San Diego with a clear mind?"

But what does she *really* want to say? "Damn it! I'm spending this dough on you to help you over some hurdles in your management style. You babble too much and you need to focus on outcomes, and that is what this seminar will do. Now get your ass out there!"

The enactment is simultaneously witty and scathingly to the point: Manning contends that women in leadership positions are held "hostage" by how people treat them. "People think I'm nice, for example, and I'm not sure that's true. They don't give me any

Manning contends that women in leadership positions are held "hostage" by how people treat them.

choice!" She does not want to be the kind of leader who barks at employees, she says, but "it's very efficient to be perceived as a Marine Corps general. . . . Maybe more women are concentrated toward the collaborative side than the competitive side, but maybe that's also because of how we are perceived and expected to act."

In Charge

Even though Sherry Manning is exasperated that women in business still must contend with the presumption she so brilliantly describes, she says she would never trade in the freedom of being an entrepreneur and president of her own prosperous company. She is one of the number of women business owners I spoke with who relish the independence of creating their own cultural and political climate. The National Foundation for Women Business Owners estimates that over one-third of all U.S. businesses are owned by women. These eight million firms employ an estimated 18.5 million people, over a quarter of the nation's workforce. By the year 2000, women are expected to own 40 percent of the nation's businesses.

These range from companies that have annual revenues of $10 million or more, to those businesses that have started up with small loans of ten to twenty-five thousand dollars from the Small Business Administration. Their owners have launched them after a divorce, or to provide a second income, or to stay closer to home, or to be independent, or to circumvent the corporate glass ceiling. They may have chosen to become entrepreneurs to escape strict reporting structures, bureaucratic procedures, or policies and rules that constrict them from functioning freely at what they do best. They have strong beliefs about the best way to lead their own business and are very willing to share what they know. Not all of them have begun with a clear business plan, but they have seized opportunities for moving ahead.

Waitress Station as Launching Pad

"Entrepreneurial stuff is great only if it's you," says Bobbi Gutman of Motorola. "But it won't be successful for you if you're doing it because it's a trend, or your friends are doing it." Linda Weister started Cleany Boppers, Inc., in Baltimore because she had customers, not an organizational chart or a credit loan. One day, as a favor, she cleaned the house of the owner at whose restaurant she was waitressing. From then on, the requests kept rolling in.

Cleaning homes and offices when she was not waitressing hardly promised a new spin on life, but Weister's eyes were open to the need that dual-career couples have for cleaning services. At the time, she knew "absolutely nothing" about starting a business, but she had the savvy to not dismiss what she had learned in setting up her waitressing station. "I didn't know it, but a station is your small business. . . . You make sure everything is there so you don't have to run for whatever it is that isn't on the table . . . ashtrays, for example, Sweet 'N Low. Salt and pepper shakers are filled. . . . So you make sure when you go in at night that everything that you're going to need is ready. If it's summer, you cut up lemons for iced tea. . . . It's like with most businesses: It's not actually the doing of the job, but the preparation."

Giving Up a Paycheck

When you give up a regular paycheck, then you know you are taking a risk.

Weister realized she was growing a business when she began to hire other people to help her clean houses and told them the standards she expected them to meet. Within a short time, she decided to quit her night waitressing job and focus on starting a *real* company. "When you give up a regular paycheck, then you know you are taking a risk," she says.

She was shy about asking for advice because she felt sure everyone knew how to start a business except herself. But one day the truth hit her hard: "All of a sudden I realized I wasn't born knowing everything. If I don't ask, I'm not going to know; so then I didn't have a problem."

Weister says she learned about business the same way she learned the right way to clean houses. She consistently adapts her skills to new challenges. "If I had to clean a cork floor, I would call a tile place and find out. . . . You think when you buy Scotch Guard that no matter what spills on it you just dab it up and it will never stain. Well, it's like hairspray. Once you wash your hair, the hairspray is gone. Once you've washed the spot, the Scotch Guard has to be reapplied. . . . But there's no way you know this stuff. . . . So you have to call and ask people." The most difficult part of going into business, she claims, is learning that nothing is wrong with asking questions of somebody who knows the answers or can point in the right direction.

The resources of the National Association of Women Business Owners (NAWBO) were invaluable to Weister during the critical early years when she was starting Cleany Boppers, Inc. In appreciation of this support, she became an energetic member of the Baltimore Chapter of NAWBO, and eventually served as its president. She also devotes time to counseling women business owners in rural areas.

Dreams Are Goals

During her first year in business, Weister accumulated customers and concentrated on learning the cleaning trade. Halfway through the second year, she wrote down her short-term and five-year business goals. As she recalls them, she wanted to have in place responsible uniformed workers with fine references; effective training programs; and perks for employees, such as Christmas bonuses. Now she is considering adding a building for day-care facilities and an exercise room for employees. "I used to think dreams were nothing more than dreams; then I realized that dreams are goals and dreams are your

I realized that dreams are goals and dreams are your vision.

vision. We started out cleaning houses, and all of these things happened. A year ago we became computerized. I never thought my industry needed that. Then we got a fax machine, which I never thought we would use. . . ."

Having a written business plan keeps Weister motivated and focused, she says. It proves that she believes in herself and knows what she is trying to achieve. "It's not etched in stone. You can also change your mind about going in a certain direction, but it's good to stay on the same path. If something doesn't work, you learn more from where you've made a mistake. Hopefully, it won't cost you a lot, but sometimes it will."

Early on, Weister made costly mistakes in underestimating the price to clean a residence or commercial establishment. Now she is efficient in estimating the time and the cost of materials, and she is able to project annual revenues. Cleany Boppers, Inc., now employs a crew of twenty-four with an office staff of three. The annual revenue is $400,000.

Streamlining the Details

By setting goals for herself, Weister sets expectations for employees and rewards them with bonuses. Her inclination to nurture them often backfires, however. She agrees with Christine Toretti and Sherry Manning that a disadvantage women have as business owners is that "employees think you're their mother. You're their family away from home, and they expect things that families expect of other family members. I'm extremely sensitive to people's feelings. I don't believe in cracking the whip and saying, 'I said it, so you do it.' But I have had to become firmer. People tend to walk all over you and think 'Oh, Linda won't get mad.'"

Weister says she had to draw a line, for example, when drivers for crew trucks kept forgetting to retrieve their gas caps and expected her to replace them. Now she takes the cost out of their paychecks. Babysitting is another issue that plagues her when workers cannot commit because of problems with child care. "I used to sympathize and offer suggestions, but now I say 'We can't get you on the schedule if you can't find a babysitter. So you call me when you've made arrangements.'"

She has learned to toughen her management style by networking with other entrepreneurs at conferences. She prefers to explore business strategies from others like herself rather than by reading conceptual studies. "I don't care how different their business is

She prefers to explore business strategies from others like herself rather than by reading conceptual studies.

from yours—they could be making circuit boards for B-52 bombers—but they have the same problems because people are working for them." Being tough about protecting the bottom line does not mean that you have to be uncaring or callous about the day-to-day needs of employees, Weister says, but you have to draw clear distinctions for those who expect friendship.

A Social Conscience

Cleany Boppers, Inc., often cleans the homes of persons who are ill or hospitalized. "If my home is neat, it gives me a lift," Weister says. "So when I know of somebody who's gone through a tough time, I try to offer a solution. . . . Other people start doing things, and it's like a rippling effect. If would be so much nicer if everybody was busy helping each other instead of saying 'What is it that you can do for me?'"

The freedom to connect with the lives of others and create the social values of their own companies is very rewarding for entrepreneurial women. As in the case of Linda Weister, gender is often basic to why they are in the businesses they are in.

All Business Is Serious

Quilt making has long been a unique female art form. Making quilts has connected women to their own lives, to each other, and to a common historical past. Lynda Milligan is president and cofounder of The Great American Quilt Factory, Inc., which has an international market in Denver. She was a university graduate who had no business background. Because she always prized the quilt her grandmother had made for her, Milligan would routinely check out the window of a local quilt shop on her way home from a day of substitute teaching. She finally enrolled in a quilting class and worked at the store during the summer.

Milligan shared her dream about owning her own quilt and fabric store with Nancy Smith, a regular customer. They attended a quilting symposium together in Oregon and began to meet every week to shape a business plan. When they applied for a loan, they were dismayed to learn that the bank wanted the co-signatures of their husbands before it would give them financing. This was impossible for Milligan, who was in the process of a divorce, and Smith knew her husband would not agree. In order for them to open the store, Milligan's father-in-law, an entrepreneur himself, agreed to give them a small loan.

Sometimes when we said we had a quilting business, men would just ignore us.

From the very beginning, Milligan considered the store to be a serious business. But because quilting is typically perceived as a quirky feminine hobby, her vision of developing a major enterprise was often dismissed or patronized. Both men and women often said to her, "'Quilting . . . that must be a tax write-off for your husband'. . . . Sometimes when we said we had a quilting business, men would just ignore us." She warns that women need to be particularly vigilant about "continually projecting their businesses as businesses," especially when their enterprises grow out of a hobby or interest that they enjoy. To counteract this attitude, Milligan and Smith undertook a concerted campaign in Denver to show how they were supporting the community by employing people, bringing visitors to the city, and exporting Denver to a global market.

From an initial investment of $35 thousand, The Great American Quilt Factory, Inc., has annual sales of over $2 million, employs a staff of thirty, and exports products to Europe and Canada. They have diversified with DreamSpinners, which sells patterns for baby quilts, soft dolls, teddy bears, and home decorating items. "Possibilities," the publishing arm of their company, has won major national awards for its colorful manuals, which shatter stereotypes by teaching girls and boys creative sewing skills. Milligan and Smith are indefatigable leaders in having transformed a woman-oriented art and skill into a business that teaches others the pleasures and companionship of quilting and sewing.

Partners Must Click

Milligan attributes their success to a willingness and ability to "change and move along and not get stuck in one thing." She also stresses that she and Smith respond intuitively to each other. "We never sit down and say 'My goal is this,' but when we start talking about goals and where we want to go, we both want to be success-ful and we still like what we're doing. We want to stay in this busi-ness and like employing other women. . . . We have never actu-ally written down our goals, partly because we are always headed in the same direction. . . . If you're going to have a partner, the secret is that at the very beginning you have to find the person that you can really work with and then go for it."

They also recommend hiring an accountant who is involved with the business as more than simply a number cruncher. Theirs, Dick Rogers, helped them over many rough spots by giving them advice about management. "He knew what we didn't know," Mil-ligan says, "but he also helped us to see that we needed to hire help if we were going to spend our time expanding and developing the business instead of micromanaging."

Friendships on the Job

When they opened their door seventeen years ago, Milligan and Smith had only one employee; as their staff grew, the employees worked flexible hours and often brought their children with them. "We tend to get really involved with the people who work for us. That is a plus but also a liability," Milligan says, "because when changes have to be made which are best for the company, it's a real tough thing to handle. . . . We've let a lot of people bring their problems to work that in most places they'd be expected to leave at home, but that is part of the reason we like what we do. . . . It's not always been the best policy for the company in terms of profit margin, but in terms of people, it's great!"

Nonetheless, as the company expanded, Milligan and Smith hired a store manager, who has been a "godsend for taking care of

The people who have been here the longest complain that we're not the same company we used to be. problems. The people who have been here the longest complain that we're not the same company we used to be. We don't have the times where we just sit around and talk and laugh after work and let steam off."

Camaraderie has also changed at The Great American Quilt Factory because the space has been divided into a retail store and a shipping department. People who were recently hired from corporation jobs expect rules and procedures, but long-term employees are frustrated by them, Milligan says. She wants the atmosphere for employees to remain communal rather than competitive, a balance that is difficult for any business to achieve. It is particularly challenging for companies like The Great American Quilt Factory, where the owners want their leadership style to be compatible with the community-oriented heritage that the business also celebrates.

Forging New Solutions

When women business owners want to find new ways of collaborating with employees, it is sometimes hard for them to break through conventional procedures to figure out their own answers. Some answers are provided in *Thunderbolt Thinking* (Bernard-Davis) by Grace McGartland, former president of the NAWBO and the founder and president of GM Consultants, which serves Fortune 500 organizations, national trade and professional associations, and entrepreneurial companies. *Thunderbolt Thinking* is a treasure trove of creative and practical ideas for jolting employers into finding new solutions to organizational problems, as well as improving the bottom line. The exercises, which are humorous and engaging, stimulate creativity and innovative thinking. McGartland also offers suggestions for integrating a social conscience with business practices and projects.

Cottage Industries Take Off

Many women have started successful businesses at their kitchen tables, and many continue to do so, propelled by either financial need or a conviction about a demand they perceive in the culture. Two of the most successful entrepreneurial businesses in the country, Carolee Designs, Inc., and Chinaberry Book Service, Inc., were started by women who followed their talents, personal interests, and intuition in this way. Carolee Friedlander wanted to stay close to her young family, and Ann Reuthling wanted to connect with other parents who cared as much about what their children read as she did. Each began her business from inside her home.

Literally working from a kitchen table in her Riverside, Connecticut, house as a designer of upscale fashion jewelry, Carolee Friedlander began a business that has become a household name. Carolee Designs, Inc., is a multi-million-dollar business, and its jewelry is sold in boutiques and prime stores on both sides of the Atlantic. "Men start in their garages and women in their kitchens," Friedlander says.

Men start in their garages and women in their kitchens.

"In 1972, I was considered revolutionary, but I just reflected the times," Friedlander says. "I wanted to aggressively find something within me that could create income because it was harder for me to go outside of the home." Having enjoyed designing jewelry while she was a student at Bennington College, she turned to it again. "I didn't have very many other choices, I guess, in my own mind. To me it was almost like a natural. It was a skill and an art expression."

At the beginning, Friedlander spent a good deal of time experimenting with her products' appearance and durability. She recalls using Oreo cookies to test the density of different waxes for casting jewelry on her kitchen stove. Her first buyers were friends; the small accounts at stores in Connecticut she acquired by pounding the pavements. She says that her immediate goals were very modest, but even as a child she had been fiercely competitive with herself. In a short time, she was out of the kitchen and making her jewelry in a cabin studio in her backyard, for she wanted to expand but without having to stray far from her family. "Although my company might be twenty-three years old, in my mind it's only twelve," she says, "because for the first ten years I was really very focused on the children and making sure they were getting off to the start I felt was important for them."

Find Your Niche

During those years, Friedlander also was developing her business acumen. "What I learned then is key to where we are today, and that is what I try to pass on to entrepreneurial women. You have to find a niche which separates you from everyone else out there. At some point my vision was to realize that the types of jewelry that I would love to own were far out of my reach. . . . They might be in auction houses or museums, but I couldn't afford them. So my desire and my vision was to figure out how to make them. . . . I'm not the kind of person who would want to have a diamond ring, but to own something that looks as if it's from an Etruscan tomb would be very interesting to me. If I couldn't own the original, there was something amusing and satisfying about creating it. . . . I was driven by needing money but also by the need to express my creativity."

Friedlander got her first major break in 1976: a big order from Bloomingdale's, where she had personally convinced a buyer that Carolee Designs would attract an energetic new market. The account helped her to secure a $50 thousand loan from a local bank to buy more sophisticated equipment for her backyard studio. Oreos were definitely a part of her past—now she was landing accounts with Neiman-Marcus and Talbot's.

While she was able to manage well by doing everything herself when she started Carolee Designs, Friedlander's background was fine arts, not business. The second lesson she learned during her first decade in Carolee Designs was: "Be honest about your weaknesses and when you can afford to hire them, gradually surround yourself with a strong group of people."

Be honest about your weaknesses and when you can afford to hire them, gradually surround yourself with a strong group of people.

The Right Decision

By the mid-1990s, Friedlander had become president of the distinguished Committee of 200, the professional organization whose membership is composed of female entrepreneurs "whose companies generate an annual revenue of $10 million or greater, and corporate executives managing divisions that produce more than $50 million in annual revenue." Based in Chicago, the Committee sponsors regional and international activities that promote its members' business interests and constitute an important support network for them and others.

As the Committee's president, Friedlander has traveled across the United States speaking to diverse groups of entrepreneurs, sharing the experiences she has had and the decisions she has made along the way. For example, her early goal was to become a world-class manufacturer in fine jewelry, but she soon realized that the key to her success would be creating a brand and then a distribution network that would identify the brand worldwide. "This was a major decision," she stresses, "because manufacturing today in this country is not where it's at. That would probably have led us down the wrong path."

Today she guards the name and reputation of her jewelry by controlling how it is merchandised in department stores and boutiques throughout the world. She hires many of the sales staff who work behind the Carolee counters directly, paying their salaries and commission.

"When I began I didn't think about all of these things. . . . I was just trying to get something off the ground," she says. "I was not thinking about my management style or if I were a leader. I was trying to buck everything that was saying I couldn't do it. . . . I was just trying to get from A to B. It's only recently that there has been a focus on women and leadership. There will be a lot more women who will have gone through the same path I have, so that more stories and materials will be available."

Mentoring Employees

Friedlander is proud of providing opportunities for high achievers within her company, particularly women, to "rise above their expectations and fulfill their potential." Even when she was a fledgling entrepreneur, her impulse was to create an environment where employees were "free to give input with questions and ideas." As a woman in a business world largely populated by men,

Staying flexible is vital to business. . . . she always felt a "little offbeat" for encouraging consensus building among her employees and encouraging them to take ownership for their own ideas. "We have rules and standards but the company has always been nonhierarchical because flexibility is key to being creative," she explains. Staying flexible is vital to business, she notes, for adaptable, smaller companies are able to react more immediately and creatively to market changes than highly structured systems.

Success Is Calculated

Consequently, Friedlander knows that her success is not a matter of luck. She tries to stay ahead of opportunity by taking risks that are based on full knowledge and projected against their rewards. She is as flexible in spotting new advantages as she was when she was moving her jewelry equipment from the kitchen table into her backyard work studio. She has introduced jewelry on the QVC shopping network, and was the first to combine cosmetics with jewelry by joining with Estee Lauder cosmetics to mount in-store promotions. While other companies might be conservative in today's economy, Friedlander says she likes to "buck the crowd and follow hunches," introducing new designs with the kind of creative marketing that cuts into her competition. She is quick, however, to credit her business success to the 250 employees of Carolee Designs, who are mostly located in the company's factory facilities in Greenwich, Connecticut, and Providence, Rhode Island. Since 90 percent of the employees are women, "we have an ear to the ground and know what women want."

Choosing a Cause

The company has also demonstrated that social conscience and good business are synergistic. Each year's collection and marketing campaign are tied to a social cause. Rather than contribute company funds to charities in an impersonal way, Friedlander uses woman-to-woman empathy and involves her employees in the decision. The gift is then a unified expression of their skills for a cause they care about. In recent years, Carolee Designs, Inc., has donated time, talent, and a share of the profits to wildlife conservation, the Actors' Fund of America, and breast cancer research. To benefit the Susan G. Komen Breast Cancer Foundation's "Race for the Cure," Friedlander designed a pin featuring a female runner holding a pink ribbon, the symbol of breast cancer awareness. Five dollars from the sale of each pin at $12.50 were donated to the foundation, and Friedlander publicized the foundation's goals when she launched the campaign, as the company does with each of the social initiatives it supports.

Another Kitchen Story

Just as Carolee Friedlander is synonymous with upscale costume jewelry, Ann Reuthling is revered in children's book publishing. When Reuthling started a business from her kitchen table, she was acting purely on social conviction; she wanted enough money only to cover her mailing costs, for she lived in Port Orford, Oregon, a small fishing village where "you had to mail away for practically everything." From a stack of postcards, she grew Chinaberry Book Service, Inc., which quarterly sends throughout the world 250,000 Chinaberry catalogs that offer "books and other treasures for the entire family."

Wanting a change from the corporate pace, Reuthling left her position as a marketing manager for a regional airline in Denver and moved with her husband to "the fartherest point west in the continental U.S." Port Orford, with a population of one thousand, seemed the perfect place for Ed to make a good living as a carpenter while Ann worked inside their home. When their first child was born, most of their time was spent indoors because the weather was so bad. "Elizabeth loved being read to, but I was taken aback by the violence and the sexual stereotyping in classic Mother Goose: 'Peter, Peter pumpkin eater had a wife

Elizabeth loved being read to, but I was taken aback by the violence and the sexual stereotyping in classic Mother Goose. . . .

and couldn't keep her,' and the old lady who had so many kids that she beat them and put them in a shoe. I did not feel we should plop one- and two-year-olds down on our laps and tell them that people are violent and sexist and lack respect for each other. They're going to find out how messed up the world is soon enough."

As she read aloud to Elizabeth, Reuthling often found herself changing words and sometimes skipping pages because she wanted to show her daughter positive examples of people caring about each other. So when the Reuthlings left Port Orford to visit larger cities, Ann spent time in libraries, taking notes on as many children's books as possible. Before long, she had a stack of index cards three inches tall, filled with notes such as, "When Elizabeth is four, I should try to get my hands on this book."

Reuthling was certain that other parents also cared about their children's reading, and she compiled her notes in a brochure that she began to advertise in parenting magazines: "Positive and uplifting books. Send for free catalog." She worried that families living in small towns would lack access to the books she recommended, so she "became a bookstore" herself and arranged to buy books on credit with a few publishers. That way, if parents read about *Good Night, Moon* in her catalog, they would be able to get it through Chinaberry.

At first, Reuthling's "bookstore" contained about forty books, which she kept stacked on a very high shelf in her toddler's bedroom. In a good week, she would have five orders to fill. For two years she worked from her kitchen table, packing books into boxes and enclosing handwritten thank-you notes. "It certainly was not a moneymaker, but a money loser. We were using grocery money on it," Reuthling says. "But I was in it for the service and because I found it very, very interesting and loved connecting with people."

No Way People Will Read These Things

Reuthling says the business turned a corner when they moved to San Diego and she and her husband began working together as a real team. "We just sort of did things by the seat of our pants. . . . We found out later that some of the things we tried were just basically unheard of in mail order, but they worked for Chinaberry. Our catalog is not a classic, glossy, four-color catalog. And our customers just really appreci-

I guess the secret to our success is that we cared about making the world a better place.

ated connecting with other concerned parents and loved reading about the books. I guess the secret to our success is that we cared about making the world a better place."

For example, the Reuthlings went against the advice of a representative they consulted from the Service Corps of Retired Executives (SCORE), who told them, "'You can't put out this funky newsprint catalog with no color pictures and all this text. . . . There's no way people are going to read these long things you've written. . . . You have to get some visuals and then rent name lists according to where all the money is.' When he left, we just looked at one another and said, 'No way. That feels too yucky.' And from then on, we just do what in our hearts we feel is right. It would have been the kiss of death if we had followed his advice, but we've since found out that they are really givens in the world of mail order. . . . We did not go where the money was, but where people of like minds would be."

In fact, Reuthling claims that the secret of her success has been in "following my heart rather than my head. And that says it all. If I would have followed my head I would have looked at the numbers and thought, 'There's no way Chinaberry can ever put food on our table,' but I just knew what I had to do for my firstborn—you know how those firstborns sort of turn into our projects. And we did it, and here we are!"

> *If I would have followed my head I would have looked at the numbers and thought, 'There's no way Chinaberry can ever put food on our table.'*

Since 1982, Chinaberry has accumulated over 120,000 active customers. Ed Reuthling (he is left brained and she is right brained, Ann says) manages the fifty staff members and "runs the show at the warehouse. He sits in his office and looks at numbers a lot," she notes. She describes herself as "the keeper of the spirit. . . . We really aren't in this just to make money . . . but to provide a service and to continue to try to make the world a better place just from our efforts."

Still Personal

Reuthling herself still selects the books, writes most of the notations for the catalog, and participates in the design with artist

Louise Popoff, a former neighbor from Orford. The catalog remains anti-glitz, filled with watercolor illustrations that kindle a sense of wonder. Why "Chinaberry?" "It wasn't because there was a big chinaberry tree in our front yard," Reuthling says. The title is also an Orford import, from a good friend who was an early supporter of Reuthling's ideas about a mail-order bookstore. Reuthling recalls how she spurred her to create it: "If you go home tonight and think of a name and come back tomorrow, I'll feed you a huge breakfast of toast and waffles until you're full," she promised. The friend returned with "Chinaberry" because her favorite story as a child was *Under the Chinaberry Tree,* and she had always thought chinaberry was a pretty word.

Despite her invisible ties with the many readers who relish the Chinaberry catalog, Reuthling does not consider herself a "people person." But "I know I can write powerfully about the things I feel deeply about," she says. "If I find a book I like, I have powerful thoughts about it and it's a gift of mine to be able to express that in my writing."

No narrow-minded idealogue, she is clearly professional. ". . . I would never stand up and say 'This is right; this is wrong.' But if I find a book that propounds or gives an example which I think is right behavior, then I will carry that book. . . . I will just say 'Here is a good book and here's why, but you may not agree with me.' . . . I don't preach about my values." What are her favorites? *Miss Rumphius* by Barbara Cooney is a story that she observes "pretty much says it all." Margaret Wise Brown's *Good Night, Moon* is also among her favorites.

Time to Change

As her daughter and son grow older, Reuthling finds herself less interested in books for little children, but she says she knows her staff will carry on her tradition because of the young mothers among them. Now she is more attracted to books on relationships and those that express women's spirituality. "I'm beginning to see that first and foremost I'm a woman rather than a mother, but for ten years or so I felt mostly like a mother. That identity is falling away now," she says. "Chinaberry could branch out to cater as much to women as it has to families."

Indeed, recent Chinaberry catalogs have included pages titled "Tapestry, books and tools for the crafting of the spirit." Among the books annotated with Reuthling's comments are *The Couple's Comfort Book* by Jennifer Louden; *Care of the Soul* by Thomas Moore; and *Coming Into Our Fullness: On Women Turning Forty* by Cathleen Rountree.

I'm beginning to see that first and foremost I'm a woman rather than a mother, but for ten years or so I felt mostly like a mother.

Bicoastal Marriage

For the past nine years of their thirty-year marriage, Maxine Coleman, vice president of personnel and organization with Kal Kan Foods., Inc., and her husband have lived on separate coastlines. "People can't seem to fashion how we manage this, but many things were in place beforehand. Number one is having unbelievable trust. If you don't have trust, forget it."

After college, the Colemans postponed having children because of economic factors, but then decided that their "lifestyle was such that we would resent kids, and that would not have been fair to them. . . . But I had to say, how do I really feel about that? Do I feel I've let down the human race by not fulfilling that responsibility? I really don't believe that. I'm comfortable with my life and the way it has worked," Maxine Coleman explains.

When she was asked to go to California for Kal Kan, she and her husband "didn't have to think about it very much at all," even though his work would keep him in Philadelphia. "He's my best friend and we are very strong supporters of each other. We have always understood what was important to each other's careers. It was not fair for me to ask him to give up everything that he had worked for to watch me get on an airplane, because I'm gone a lot. And so we just said, we're going to figure out how to make this work."

While business trips often bring them together, the Colemans also travel back and forth for weekends and take long vacations together. "Planning is key," Maxine Coleman says "and we know that our lives can't be very spontaneous."

Planning is key, and we know that our lives can't be very spontaneous.

Frequent telephone conversations keep them involved in each other's daily lives. "When he's in Philadelphia and I'm in California, we use the telephone as if we're in the next room. . . . He's my wake-up call at five A.M. Sometimes it's just hi and other times we have a long conversation. . . . We found out very quickly how unimportant some things are that used to seem like the end of the world. You don't spend a lot of time arguing and pouting. You get right to the heart of an issue, get it over with and on to the next thing. We just simply don't have the luxury of letting things go on and on . . . and that has been very good for us. It's helped both of us grow."

Even when she and her husband are separated, Coleman says she keeps her work distinct from her private life. "In the personnel field, you take it home in your head anyway and can't easily let go of it. So I have to try to maintain a dividing line by not taking paperwork home with me. . . . If the pile gets high, I try to at least have a Saturday to myself and come in on a Sunday morning when no one is here. Then at least the bulk of the day is mine."

Up From Junk

Now president of Western Industrial Contractors, Denver, Colorado, Barbara Grogan became an entrepreneur after a divorce when she had young children and not much money. From modest savings and a small loan, she started a construction business; she bought an old pickup truck and rented an office across from a junkyard, and eventually began to specialize in the building and installing of heavy industrial equipment. Today the company has an annual revenue of $5 million and employs more than eighty people.

Grogan describes her decision to go into business as an "act of lunacy that should never have worked. At that time I wasn't thinking 'Won't this be fabulous—a woman in a pioneer role'—or that I'll be entrepreneur of the year. I just knew I had to figure out something I could do that would work and allow me to support my kids.

"For a while, I sat around waiting for a white knight to show up," she recalls. Marilyn French's *The Women's Room* was her "wake-up call," she says: It made her realize that she had to take responsibility for her own life, "however scary. There are many opportunities out there, and generally the boxes we've built around ourselves are of our own building. It doesn't make any difference whether you're in a small town, a medium town, or a big city. We each have skills and talents, and we can use them."

Business and Community

Grogan is as committed to responding to social needs as she is to growing her company. She estimates that 25 percent of her time is given to the community. In 1988, she headed a ragtag team to reverse the decline of the Denver public schools. Ignoring those who said it couldn't be done, she managed to spearhead efforts that resulted in a bond issue of $199.6 million, the largest in Denver history, marked for deferred maintenance and capital improvement projects. She became the first woman in the organization's 108-year history to become chairperson of the Greater Denver Chamber of Commerce. She started a community program to prepare women and minority members to become entrepreneurs. "Leadership is about convincing others to believe in their dreams," she says.

Leadership is about convincing others to believe in their dreams.

More to Life Than Work

"Western Industrial Contractors is a big part of my life, but not my life," Grogan says. "I want to leave the world a better place by providing a company where people are happy and can thrive. And having my own business also allows me the luxury of being involved in the community and helping to be a catalyst for change."

For Grogan, it is impossible to not integrate politics with daily life and work. "I don't believe that you can segregate your life," she observes. "And when you're involved in parenting, you can't help but see all the ancillary issues that are impacting our children and the future. I don't know how you ignore them, and so women in

It's frightening that national policy is being made without us at the table.

business do have a social conscience that makes them want to make the world a better place. Lots of men are doing the same thing . . . [but] it's very frightening that women are not taking over leadership positions in either the Congress or Senate. . . . It's frightening that national policy is being made without us at the table."

An employer's commitment to nurturing employees is the key difference between being a leader and a manager, she asserts. "Leadership is about inspiring and empowering people to do what they would normally do anyway once they had that awareness."

Without the Charts

As a function of Grogan's business style, the new building for Western Industrial Contractors contains few interior doors. She had specified that she wanted open spaces, so in the architect's first plan, all the offices were designed without doors—except her own. "He couldn't believe that I did not want a door on my office," she says. "But I think the most important person in the company *not* to have a door is me. . . . People know they can walk in and see me any time and not wait for decisions."

She says she prefers to bring staff together quickly to solve problems as needed rather than to wait until some regularly scheduled meeting. This ability to respond rapidly is crucial to the success of her company, she points out.

She has not always commanded such a degree of certainty. As a new entrepreneur, she read numerous books on how to manage a business and absorbed much advice on setting goals and writing job descriptions. "But all the time I hated it," she says. "I would have these stupid meetings and we would write all this stuff, and I thought 'I can't do it this way. It's wasting energy that I need to be using to make this company work.' So I just threw out all those books and started listening to tapes like Robert Schuller and Brian Tracy that were much more empowering and gave me the inner strength and courage to follow what intuitively felt right."

As a result, Grogan abolished conventional flowcharts in favor of achieving open communication. She focused on creating trusting relationships with her clients and instilled her staff with the intention of delivering the highest level of service possible. "We didn't do a lot of the things that other companies were doing twelve years ago, but now they are interested in our management style and writing about it. When people call up and say 'Do you have a TQM [Total Quality Management] program?' I say, 'We've focused on *quality* since the day we were born. . . . It would never occur to us to focus on anything else.' So when someone says, 'You need a TQM program,' I say, 'Give me a break. . . . If you provide top service, customers come back. Giant industry is trying to figure out how to have the entrepreneurial role model. What is corporate America thinking about? If they weren't doing TQM, help me understand what they *were* doing!'"

Women in highly responsible positions are often asked how they balance the priorities of work and family, though this would certainly seem an odd question indeed to pose to a man. Grogan has little patience with stereotyped attitudes about family life and professional achievements. "I don't think anyone should look at my life, whether they are 20 or 80, and say, 'Well, her life isn't in balance,' she says. "They have no idea unless they've walked in my shoes." She turned down an invitation to speak on a panel called "The Sacrifice of Success," explaining to the sponsor that "sacrifice" is a victim word. She seldom attends black-tie dinners and late-night receptions, she adds, because she has a teenager at home. "He's over six foot, but still needs my love and attention. Is that a sacrifice?" she asks. "I don't think so. That is a life choice. *Sacrifice* is a cop-out word to me."

Chapter Six

Women in Arts Management: Out on Thin Ice

Whether they are engaged in the arts as producers, managers, funders, or policy makers, these professionals are kindred spirits who share a genuine passion for bringing the arts to public attention. Despite sometimes grueling hours and persistently tight budgets, they seldom yearn to be elsewhere, they say.

Passion Is Indispensable

Karen Brooks Hopkins, the executive vice president of the Brooklyn Academy of Music (BAM), the oldest performing arts center in the United States, says she remembers the magic of attending Broadway plays with her parents. "I've really been single-minded from junior high school and couldn't tell you that I've done much else. It's always where I've been comfortable and where I wanted to be."

Since 1979, Hopkins has completed many profitable fund-raising campaigns for BAM. She also published *Successful Fundraising for Arts and Cultural Organizations,* a basic text for arts management masters programs.

Her first love was not administration, but theater. As a student at the University of Maryland, she acted and directed plays. When she graduated, she joined the theater department of the Jewish Community Center and the New Playwrights Theater in Washington, D.C.; she turned to development as a way of remaining in the theater, but in a capacity that offered security. Hopkins says that her firsthand knowledge of the stage has helped her to become a more effective professional: "You're a much better advocate when you really understand and have a passion for what you're selling," she notes.

You're a much better advocate when you really understand and have a passion for what you're selling.

Alliances Needed

Enlarging the role of the arts in mainstream U. S. culture means that arts professionals must persuade larger audiences that art is essential to the quality of life—for them and future generations of U.S. citizens. Making this transition from having a private vocation to setting a public agenda is daunting, even for those arts administrators who clearly address the issues.

"It would be better for the arts if we weren't so isolated from other fields, and even from each other," Hopkins says. "For the more the arts connect with mainstream audiences, the more the arts will be invited to participate in all kinds of discussions about all of the critical issues of society." But when finances shrink, day-to-day problems are often so consuming that even a visionary leader is detained from outlining a broader public agenda.

"My job here is just to keep moving, keep changing strategies for fundraising," Hopkins says. "Whether it's government or corporate or private fund-raising, the challenge here is to adapt a campaign to deal with an unfriendly climate."

Museums, theaters, orchestras, and other institutions need to find the money to present new work and new programs for attracting and keeping audiences, while simultaneously remaining fiscally sound. Hopkins lists the problems in doing that: "How will we build audiences for the future," she asks, "when arts education has met its demise in the schools? What happens if we don't build audiences for the future? How do we give culture a value in this country? What can we say about developing a passion for the arts and their intellectual value? How do we get it across that the arts are a tool for the economic development of America? . . . How do we keep our edge? How do we continue to push the envelope of human experience and communicate it artistically as well as keep alive great classical works so that people have a sense of their tradition? There's a lot we have to figure out and deal with [but] how are we going to meet the payroll this week?"

Passion and Trust

"It's easy to get up in the morning, knowing that the people around you are equally challenged and committed," says Alice C. Walsh, president and chief operating officer of the Alaska Center for the Performing Arts in Anchorage. As a student at the experimental John Dewey High School in New York City, she was required to carry out every task involved in a theater production, and she learned then that she preferred working behind the scenes to being on stage. But since few undergraduate interdisciplinary programs in the arts were available in 1976, she enrolled in New York University (NYU) as an acting major. While she was not happy as an actor, she loved the performing arts and theater and considered getting a degree in accounting as a wedge into theater administration. Rather than have her forsake her work for a bachelor's degree in fine arts, the NYU faculty encouraged her to design a program that integrated the liberal arts with practical internships. So when other students were taking their acting classes, Walsh reported to off-Broadway theaters to learn management. A few years later, she finished a master's degree in public administration with a specialization in nonprofit management.

"It's very rare that people in the arts aren't giving 110 percent," she says. "That drives you because you want to do a good job for them, because they are busting their tails for you. And in the end, we all want to do a good job for the artists who are on stage and also for the community. . . . In the arts, you never feel like you're by yourself. You've always got a whole team of people around you pulling."

The relationship that Alice Walsh has with the staff at the Alaska Center for the Performing Arts is largely the result of her early experiences in the theater, she says. "I can't describe my style with any kind of buzz words, but it's a natural outgrowth of my passion for what I do. . . . I've worked in almost every capacity in the theater. Now technology has changed considerably, and if somebody asked me right now to go downstairs and run the light or soundboard, I probably couldn't do it because now it's all computerized. . . . But the point is that my staff knows that at some point I have swept the stage, sold tickets, painted sets, sewed costumes . . . and so there's a certain camaraderie."

For Walsh it feels only natural to seek staff opinion and encourage discussion. "But there are some times when you either don't have the time or it's not appropriate to bring an issue to the staff. The key to leadership is that the staff trusts you are treating them fairly and making the best decisions that you can in their behalf."

Calculating the Audience

As Karen Hopkins's questions imply, governmental and many sectors of the public may believe that the creative and performing arts are a dispensable frill, but the staff of an arts organization is bonded by their passion for the arts. Alice Walsh says she interacts with the staff intuitively because they share her commitment and "we all love what we're doing." Walsh is also comfortable with her board, which she says is very clear about its mission and about giving her direction.

People in the arts are very good at pulling rabbits out of hats, but not as good at writing a press release or announcing the next day, 'Hey, look, we pulled this rabbit out of a hat.'

Her external leadership is more calculating. "It's really about developing a plan and carrying it out to educate people about what we do in the arts and humanities," she says. "People in the arts are very good at pulling rabbits out of hats, but not as good at writing a press release or announcing the next day, 'Hey, look, we pulled this rabbit out of a hat'."

To acquire and apply this kind of expertise, she believes that professionals in the arts need to organize. The message to be expressed is that the arts are fundamental to society, a fact that seems especially elusive in an era when they are often suspected of being subversive. Because she knows that this understanding starts in communities, she takes every opportunity to speak to local organizations. "I love to raise money because if I speak to a Rotary group and convince somebody how important my organization is to the point where a week or a month later they write out a check, that means they have not only been persuaded by my project, but also to the importance of the arts in general."

Now in her late thirties, Walsh is determined to explore her own personal creativity. She credits the demands of family life with helping her become a better theater manager: Marrying at age 30, she became an instant parent with a stepdaughter. Then she had a baby. "So different personal factors affect the way you spend your time and decide what is a priority and what isn't," she says. "There's no question that I have not lowered my standards, but I have changed the way that I work in the past few years. . . . I promised I wouldn't use buzz phrases, but I can't escape this one: I definitely work smarter now than I did. That's the result of being older, but also external factors force you to work smarter."

Two years ago, Walsh started lessons in singing and photography. It tickled her not to be recognized when she sneaked on stage to join the chorus for an Anchorage Opera production of *Madame Butterfly*. "It was a wonderful personal experience," she says, "but it also gave me an opportunity to experience my own facility from the other side, as a performer."

Getting It Real

Lee Grant has a formidable reputation in film, theater, and television. As an actor, she won an Academy Award for her performance in *Shampoo* and nominations for those in *The Landlord* and *The Voyage of the Damned*. She received an Obie Award for her role in Jean Genet's *The Maids*, and Emmys for performances in *The Neon Ceiling* and the television series, *Peyton Place*.

In midlife, Grant's interests started shifting toward directing, she says. "I don't know if *enjoy* is the word I'd use for it," she observes. "I have to be obsessed with something or impassioned by it, or else I have no ambition or gumption—no anything. . . . I took on another career where women were not particularly welcome and stepped into really hostile territory, but it was something that I just needed to do."

She is drawn to direct documentaries because of her sense of justice and her exasperation that the reporting of daily news is "slanted, distorted, or made into entertainment. . . . The news, which is the life around us, is becoming a joke," Grant says, "and has nothing to do with fairness or having any feeling about the world and what it should be, or about the people in it and what they desire."

Her earliest perception of *injustice* occurred in a very private moment. "It was nothing I voiced as a kid. But when I was about 8, I saw a man moving in on a woman on Broadway. . . . She tried to get away in a bus, but the driver closed the doors in her face. People stood in a kind of circle around her, but didn't do anything to help. I ran and got a policeman, but when we returned, they had gone. The policeman said to me, 'Oh, it's just a couple fighting. They're probably sitting in a bar someplace talking it out.' But even as a little kid my mind kind of flopped at this man in uniform who I thought would save the situation, not seeing that somebody was in danger or scared. . . . Nobody was helping her."

Collaborating

Grant's documentaries address burning social issues. *Down and Out in America*, which deals with homelessness, won an Academy Award in 1987. Among her other documentaries are *Willmar 8, When Women Kill, Battered,* and *Women on Trial. Willmar 8* tells the powerful story of women bank employees who went on strike against a bank in Willmar, Minnesota, because the president hired men, had the women train them, and then made the men their bosses. In protest, the women picketed the bank in all kinds of weather for a year. "More banks bought that documentary than anyone else," Grant says, "and it's brought about some important changes in banking."

I carry in my heart a great sense of unfairness, and I don't think it has a label on it or a political name.

Grant also took chances with *Women on Trial,* a 1993 film. It depicts the dilemma of two women in Houston, Texas, who raised the question of abuse when a judge in divorce proceedings ruled against their seeing or having communication with their children for three years. "I carry in my heart a great sense of unfairness, and I don't think it has a label on it or a political name," Grant says. "It's something I've always had, and the documentaries give me an outlet for it."

Asked to describe her style as a director, Grant observes that while the decisions about selecting, casting, and shooting are vital ones, her day-to-day instincts for her work are partly the result of her own acting experience. "I've worked with many directors myself as an actor, and I trust them as kind of paternal or maternal figures who will keep my best interests in mind. And I think that's what I have to be to the actors and writers who work with me. . . . I have to be that figure who makes everything comfortable, easy, who makes it nice for cameramen and actors and the director of photography and production designers to come to work. I have to create the atmosphere so that the best things can happen. Being a director is endless responsibility. It's a great collaborative experience."

Grace and Joy

The exuberance of participating in an artistic production extends beyond those who take an on-the-scene part in performing it. The grant makers and funders I spoke with all assert their own pleasure in the performing arts as a continual inspiration to them. Marian A. Godfrey, program director for culture at The Pew Charitable Trusts, says: "I'm driven personally and reinvigorated by experiences I feel lucky to have once in a while sitting in a theater. Most recently I had it at the Los Angeles Philharmonic, listening to a Beethoven symphony. I thought I was jaded about symphonies playing the dramatic repertory of the nineteenth century, but I had an epiphany. . . . I was swept away. Sometimes this happens in the theater or at a dance concert or at a museum. I know myself at those moments and have some kind of understanding about grace and joy in the world. And that's priceless to me. That might seem corny, but it's very true and keeps me committed and believing and trusting in what I do."

Tough Questions

At the Pew Trusts, Godfrey manages a program budget of $18 million a year. She is responsible for developing and recommending programming policy to the executive leadership and to the board. She also defends every grant the Trusts decide to make at quarterly meetings of the board.

The skills she uses at the Trusts were acquired and refined during the twelve years she spent as a performing arts manager and consultant in New York City. She was manager of the theater collaborative Mabou Mines, for which she also produced a feature film, *Dead End Kids: A Story of Nuclear Power*. She also worked as theater consultant to AT&T, and was New York representative to the La Jolla Playhouse.

She sees herself as a facilitator within a broad societal effort on behalf of the arts, working within a system—philanthropy. As arts advocates have been forced to intensify their efforts for financing, grant makers, funders, and arts administrators have had to assume responsibility for attempting to influence or shape public policy. During the eight years that Godfrey has been with the Pew Trusts, she says she has learned a great deal about this process from colleagues in other fields, such as education or health and human services.

*T*hose of us in the arts need to think more systematically about policy issues.

"Those of us in the arts need to think more systematically about policy issues," Godfrey says. "We need to have a lot more research and data and analysis of research to really understand how culture fits into the American system. There is a sense of urgency about this that we didn't have even six years ago. . . . So all of this together has caused me to arrive at the point where I am now. I'm trying to combine the practical work of supporting the arts with the intellectual work of making a case for the arts in order to influence policy discussions that need to take place."

The perception that the arts are indispensable to society begins at a grassroots level. But the struggle to find the right words for making a persuasive case is often so difficult that arts administrators retreat to the cocoon of like-minded people.

Even when foundations are proactive or interventionist, they can merely facilitate leadership, Godfrey says. "We can lead with an idea and bring people to the table and make resources available, but the actual leadership happens on the ground."

For example, if locally elected government officials, including school boards, are not convinced of the necessity of the arts, a foundation has little clout for being able to integrate an art curriculum into the school system. "Children are growing up without any sense of what the arts can do for them," Godfrey says. "You don't have to be a practitioner to be passionate about your experience of music, and yet most people don't even have enough access to music when they are young to have it influence their understanding about things they have an ability to do. . . ." Raising consciousness about such issues is beyond what a single individual or foundation can achieve. Consequently, arts advocacy groups are moving out of their private compartment and working together to offer more focused leadership on the value of integrating the arts into the life of a community.

Mainstreaming the Arts

When Congress gutted the Arts and Humanities Endowments, a number of women reinvented themselves as public arts advocates. Anne Bogart is well-known as the director of the distinctive Saratoga International Theatre Institute (SITI). "More and more," Bogart says she sees herself acting as a leader, "not because I feel motivated to be that, but I sense that people who feel passionately about the arts need to speak out. I have a great love for the role of the theater and I'm very committed to young people going into theater, so I'm beginning to feel a little bit like a spokesperson. . . . I don't feel that I represent the theater, but I should speak out about it and try to articulate what I understand."

Bogart says that many local artists who work in the theater, especially those who offer their talents as freelancers, "are protected by regional theaters and are not expected to have any responsibility to the audiences that we serve. I think it's time to go through the uncomfortable process of getting to know our audiences," she observes, "and to share our thoughts with them."

As often as she can, Bogart speaks at symposiums throughout the country about the urgency to support the arts: "I try to articulate from my own perspective where we come from and where we might be going." As the advisor to the graduate directing program at Columbia University, she also encourages "young people to look at the tradition out of which they come and ask questions about what the responsibilities are to serve. Most young people are encouraged to become stars, and that's what their values are based on. But once you start questioning that, they can change their minds. . . . They start realizing that there might be more to life than their individual successes as entertainment stars."

Great theater is both entertaining and life-altering, but since the McCarthy era when actors and playwrights were blacklisted, Bogart says that U. S. drama has backed away from exploring social issues. Tony Kushner is a playwright she greatly admires for courageously writing about contemporary problems. *"Angels in America* was highly successful, and it's made money, which makes everybody happy," Bogart observes.

Art Weathers

. . . artists also need to keep doing what we do to the best of our abilities because [art] will find a way.

Now that artists themselves are articulating the case that support for the arts is in the self-interest of the nation, Sharon Ott, artistic director of the Seattle Repertory Theatre, stresses the long-term perspective: "Art weathers whatever storm. . . . I do feel that we need to be better advocates for what we do, but artists also need to keep doing what we do to the best of our abilities because [art] will find a way."

Ott also notes the catch-22 of her argument: "Those who grant federal funding can also say that Herman Melville wrote *Moby Dick* without an NEA [National Endowment for the Arts]. Of course, some solo person will always figure out a way to write a great play, but those of us who aren't the geniuses may not figure out a way to do it. Also there may not be the environment to foster an appreciation of the great play once it is written. . . . The arts really contribute to a climate, a general humanist quality of life that enlightened societies understand, and that's what we're in danger of losing."

Before joining the Seattle Repertory in 1997, Ott was artistic director of the Berkeley Repertory Theatre for twelve years and, before that, the Milwaukee Repertory Theater for four years. "As director you lead the ensemble, but the artistic director of a theater is a whole level of leadership that is in many ways a trial by fire," she says. At BRT, the San Francisco Bay audiences did not give her "much time to float around. I was expected to be a leader the minute I got there. . . . I wouldn't have been able to stay in the job if I weren't able to quickly decide where I wanted to lead the theater, and then get it there."

With her vision, the Berkeley Repertory Theatre grew from a budget of $1.5 million to $4 million. It has a national reputation for presenting experimental plays as well as new adaptations of the classics. Ott is particularly well-known for her pioneering efforts in multiracial casting and expanding the BRT in relation to the Asian-Pacific culture surrounding it.

She says that her 1994 original production of *The Woman Warrior*, based on the narratives of Maxine Hong Kingston, was the most "rewarding piece of theater" she has done as a producer and director: "I was proud that in times that are this difficult we [the BRT, The Huntington Theatre Company, and the Center Theater Group of Los Angeles] were able to support a work of art of that scope, size, and dimension, and it was genuinely cross-cultural by representing Chinese America as a developing American culture."

A Transformation

Ott's perspective was shaped as a student of theater and structural anthropology at Bennington College. "I know it's partially my training as an anthropologist that causes my proclivity to stand back and watch how a situation

T heater is not just about producing plays . . . but about the dynamics of life within a community.

is developing and to observe in a rather detached fashion the underlying rules of how a society really operates. . . . I'm aware of change and look beyond what's happening on a daily basis to the future. Theater is not just about producing plays . . . but about the dynamics of life within a community."

Ott is quick to say that she does not place herself in the company of the pioneering generation of women in theater like Zelda Fichandler, founding director of Arena Stage in Washington, D.C., or Sara O'Connor, the managing director of the Milwaukee Repertory

Company. She notes that because of their example, more women were able to become managers, artistic directors, and directors. Though while more women are now in leadership positions in the performing arts, Ott thinks that succeeding generations of women will have a "very, very, very hard time finding their way [because] the venues just don't exist now for working in small theaters."

Government cutbacks have eliminated the small theaters and the publicly funded programs that helped young people get started in the arts. "I bopped around in small theaters for eight years before I was hired by Milwaukee Repertory. . . . I wouldn't hire somebody right away [without sufficient experience]. So when young directors come to me and ask how I did it, I don't know how to tell them that there's nothing like that open for them. They can't imitate what I did."

Scranton Was Important

Thirty years ago, Sondra Myers began her career as a volunteer for an arts project in Scranton, Pennsylvania. That was the first step toward her position with the National Endowment for the Humanities (NEH) as special assistant to the chairman for institutional relations.

After the creation of the National Endowments for the Arts and Humanities in 1965, arts projects in small communities increased. Wanting to expand and enrich the arts in Scranton, her hometown, Myers, a Phi Beta Kappa graduate from the University of Pennsylvania, talked with administrators at the University of Scranton about sponsoring a concert program that had a "little more depth, substance, and diversity." In particular, she wanted to bring in an African-American dance company from New York City. She was persuasive, and her campaign was a success. From then on, she became more aggressive in trying to create a friendly environment for the arts.

"It's important that I was in Scranton," Myers says, "because in a small city if you've shown your colors, people will trust you and you develop a reputation easier. I was able to get my training in making decisions and presenting ideas and persuading people.

If I had happened to live in a big city, I probably would have gotten a job and maybe wouldn't have felt confident about my leadership skills."

Her work was so visible and appreciated that Myers was one of the first people appointed to the Pennsylvania Humanities Council: She became a player in its development and soon became chair. Her entrepreneurial spirit has continued to advance the arts. With each move, from local to state to national, she has increased her knowledge, confidence, experience, credibility, and contacts.

When Robert Casey was elected governor of Pennsylvania, Myers proposed a new position that would work toward integrating culture into public policy at all levels of government. He accepted the idea and named her as cultural advisor, a post she held until her appointment to the NEH with the Clinton administration.

Using Her Bully Pulpit

Myers was not drawn to the arts as a performing or creative artist herself, but when, as a philosophy major at Penn, she became interested in visiting Philadelphia's museums, attending concerts, and going to the theater. "I

I guess I would have to say I came to the arts more through my intellect than a personal affinity.

guess I would have to say I came to the arts more through my intellect than a personal affinity. . . . I took studio art but am very inept at it. . . . It was what I thought and felt about artistic expression that attracted me and trying to understand the impact that art has on the individual as well as society. Later, as an extension of my civic interests in Scranton, I wanted the arts and humanities to be more available and integrated into the community."

Thirty years later, Myers's commitment is much the same, but from her NEH "bully pulpit" she has more clout "to change the landscape." Her talent has always been in creating new audiences for the arts. Her dream is a cabinet-level position for culture. "I think this will eventually happen," she says, "but probably not in my life. It will evolve if we don't receive absolutely draconian cuts which would render us ineffectual." She sees establishment of such an office as the natural outcome of the success of the endowments in creating art programs across the country. "A steamroller cannot be run over the process. We cannot set back the clock because communities and citizens have come to respect more and more what the government/cultural enterprise can do." She is certain the results will "bubble up" into a more coherent cultural policy for the nation, and that the cabinet-post-to-be will ensure that the arts will be an integral part of U.S. public policy.

For Sondra Myers, art is an essential manifestation of the spirit of the country. For Sondra Myers, art is an essential manifestation of the spirit of the country. Art creates a context for defining all aspects of our national aspirations, including the most pragmatic concerns. "What drives me," she says, "is that I want to live in a society that I am proud of and a society that is appropriate to what our founding documents say. We were the invention of creative minds."

If she were to begin her career now, how would she go about arriving in the position she presently holds? She describes herself as "self-taught and going on intuition," and in today's world, she says, she probably would have studied for an advanced degree in arts management or policy. "It's hard to recreate myself . . . but if I wanted to run a major arts agency or facility now, I certainly would like to have the management skills." But more important, she says, is having an "appetite for trying to understand the role that art plays and what impact it has on the individual as well as society."

Wrong Address

Sandra A. Kimberling says she loves her job as president of the Music Center Operating Company (MCOC), the enterprise that runs the Music Center of Los Angeles County (MCLAC). She is responsible for one of the outstanding performing arts centers in the United States and oversees a twenty-four-hour operation. The Music Center includes the Dorothy Chandler Pavilion, which houses the Los Angeles Opera, the Los Angeles Philharmonic, and the Los Angeles Master Chorale. The Center Theater Group, also included in the Music Center, is composed of the Ahmanson Theatre, Doolittle, and Mark Taper Forum.

At the beginning, Kimberling says, she almost literally stumbled upon the position that would lead her here. She thought she was applying for a job at a small record company when she pulled up in front of the MCLAC, which was still in the process of construction—at the time. She had been unhappy as a student preparing for a teaching career and decided that she would get a taste of the business world. She was conscious of being without any business experience and was delighted when her astrological sign got her hired—even for an entirely different organization than the one she had assumed she was applying to. "The woman who interviewed me had bright red lipstick, dark, dark black hair, and was wearing fishnet hose. She looked at me and said, 'What's your sign?' I said, 'Capricorn,' and I was hired. That's the literal truth," she laughs. "She was very into astrology and a Capricorn herself, so she felt I could do it."

As Kimberling advanced through the MCOC, she had not imagined that she would become the organization's leader. "I never had the gall to think that way," she said. "Not because I didn't think I could do it, but it was just remote. I don't put goals in front of myself. I literally put my nose down and did the job. I never thought if I do this, and this, and this, maybe I'll get to be president."

She describes her ascent to the presidency as "being in the right place, doing the right thing, and working hard. I moved offices until I got to the end of the hall, which was the [office of the] president." She adds that when the previous CEO retired in 1984, when she was general manager, the job was not offered to her, but to a man "who lasted about eighteen months." Then it was divided into three parts, another attempt that did not work. Finally, Kimberling was named president.

She describes her ascent to the presidency as "being in the right place, doing the right thing, and working hard. . . . "

"Outside of that, I've never really gotten involved in thinking, I'm not where I should be because I'm a woman; or I am where I am because I'm a woman," she says. "But there were some elderly Pasadena gentlemen on the board who had a hard time relating to me as a potential executive. . . . It was very difficult for them to say, 'Hey, we'll let her do it.' . . . I have a tremendous relationship with them now and they have respect for me, which is very gratifying."

Entrepreneurial Pride

Because she always felt not "quite as good" for not having completed college, she gave special attention to watching and listening to others, Kimberling says. Ironically, her major growth took place when she left the Music Center after eight years—briefly, it would turn out—and became an entrepreneur. She worked as the assistant to the president of a Hollywood film company, but, more important, she bought a dog kennel, a business that demanded twenty-four-hour attention. "I understood that I was the one who had to put the dog food in the bowls and make sure the staff was paid. It was rewarding to know that people were making their living out of something that I had bought and was managing. I had a sense of pride in that."

Three years later, when she was asked to return to the Music Center, she felt a greater degree of confidence as a result of having developed her own business. It was soon after that she became president.

At MCLAC, Kimberling is responsible for running everything from the top of the roof, where the restaurant is located, down to the eighth level, the garage. "We are responsible for the theaters, the patrons, and the art work," she explains. "We are responsible for making good business decisions because we manage this seventy-acre property which has five artistic groups that are a blessing for this community. I am very committed to the arts; I love the arts, but I'm not the artist. . . . To have this job, you need to provide an environment so that the arts can thrive and the public will come. I'm very fortunate to be an overall part of that effort."

Never Say "My People"

Kimberling has a management team of ten, but a staff of hundreds. They include accountants, stagehands, and archivists. She believes in surrounding herself with competent managers because she says she has seen too many administrators fail because of being too threatened to hire personnel with superior skills. Giving others a chance to excel is her best leadership trait, she says.

"Leadership is really knowing how to coordinate and work with people as opposed to being *the leader*," said Kimberling. "I know a lot of leaders who are so busy leading that they lose total

They're into saying 'my people' or 'my staff,' and their eyes are too close together.

reality about their relationships. They're into saying 'my people' or 'my staff,' and their eyes are too close together. They're constantly taking credit for whatever has been achieved, when, in fact, everybody knows that if something good happens, it took ninety people to back you up to make it work. And you need to give credit above all to those people, or they don't do it again."

In the late 1950s, the board of supervisors of Los Angeles County appointed Dorothy Buffum Chandler to lead a campaign to raise the private and public monies necessary to build the Music Center. Kimberling respects Chandler for "getting a force of women together and arm-twisting bank presidents and coming up with over $17 million." Public money matched that. "So the Music Center was a real communal effort. That's why it's so important in the present environment with government cutbacks for the community to understand that the Music Center is really their facility."

Kimberling is proud of being in an influential executive position without having finished college, but she advises young women today not to sacrifice an education if they hope to head an arts facility. She does emphasize the benefit of common sense and practical experience, however: "Starting in the mailroom is not the way to the executive office," she remarks, "but getting a job inside a company and learning and observing as much as possible is invaluable." Her current concern is to increase community involvement in the Music Center and in general to promote the arts as having "an incredible impact on the economy."

Avant-Garde in Hiring

On-the-job training was once the only way for women to advance in arts administration. Marie Nugent-Head, the director of development at New York City Ballet (NYCB) for eleven years, identifies herself as "one of those old-fashioned directors of development who began from the ground up. Now they all have masters in arts administration. But we all learned on the job."

Nugent-Head was teaching Romance languages at the University of Washington when she moved to Boston because of her husband's work. She knew that changing locations would always make it hard for her to acquire academic tenure, so she was ready when serendipity gave her her first job in development.

Hearing about her arrival in Boston, a family friend who was the founder of the Musicians' Emergency Fund, a nonprofit organization started after World War I to benefit veterans, told Nugent-Head about ongoing efforts to expand occupational therapy programs in Greater Boston Veterans Administration hospitals. Was she interested in joining the effort? Sympathetic to the psychological and physical problems of soldiers returning from Vietnam, she accepted a position as the organization's regional development director and had great satisfaction in successfully funding programs that helped the wounded.

Nugent-Head moved again when her husband was hired to join the staff of *Mr. Rogers' Neighborhood* in Pittsburgh. Her successful five-year track record with the Musicians' Emergency Fund impressed the board of directors of the Pittsburgh Public Theater (PPT), and they hired her as their first director of development.

"Twenty years ago it was very unusual to see a woman in a management position in an arts organization," says Nugent-Head, "and unfortunately it still holds true today." At that time, the PPT was avant-garde in even hiring a development head, for development in arts organizations was still generally practiced as a board activity. The development department at the PPT *was* Nugent-Head, until Ben Shaktman, the theater's executive director, found her at two in the morning sitting on her office floor in tears surrounded by papers for a proposal she was writing. "Okay," he said, "you can have an assistant."

Developing People

From Shaktman, Nugent-Head learned a basic lesson in leadership strategy that she still practices. An appointment was arranged for Shaktman and board officers to meet with the head of the R. K. Mellon Foundation, but Nugent-Head was not included. After she told Shaktman that it was appropriate for her to be there, he commented, "The only appropriate thing, if you're going to go, is that you be a contributing individual."

"That taught me one of the most important lessons," Nugent-Head says. "Today I have nineteen people on staff, and they always want to accompany me someplace. But if you're going to include them, you have to know how to delegate and be generous enough to

Unfortunately, at a certain level, it's like God wants to talk only to God, not to vice-God. . . .

bring the person into the conversation. Unfortunately, at a certain level, it's like God wants to talk only to God, not to vice-God. . . . I never forgot that lesson for myself. If you want to push somebody and encourage them and take them to meet a CEO, generally the CEO will respond only to the senior person, and the other person sits there like a dodo. So you really have to give them a place in the sun by turning to them and including them. That's the best way to build their confidence, not just by having them drag along."

The Legacy of the Past

After six successful years at PPT, where the contributed income tripled, Nugent-Head was in a prime position to become executive director of the National Corporate Theater Fund. The job "was mutually beneficial," she says, for it positioned her, after a divorce, in Manhattan and propelled her to the highest level of fund-raising. From there, she became director of development at NYCB. Over the next eleven years, she would make more than $100 million for her new employer.

Nugent-Head's gamble to accept her first development position with the Musicians' Emergency Fund paid in spades, for it was the beginning of a lucrative career. Development is enormously demanding, she warns, but anyone who wants to be in arts management should not avoid it. "If you are going to be successful, then you have to pay your dues. There's no halfway with development. . . . Development is paramount to any successful director in any area of the arts," she says.

Nugent-Head refers to her first year at NYCB as "learning on the job." Shortly before she began conversations with the NYCB, George Balanchine, the revered founder, died. "I was coming into a distinguished organization, but nothing much had changed in a long time. . . . I knew my job from the beginning was to fire people." Within eighteen months, only one person was left from the original staff. Without being explicit, Nugent-Head claims to have made "every mistake in the book." In retrospect, she says she would have taken a course in management before she began the job.

"At the time, I did the best I could, but I was too tough too often and not patient enough. . . . I had come into an organization which had been dominated by one man, and the people working there were so entranced by his genius and how extraordinary the place was—but they had done things in only one way. I was hired to bring about change. But change is very hard to implement wisely and sensibly. It takes a certain maturity. I learned on the job."

After making those mistakes, Nugent-Head learned to work better with staff and also with the artists. "[Artists] are strange creatures, and you need to convince them that you care deeply about the company and the artistic product. I'm very proud of the trust I've built with the artistic management, the board, and the funding community."

Nugent-Head says that operational management is neither her first love nor her strength, but that she learned to delegate responsibilities and to use her skills to motivate, inspire, and galvanize others. She says with pleasure that many from the NYBC development staff have gone on to work in arts organizations across the country as executive directors or directors of development; some are now employed in the private sector.

Passion Is First

"When I want passionately to do something, I find a way to do it," says Sara O'Connor, recently retired managing director of the Milwaukee Repertory Theater, former head of the League of Resident Theatres (LORT), and a dynamic force in promoting theater exchanges between countries. Directing a play, producing a documentary film, or raising funds for a museum have been a vocation for her. Being a leader is "a skill you develop because you need it to get whatever you want to get," she says. "You edge out on thin ice, giving name to what it is you want to do. The possibility of failure or embarrassment or ending up with egg on their faces keeps some women from edging out on the ice."

The possibility of failure or embarrassment or ending up with egg on their faces keeps some women from edging out on the ice.

Now in her early sixties, Sara O'Connor is widely acknowledged as a multifaceted dynamo in the theater. In addition to her LORT work, she is credited with creating the Milwaukee Repertory's Theater Center in the elaborately planned Milwaukee Center. She is also the talented translator of many classical and contemporary French dramas produced in the United States. She has been a driving force in organizing international exchanges between regional theaters in the United States and theaters in Japan and Russia. In July 1994, she was ordained as a priest of Soto Zen Buddhism, and she now serves at the Milwaukee Zen Center.

"When I get brochures and letters about workshops and courses on leadership, I just throw them away," O'Connor says. "That's all garbage. What's more important is developing an ethic of behavior that makes you confident about the way you approach the world. Whether you write or produce a documentary film, fund a business, become a

What's more important is developing an ethic of behavior that makes you confident about the way you approach the world.

judge, or get a law passed—those are all active verbs, actual activities. A leader is a leader by what she accomplishes. Only in sports do you set out to lead, or set a goal, or run a mile better than the last person."

Sara O'Connor's sensibility about these matters was first developed when she was an undergraduate at Swarthmore College, a school founded on Quaker values. "The college doesn't really teach Quakerism," she explains, "but there was always the underlying assumption that you discover your interests and talents and then serve society with what you do."

As an example, O'Connor refers to the theater exchanges she has negotiated between Japan, Russia, and the United States. "I have an enormous interest in cross-cultural encounters, but I didn't set out and say, 'Now hear this. We're going to do X.' But I had real enthusiasm for the Japanese connection and the possibilities of tours back and forth and the same thing with Russia—I had enough interest to fight my way through the jungle of difficulties that it takes to bring about a large-scale international change."

No Master Plan

How has O'Connor managed so many responsibilities within such a rich life? She recalls a comment that was thrust at her at an opening night party after a theater production in Korea. "A brilliant woman, a stage designer, turned to me and said, 'You look very serene. You must not have suffered much in life.'

"It was an insult, and I said, 'Well, the truth is, I don't know that I got to design my life, but when bad things happen, you have a choice about how to react.' I never had felt that I was a victim. I have lived through perfectly hideous times. My husband left me and I didn't want him to. I was raising kids and living on less than welfare in Boston, still determined to work in the theater and guilt-ridden that I was making life difficult for my children. But I had made that choice to respond in that particular way. So the issue of balance has to do really with whether you feel free to respond as you choose. You're not free to decide what happens. . . . We didn't get promised anything. We just got to come here, that's all. So balance for me is a matter of keeping things on a more or less even keel, moment to moment, not in terms of a master plan. . . . Any man or woman who makes a commitment to a profession they are deeply interested in and a commitment to a family is going to have to work hard to meet both commitments. There's never a magic formula that says, Gosh, you're trying to do so much. You're a good person, so we'll make it easier for you."

A Coda

"You Aren't What You Do"

Jean Yancey is in her eighties and calls herself the "crone of Denver." Among her other talents, she has inspired many women with her wisdom and commonsense. In 1970, Yancey sold the bridal shop she owned and started Jean Yancey Associates to counsel people hoping to become entrepreneurs. Soon she became a popular keynote speaker for national conferences. At a White House ceremony in 1982, President Reagan awarded her a plaque in recognition of her success in advising women in small businesses.

No matter how much in demand she was, Yancey has always been glad to return to Denver. "I guess it got to the point where I was older than anyone else here," she laughs, "so I was supposed to know everything. Gradually, I began counseling women about everything under the sun and had a marvelous time. We just talk."

On clear days, Yancey drives with her guest to a picnic bench overlooking the lake and mountains at Cherry Creek State Park. Her favorite advice is: "Remember, you aren't what you do. Because if you don't do that any longer, then you won't know who you are."

Recently, three hundred people, many from across the United States, who had been influenced by Jean Yancey, celebrated her birthday at Denver's Cherry Creek State Park. When a committee of Denver citizens asked her about a gift for her eightieth birthday, she had requested that a bench that would last for one thousand years be placed in the park she loves. When an oak bench was suggested, she persisted in asking for stone.

Today the stone bench, made in California, sits on the hillside that she visits regularly. The bronze inscription reads:

In celebration of the life and energy generated by this remarkable woman
Rest and meditate here, and know that you make a difference in the world.

Yancey confides that she cannot recall a woman who was influential in her own life: "I think that many women have just shuffled along and done it by themselves," she says. This is why she feels responsible for passing on what she has learned over a lifetime to other women.

Index

abortion, 76, 78, 139
  see also Nurturing Network
Abramson, Shirley, women as
  judges, 112
Abzug, Bella, 50
Actors' Fund of America, 213
Adams, Paul, healthcare for
  women, 73
Addams, Jane, social change by
  women, 93
affirmative action, 157
African Americans
  Avery, Byllye Y., 72–76
  Belton, Sharon Sayles, 33–36
  and feminism, 35
  Gutman, Roberta W. (Bobbi),
    187–190, 202
  Ifill, Gwen, 144–148
  McCabe, Jewell Jackson,
    87–88
  Norton, Eleanor Holmes,
    19–23
  Reynolds, Barbara, 153–155
  Tolliver, Melba, 146
  Walker, Liz, 155–157
  and women's movement, 21,
    35
Agee, Mary Cunningham,
  social change by women,
  76–81
Agee, William M., husband of
  Mary, 77, 80
Agosti, Deborah, women as
  judges, 98–100
AIDS
  Atlanta Gay Center, 64
  legislative work on, 17
  treatment for homeless
    people, 89–90
Alaska Center for the
  Performing Arts in
  Anchorage, Walsh, Alice
  C., 225–227
Alaska Teamsters Union, 162
All Things Considered (National
  Public Radio), Stamberg,
  Susan, 86
alternative sentencing
  programs
  Normandin, Sister Jeannette,
    88–89
  Temin, Carolyn Engel,
    100–103
American Bar Association
  (ABA)
  code of judicial conduct, 101
  Report on the Status of
    Women, 134

statistics on women general
  counsels, 129
statistics on women in the
  law, 111
American Board of Trial
  Advocates (ABOTA), 99
American Corporate Counsel
  Association, 129
American Indian Ambassadors
  Program, 71
American Judicature Society's
  Center for Judicial
  Conduct Organizations,
  101
American Society of
  Newspaper Editors
  (ASNE), 163
Americans for Indian
  Opportunity (AIO),
  Harris, La Donna, 68–72
AmeriCorp national service
  program, 15
Anchorage Daily News, Fanning,
  Katherine (Kay)
  Woodruff, 159, 161–164
Anderson, Susan, women in
  journalism, 142
Angels in America (Kushner),
  232
anti-Semitism, 22
Apple, R.W., Jr., *The New York
  Times*, 12
appointeded versus elected to
  office, 10
Arena Stage in Washington,
  D.C., Fichandler, Zelda,
  233
Armed forces, women in the, 5
Arsht, Roxanna, women as
  judges, 96–98
arts education, 224
arts management, women in,
  223–244
  Bogart, Anne, 231
  Chandler, Dorothy Buffman,
    239
  Fichandler, Zelda, 233
  Godfrey, Marian A., 229–231
  Grant, Lee, 227–229
  Hopkins, Karen Brooks,
    223–224
  Kimberling, Sandra A.,
    236–239
  Myers, Sondra, 234–236
  Nugent-Head, Marie,
    239–242
  O'Connor, Sara, 233–234,
    242–244

Ott, Sharon, 232–234
  Walsh, Alice C., 225–227
Asians, 35
associates in law firms, 121–122
Atlanta Gay Center, 64
Avery, Byllye Y., social change
  by women, 72–76

Balanchine, George, founder of
  New York City Ballet, 242
Balser, Barbara, women in
  business, 176–179
Bank of American National
  Trust and Savings
  Association, 131
  diversity initiative of, 132
banking industry, 228
Barnes, Teveia Rose, women as
  lawyers, 131–133
Barnett, Ida B. Wells, social
  change by women, 93
Beck, Phyllis, women as judges,
  105
Beijing World Conference on
  Women, 50
Belton, Sharon Sayles, women
  in politics, 33–36
Bendix (company), 76, 80, 81
Berglin, Linda, women in
  politics, 25–26, 50–51
Berkeley Repertory Theatre,
  Ott, Sharon, 232–233
Berrigan, Daniel, Jesuit peace
  activist, 59
Betsy Coalition, 37, 38
Bickett, Mary Kay, women as
  judges, 108–109
Bingham, Jeff, senator from
. New Mexico, 39
biomedical ethics, 138
birth control, 136
Bitter, Carole, women in
  business, 197–198
Blue Cross/Blue Shield, 38
Bogart, Anne, women in arts
  management, 231
Boggs, Barbara (sister of Cokie
  Roberts), 140
Boggs, Lindy (mother of Cokie
  Roberts), 140
book catalogs, Reuthling, Ann,
  213–217
Born, Brooksley, women as
  lawyers, 118–119
Boston Food Bank, 61
Boston Women's Fund and
  Communityworks, 62
Brady Bill, 39

Brady, Jim, 39
Braver, Rita, women in
journalism, 142–144
breast cancer research, 213
breast implants, 144
Brooklyn Academy of Music
(BAM), Hopkins, Karen
Brooks, 223–224
Brown, Margaret Wise, *Good
Night, Moon*, 216
Buck, Smith, and McAvoy,
Smith, Julia, 92
Buckner, Jennie, women in
journalism, 159
Bullard, Marcia, women in
journalism, 159
Bunda, Sue, women in
journalism, 166
Bush, George
administration of, 10
in China, 50
business, women in, 171–221
Balser, Barbara, 176–179
Bitter, Carole, 197–198
Coleman, Maxine, 217–218
cross-training, 185
Davis, Susan, 175–176
De Dominic, Patty, 186
Fertel, Ruth, 171–173
Friedlander, Carolee,
209–213
Grogan, Barbara, 218–221
Gutman, Roberta W. (Bobbi),
187–190, 202
LoRé, Linda, 179–183
Macaskill, Bridget, 190–192
McGartland, Grace, 208
Manning, Sherry, 198–202
Milligan, Lynda, 205–208
Popoff, Louise, 216
Reuthling, Ann, 213–217
Rothman, Clare L., 173–175
Schapiro, Mary, 294–197
Smith, Nancy, 206–208
Tarr, Whalen, Linda, 171
Toretti, Christine, 197–198
Weister, Linda, 202–205
Woods, Sandra, 192–194
Yancey, Jean, 245–246

California Forum, Rothman,
Clare L., 173–175
Caliguiri, Richard, mayor of
Pittsburgh, 40
Campbell, Nancy Duff, women
as lawyers, 116–117
Capital Missions Company,
Davis, Susan, 175–176
Care of the Soul (Moore), 217
Carnegie, Andrew, 55
Carolee Designs, Inc.,
Friedlander, Carolee,
209–213
Carroll, Luke, 149

Carter, Jimmy, administration
of, 42, 104, 154, 167
Casey, Robert, as governor
of Pennsylvania, 235
Catalyst award, 188
Catholic Worker Movement,
Day, Dorothy, 60
CBS, 149, 151
CBS *News*, Braver, Rita, 142–144
Center for Law and Social
Policy (CLASP), 115–116
Women's Rights Project, 116,
117
Center for Policy Alternatives,
42
Tarr, Whalen, Linda, 171
Chandler, Dorothy Buffman,
women in arts
management, 239
Charlotte Observer, Buckner,
Jennie, 159
Chesed House in Westfield, for
homeless AIDS patients,
90
Chinaberry Book Service,
Reuthling, Ann, 213–217
Chinese Americans, 233
Chisholm, Shirley,
representative
from New York, 31
The Christian Science Monitor,
Fanning, Katherine (Kay)
Woodruff, 159, 161–164
Civil Rights Act of 1991, 113
Civil Rights Act of 1964, 113,
138, 193
civil rights movement, 21, 23,
33–34, 156
Civil Rights Restoration Act of
1988, 113
Clabes, Judith G., women in
journalism, 162
Cleany Boppers, Inc., Weister,
Linda, 202–205
Clinton, Bill
administration of, 12, 15, 235
campaign of, 146
Coalition for Women's
Appointments, 24
impeachment vote on, 18
signing Family and Medical
Leave Act of 1993, 113
CNN, Evans, Gail, 166–169
CNN and Company
Bunda, Sue, 166
Tillotson, Mary, 166
Coalition for Women's
Appointments, 24
coalitions
in Comanche culture, 69
with men in politics, 50
of women in politics, 27,
28–30, 38, 47

code of judicial conduct,
American Bar Association
(ABA), 101
Coleman, Maxine, women in
business, 217–218
Collaborative Fund for
Women's Economic
Development, 66
Colorado Women's Bar
Association (CWBA), 119,
121
Columbia University, Bogart,
Anne, 231
Comanche tribe, "giveaways,"
68–69
*Coming Into Our Fullness: On
Women Turning Forty*
(Rountree), 217
Commission on the Status of
Women
Peterson, Esther, 31
Roosevelt, Eleanor, 31
Committee of 200, 210–211
Communism, 23
community involvement, 219
community organizing
Metropolitan Atlanta
Community Foundation,
64–65
Mon Valley Intiative (MVI),
53–57
see also social change by
women
community service, 121, 122
confidential sources, Torre,
Marie, 148–152
consciousness raising, 74–75
consensus, 186, 190
in Comanche culture, 69
downside of, 191–192
as leadership style, 179
process of, 116
construction business, Grogan,
Barbara, 218–221
Contact (television call–in
show), Torre, Marie, 148,
153
Cooney, Barbara, *Miss
Rumphius*, 216
Coors Brewing Company, 128
Woods, Sandra, 192–194
corporate law, 128–134
see also law firms; sole
practitioners
corporate social responsibility,
175
Correa, Mathias F., 150–151
The Couple's Comfort Book
(Louden), 217
Cowan, Belinda, National
Women's Health
Network, 74
Coyne, Jeanne, women as
judges, 110

Cranston, Mary C., women as lawyers, 133–134
Cromer, Diane, women in politics, 15–16, 29–30, 47–48
cross-training, 193
culture, 224, 230
    see also arts management, women in

Danburg, Debra, women in politics, 28–29, 48
Davies, Susan, Women's Institute for Housing and Economic Development, 92
Davis, Ann, women as lawyers, 128
Davis, Susan, women in business, 175–176
Day, Dorothy, Catholic Worker Movement, 60, 63
De Bolt, Jo, social change by women, 53–57
De Dominic, Patty, women in business, 186
DeLauro, Luisa, mother of Rosa, 1–2
DeLauro, Rosa, women in politics, 1–4, 39
DeLauro, Ted, father of Rosa, 1
Des Moines Register, Overholser, Geneva, 159–161
Diane Cromer Enterprises, 15–16
Dilley, Marjorie, teaching law, 104
disfigurements, see facial differences
diversity initiative, of Bank of American National Trust and Savings Association, 132
documentaries, Grant, Lee, 227–229
Dodd, Christopher J., senator from Connecticut, 2, 3
domestic violence, 73, 87–88
Domestic Violence Hotline, 18
Dominguez, Cari, women in politics, 10
Domitrovich, Stephanie, women as judges, 95–96, 134
Donnell, Caithlin, women as lawyers, 119–120
Douglas, William O., 151
downsizing, 185
Dukakis, Michael
    campaign for president, 39
    governor of Massachusetts, 61
DuPont, Mrs. E. Paul, 97
dysfunctional pronouns, 107–108

Edgewood Community Gardens, 65
Education Communications Consortia, Inc., Manning, Sherry, 198–202
Eisenhower, Dwight D., administration of, 32
elected versus appointed to office, 10
Elliot, Mary O'Loughlin, mother-in-law of Kate, 106
Elliott, Kate Ford, women as judges, 105–108
EMILY'S List, 2, 32
Equal Rights Amendment
    extending period for ratification, 31
    in Illinois, 22
    need for, 118
    passed in Maryland, 17
    in Texas, 29
Evans, Bob, husband of Gail, 167
Evans, Gail, women in journalism, 166–169
Eyewitness News (WBZ–TV in Boston), Walker, Liz, 155–157

facial differences, 81–87
Family and Medical Leave Act of 1993, 113
Fanning, Katherine (Kay) Woodruff, women in journalism, 159, 161–164
Fanning, Lawrence, husband of Kay, 161
feminism
    and African Americans, 35
    and racism, 21–22
    separatist, 50
Ferraro, Geraldine, Democratic vice–presidential nomination (1984), 10
Fertel, Ruth, women in business, 171–173
Fichandler, Zelda, women in arts management, 233
Field, Marshall, Jr., ex-husband of Kay Fanning, 161
Financial services industry, 194–197
Fisher, George, 187–188
Flinn, Kelly, discharge from the Air Force, 4–5
Ford, Gerald, administration of, 32
Ford, Loretto O'Toole, mother of Kate Ford Elliott, 106
fragrance industry, LoRe, Linda, 179–183
French, Marilyn, The Women's Room, 219
Friedlander, Carolee, women in business, 209–213

Friedman's Super Markets, Bitter, Carole, 197–198
Froehlich, Fran, partner with Tiernan, Kip, 58

Garland, Judy, 149, 151
gender bias, 108–109
    see also sexual discrimination
gender equity, 87, 114
gender language, 17
Gilligan, Carol, on self-esteem of girls, 67, 68
Ginsburg, Ruth Bader, on the United States Supreme Court, 110
Giorgio, LoRe, Linda, 179–183
"giveaways," Comanche tribe, 68–69
glass ceiling
    for women in business, 175, 181, 184, 201
    for women in law, 120
    for women in politics, 48
global marketplace, 188
Global Research Services, Evans, Gail, 167
GM Consultants, McGartland, Grace, 208
Godfrey, Marian A., women in arts management, 229–231
Good Night, Moon (Brown), 216
Goodelle, Lavinia, women as lawyers, 98
Goodman, Ellen, women in journalism, 137–139
Gould, Michael, head of Robinson's, 182
Grant, Lee, women in the arts, 227–229
grassroots activists
    for the homeless, 62
    in politics, 33–37, 47, 51, 58
    see also politics, women in; social change by women
Graves, Barbara, Massachusetts state representative, 38
Gray, Cynthia, women as lawyers, 101
The Great American Quilt Factory, Inc.
    Milligan, Lynda, 205–208
    Smith, Nancy, 206–208
Greenberger, Marcia D., women as lawyers, 114–117
Grogan, Barbara, women in business, 218–221
Gutman, Roberta W. (Bobbi), women in business, 187–190, 202

Harris, Fred, husband of La Donna, 70
Harris, La Donna, social change by women, 68–72
Harris, Laura, daughter of La Donna, 69

Harry S. Truman Scholar, 15
Health Care for the Homeless,
    61
health reporters, MacLennon,
    Linda, 157–158
healthcare activists, Avery,
    Byllye Y., 72–76
Heckler, Margaret M.,
    representative from
    Massachusetts, 31
Hernandez, Antonia, women in
    politics, 49–50
Hill, Anita, sexual harassment,
    136
Hills, Carla, secretary of
    housing and urban
    development, 32
Hispanics, 35
HIV
    and healthcare preventive
        services, 74
    research in women, 17
    treatment for homeless
        people, 89–90
Hobby, Oveta Culp, secretary of
    health, education, and
    welfare, 32
Hoeksema, Mary Jo, women in
    politics, 38–39
Holland, Eddie, 136
Holmes, Oliver Wendell, on
    experience in the law, 100
Holtzman, Elizabeth,
    representative from New
    York, 31
homeless people, 57–64, 228
    see also social change by
        women
Homestead Strike, 55
Hopkins, Karen Brooks
    Successful Fundraising for Arts
        and Cultural Organizations,
        223–224
    women in arts management,
        223–224
Houses of Hospitality, 60
Hutchison, Kay Bailey, women
    in politics, 33
Hyman, Fred, Giorgio founder,
    182

I Have A Dream Foundation, 15
Ifill, Gwen, women in
    journalism, 144–148
in-house legal departments, see
    corporate law
Ingram, Frank, first husband of
    Ruth Minner, 26
insurance business, Balser,
    Barbara, 176–179
international theater exchanges,
    242–244
investment business, Davis,
    Susan, 175–176

Jackson, Jesse, and Norton,
    Eleanor Holmes, 21–22
Jean Yancey Associates, Yancey,
    Jean, 245–246
jewelry design, 209–213
Jews, 96
Johnson, Lyndon B.,
    administration of, 31
Jones, Anita K., women in
    politics, 8–9
Jones, Mary Harris (Mother),
    social change by women,
    63, 93
Joseph E. Seagram & Sons, 76, 81
journalism, women in, 135–169
    Anderson, Susan, 142
    Braver, Rita, 142–144
    Buckner, Jennie, 159
    Bullard, Marcia, 159
    Bunda, Sue, 166
    Clabes, Judith G., 162
    Evans, Gail, 166–169
    Fanning, Katherine (Kay)
        Woodruff, 159, 161–164
    Goodman, Ellen, 137–139
    Ifill, Gwen, 144–148
    Lloyd, Wanda, 159
    MacLennon, Linda, 157–158
    Meisner, Mary Jo, 159
    newspaper editors, 159
    Overholser, Geneva, 159–161
    Reynolds, Barbara, 153–155
    Roberts, Cokie, 139–142
    Robertson, Nan, 161
    role models, 135, 136,
        167–168
    Rowe, Sandra Mims, 159,
        164
    Schorer, Jane, 159–161
    Stogsdill, Carol, 159
    Tillotson, Mary, 166
    Tolliver, Melba, 146
    in top positions, 158–159
    Torre, Marie, 148–153
    Totenberg, Nina, 135–137,
        149
    Walker, Liz, 155–157
    Walters, Barbara, 157
    Wolfe, Lois Lauer, 159
judges, women as, 95–111
    Abramson, Shirley, 112
    Agosti, Deborah, 98–100
    Arsht, Roxanna, 96–98
    Beck, Phyllis, 105
    Bickett, Mary Kay, 108–110
    Coyne, Jeanne, 110
    Domitrovich, Stephanie,
        95–96, 134
    Elliott, Kate Ford, 105–108
    Ginsburg, Ruth Bader, 110
    Kaye, Judith S., 110–111
    Morrison, Phoebe, 117
    Temin, Carolyn Engel,
        100–103
    Wald, Patricia M., 103–105

Kadushin, Karen D., women as
    lawyers, 123–126
Kal Kan Foods, Inc., Coleman,
    Maxine, 217–218
Kane, John, county
    commissioner in
    Pittsburgh, 40
Katzenbach, Nicholas, as
    attorney general, 104
Kaye, Judith S., women as
    judges, 110–111
"The Kennedy Commission"
    (Peterson), 31
Kennedy, John F., 13–14, 45
    administration of, 31
    assassination of, 145
    rally for, 117
Kennedy, Joseph P.,
    representative from
    Massachusetts, 12–13
Kennedy, Michael, skiing
    accident of, 13
Kennedy, Robert F.
    assassination of, 145
    as attorney general, 104
Kimberling, Sandra A., women
    in arts management,
    236–239
King, Martin Luther, Jr., 157
    anniversary of assassination,
        22
    assassination of, 145
    marching with, 59
    Martin Luther King Day, 33
Kingston, Maxine Hong, The
    Woman Warrior, 233
Kneale, Jean, women as
    lawyers, 133
Kushner, Tony, Angels in
    America, 232

Lake, Celinda, women in
    politics, 9
language
    dysfunctional pronouns,
        107–108
    forms of address, 108
    gender, 17
    and sexism, 8
law firms
    associates in, 121–122
    owned by women, 122–124
    partnerships in, 119–122, 124,
        126, 130
    rainmaking in, 122, 124–126,
        130, 131
    see also corporate law; sole
        practitioners
lawyers, women as, 111–134
    acting on women's rights
        issues, 111–112
    Barnes, Teveia Rose, 131–133
    Born, Brooksley, 118–119
    Campbell, Nancy Duff,
        116–117
    corporate law, 128–134

Cranston, Mary C., 133–134
Davis, Ann, 128
discrimination in law
    careers, 99, 133–134
Donnell, Caithlin, 119–120
establishing their own firms,
    122–124
Goodelle, Lavinia, 98
Gray, Cynthia, 101
Greenberger, Marcia D.,
    114–117
incomes of, 120
Kadushin, Karen D., 123–126
Kneale, Jean, 133
Lichtman, Judith L., 112–114
    management style of, 131
Odel, Kathleen Ann, 121–122
Pudlin, Helen C., 129–131
Richmond, Gloria, 124
sole practitioners, 127–128
statistics on, 111
Todhunter, Marcia C., 126
Tucker, Marna, 118
Turner, M. Caroline, 128–129
Walsh, Holiday, 122–123
leadership style, 198, 220
    consensus as, 179
    and relationships, 239
    see also management style
League of Resident Theatres
    (LORT), 242, 243
Lee, Sheila Jackson,
    representative from Texas,
    12
Let's Face It, Wilson, Betsy,
    81–87
Let's Face It (Piff), 83–84, 85–86
Levy, Judith, healthcare for
    women, 73
Lichtman, Judith L., women as
    lawyers, 112–114
Lloyd, Wanda, women in
    journalism, 159
Logue, Frank, campaign for
    mayor of New Haven, 2
LoRé, Linda, women in
    business, 179–183
Los Angeles Times, Stogsdill,
    Carol, 159
Louden, Jennifer, The Couple's
    Comfort Book, 217
Lucchino, Frank, candidate for
    mayor in Pittsburgh, 41
Luft, Sid, 149

Macaskill, Bridget, women in
    business, 190–192
McCabe, Jewell Jackson, social
    change by women, 87–88
McCarthy, Joseph, 23, 117, 151,
    232
McGartland, Grace
    Thunderbolt Thinking, 208
    women in business, 208

MacLennon, Linda, women in
    journalism, 157–158
mail order catalogs, Reuthling,
    Ann, 213–217
Malave, Idelisse, vice president
    of Ms. Foundation, 68
male judges, biases of, 108–109
male mentors, 50
Management Compensation
    Group, Inc., Balser,
    Barbara, 176–179
management style, 131, 205,
    220, 221
    see also leadership style
Mandela, Nelson, on nonracial
    or nonsexist
    administration, 87
Manning, Sherry, women in
    business, 198–202
marginalized social groups, 163
Margolies-Mezvinsky, Marjorie,
    representative from
    Pennsylvania, 11–12
martial arts, 87
Mary House, 60
Masloff, Sophie, women in
    politics, 40–42
Massachusetts Correctional
    Institute (MCI) at
    Framingham, 88–89
Massachusetts for Health Care
    for the Homeless, 61
media, 148
Meisner, Mary Jo, women in
    journalism, 159
Melvill, Herman, Moby Dick,
    232
Menominee tribe, 70–71
mentors
    for employees, 211–212
    male, 50
    women judges as, 96
meritocracy, 196
Metropolitan Atlanta
    Community Foundation,
    64–65
Mexican American Legal
    Defense and Educational
    Fund (MALDEF), 49–50
Mikulski, Barbara, senator from
    Maryland, 33
military programs, 87
Milligan, Lynda, women in
    business, 205–208
Milwaukee Journal, Meisner,
    Mary Jo, 159
Milwaukee Repertory Theater,
    O'Connor, Sara, 233–234,
    242–244
Milwaukee Zen Center, 243
Minner, Ruth, women in
    politics, 26–27
Minnesota Program for Victims
    of Sexual Assault, 35

minorities
    healthcare for, 75
    pressure to hire, 157
    and veterans' preference in
    governement jobs, 26
Miss Rumphius (Cooney), 216
Mizeur, Heather, women in
    politics, 11–15
Moby Dick (Melvill), 232
Molinari, Guy, father of Susan,
    10–11
Molinari, Susan, women in
    politics, 10–11
Mon Valley Initiative (MVI),
    53–57
Moore, Thomas, Care of the Soul,
    217
Morella, Constance A., women
    in politics, 16–19, 20
Morella, Tony, husband of
    Connie, 17
Morrison, Bruce, representative
    from Connecticut, 2
Morrison, Phoebe, women as
    judges, 117
Mother Jones, 63, 93
Mother Theresa, 63
Motorola, Gutman, Roberta W.
    (Bobbi), 187–190, 202
Ms. Foundation, 65–68, 74
Murray, Therese, women in
    politics, 28, 37–38, 51
Music Center of Los Angeles
    County (MCLAC),
    Kimberling, Sandra A.,
    236–239
Music Center Operating
    Company (MCOC)
    Chandler, Dorothy Buffman,
    239
    Kimberling, Sandra A.,
    236–239
Musician's Emergency Fund,
    240, 241
Myers, Sondra, women in arts
    management, 234–236

National Asian Women's
    Health Project, 75
National Association for the
    Advancement of Colored
    People (NAACP), 34
National Association of Editors,
    159
National Association of
    Securities Dealers
    Automated Quotient
    System (Nasdaq), 195
National Association of
    Securities Dealers
    Regulation (NASDR),
    Schapiro, Mary, 294–197
National Association of Women
    Business Owners, 186,
    203, 208

National Association of Women Judges, 101

National Black Women's Health Project, 72–76

National Coalition of 100 Black Women, McCabe, Jewell Jackson, 87–88

National Committee on Crime and Delinquency, 102

National Corporate Theater Fund, 241

National Endowment for the Arts (NEA), 232

National Endowment for the Humanities (NEH), Myers, Sondra, 234–236

National Federation of Press Women (NFPW), 158–159

National Foundation for Women Business Owners, 201

National Institutes of Health, 17

National Judicial College in Reno, 108

National Latino Women's Project, 75

National Public Radio
    All Things Considered, 86
    Roberts, Cokie, 139
    Totenberg, Nina, 135–137

National Women's Health Network, Cowan, Belinda, 74

National Women's Law Center, 112, 114, 116–118

National Women's Political Caucus, 24

Native Americans, 35, 162
    Harris, La Donna, 68–72

NBC News, Ifill, Gwen, 144–148

neighborhood redevelopment, 65
    see also social change by women

New Directions for Women, 101

New Guardians of the Press, Clabes, Judith G., editor, 162

New York City Ballet (NYCB), Nugent-Head, Marie, 239–242

New York Herald Tribune, Torre, Marie, 148–153

The New York Times, Robertson, Nan, 161

Newsmakers (WILM Newsradio), Torre, Marie, 153

Nixon, Richard M., 31, 45

Normandin, Sister Jeannette, social change by women, 88–92

Norton, Eleanor Holmes, women in politics, 19–23

Nugent-Head, Marie, women in arts management, 239–242

Nurturing Network, Agee, Mary Cunningham, 76–81

O'Connor, Sara, women in arts management, 233–234, 242–244

Odel, Kathleen Ann, women as lawyers, 121–122

Oklahomans for Indian Opportunity, 70

old boys' network, 105

Oneida tribe, 72

O'Neill, Tip, House Speaker, 10

Oppenheimer Funds, Inc., Macaskill, Bridget, 190–192

Opportunity 2000 Award, 188

The Oregonian, Rowe, Sandra Mims, 159, 164–166

Ott, Sharon, women in arts management, 232–234

Overholser, Geneva, women in journalism, 159–161

partnerships in law firms, 119–122, 124, 126, 130

Paulist Seminary in Washington D.C., 88

PDQ Personnel Services, Inc., De Dominic, Patty, 186

Perkins, Frances, secretary of labor, 31–32

Persian Gulf War, 140

Peterson, Esther, women in politics, 31

Pew Charitable Trusts, Godfrey, Marian A., 229–231

Phillips, Alicia, social change by women, 64–65

physician-assisted suicide, 138

Piff, Christine, Let's Face It, 83–84, 85–86

Planned Parenthood, 98

policy work by women, see social change by women

political consultants, Cromer, Diane, 15–16

politics, women in, 1–51
    Belton, Sharon Sayles, 33–36
    Berglin, Linda, 25–26, 50–51
    coalitions of, 27, 28–30, 38, 47
    Congress (106th), 30–31
    Cromer, Diane, 15–16, 29–30, 47–48
    Danburg, Debra, 28–29
    DeLauro, Rosa, 1–4, 39
    difference from social change work, 13, 65–66
    Dominguez, Cari, 10
    elected versus appointed to office, 10
    Ferraro, Geraldine, 10

glass ceiling for, 48
    Hernandez, Antonia, 49–50
    Hoeksema, Mary Jo, 38–39
    Hutchison, Kay Bailey, 33
    Jones, Anita K., 8–9
    Lake, Celinda, 9
    Masloff, Sophie, 40–42
    men as mentors, 50
    Minner, Ruth, 26–27
    Mizeur, Heather, 11–15
    Molinari, Susan, 10–11
    Morella, Constance A., 16–19, 20
    Murray, Therese, 28, 37–38, 51
    national average for female legislators, 49
    Norton, Eleanor Holmes, 19–23
    Peterson, Esther, 31
    priority on people, 30, 51
    Richards, Ann, 43–44
    as role models, 43
    Savocchio, Joyce, 44–47
    Schroeder, Patricia, 10
    Tarr-Whelan, Linda, 42–43, 58–59
    Whitman, Christine Todd, 30
    Widnall, Sheila E., 4–7, 37
    Woods, Harriet, 8, 24–25

Poole, Alden, journalism professor, 146

Poor People's United Fund, 57, 58, 62, 63

Popoff, Louise, women in business, 216

pregnancies
    drug addiction during, 102
    see also Nurturing Network

Pregnancy Discrimination Act of 1978, 113

President's White House Exchange, 193

prisons
    Normandin, Sister Jeannette, 88–89
    Temin, Carolyn Engel, 100–103

pro bono work, 118, 121

Providence National Bank, 129–130

public housing, 145

Pudlin, Helen C., women as lawyers, 129–131

Pulitzer Prize, Anchorage Daily News, 162

racism and feminism, 21–22

rainmaking in law firms, 122, 124–126, 130, 131

rape, 159–161

Reagan, Ronald, 14, 137, 245

Reid, Ogden R., 150

restaurant business, Fertel, Ruth, 171–173

Reuthling, Ann, women in business, 213–217
Reuthling, Ed, husband of Ann, 215
Reynolds, Barbara, women in journalism, 153–155
Richards, Ann, women in politics, 43–44
Richmond, Gloria, women as lawyers, 124
rights of women, 111–112, 115–118
R. K. Mellon Foundation, 241
Roberts, Cokie, women in journalism, 139–142
Robertson, Nan, women in journalism, 161
Robinson, Jackie, breaking racial barriers, 112
Rogers, Dick, accountant with The Great American Quilt Factory, Inc., 207
role models
    women journalists as, 135, 136, 167–168
    women judges as, 96
    women politicians as, 43
Roosevelt, Eleanor
    Commission on the Status of Women, 31
    influential role as first lady, 7, 44
    Pittsburgh visit in 1936, 42
Roosevelt, Franklin D., administration of, 31–32
Rosie's Place in Boston, 60, 61, 63
Rothman, Clare L., women in business, 173–175
Rountree, Cathleen, *Coming Into Our Fullness: On Women Turning Forty*, 217
Rowe, Sandra Mims, women in journalism, 159, 164–166
Ruah House, for homeless AIDS patients, 90–91
Ruth's Chris Steak House, Fertel, Ruth, 171–173
Ryan, C.J., on women as lawyers, 98
Ryan, Sylvester J., 150

Safehouse, 121
St. Joseph House in New York, 60
St. Phillip Church in Roxbury, 59
Saratoga International Theatre Insitute (SITI), Bogart, Anne, 231
Savocchio, Daniel, father of Joyce, 45
Savocchio, Joyce, women in politics, 44–47

Schapiro, Mary, women in business, 194–197
school desegragation, 113
Schorer, Jane, women in journalism, 159–161
Schroeder, Patricia, representative from Colorado, 10, 31
Schuller, Robert, tapes by, 220
Seattle Repertory Theatre, Ott, Sharon, 232–234
Secretary of the Air Force, Widnall, Sheila E., 4–7
separatist feminism, 50
Service Corps of Retired Executives (SCORE), 215
Severens, Penny L, Illinois state senator, 14–15
sexaul assault, 35
sexism
    and language, 8
    in politics, 40
sexual discrimination, 118, 139
    see also gender bias
sexual harassment
    Hill, Anita, 136
    in the military, 5
    and sexual discrimination, 116
Shaktman, Ben, as executive director of the Pittsburgh Public Theater, 240–241
shelters for battered women, 121
shield laws, 149, 152
Sisters of St. Anne, 88, 92
Small Business Administration, 201
small businesses, Yancey, Jean, 245–246
Smith, Julia, Buck, Smith, and McAvoy, 92
Smith, Nancy, women in business, 206–208
social change by women, 53–93
    Addams, Jane, 93
    Agee, Mary Cunningham, 76–81
    Avery, Byllye Y., 72–76
    Barnett, Ida B. Wells, 93
    De Bolt, Jo, 53–57
    difference from politics, 13, 65–66
    Harris, La Donna, 68–72
    history of, 92–93
    Jones, Mary Harris (Mother), 63, 93
    McCabe, Jewell Jackson, 87–88
    Normandin, Sister Jeannette, 88–92
    Phillips, Alicia, 64–65
    Stone, Lucy, 93
    Tiernan, Kip, 57–64

Truth, Sojourner, 93
Walker, Liz, 155–157
Wilson, Betsy, 81–87
Wilson, Marie C., 65–68
social ventures, 175
socially responsible companies
    Davis, Susan, 175–176
    Friedlander, Carolee, 212
sole practitioners in law, 127–128
    see also corporate law; law firms
Soto Zen Buddhism, 243
spirituality of women, 216
sports and entertainment business, Rothman, Clare L., 173–175
Stamberg, Susan, *All Things Considered* (National Public Radio), 86
steel industry, Mon Valley Intiative (MVI), 53–57
stereotypes
    of women, 9, 107, 109
    of women in business, 184, 221
Stogsdill, Carol, women in journalism, 159
Stone, Lucy, social change by women, 93
Successful Fundraising for Arts and Cultural Organizations (Hopkins), 223–224
Susan G. Komen Breast Cancer Foundation, 213
S. W. Jack Drilling Company, Toretti, Christine, 197–198

tabloid writers, 148
"Take Our Daughters to Work Day," 67, 68
talk-show personalities, 148
Taos Pueblo, 70
Tarr-Whelan, Linda
    Center for Policy Alternatives, 58–59
    women in politics, 42–43, 171
teams, 186, 187, 189, 192, 193
television roundtables, 147
Temin, Carolyn Engel, women as judges, 100–103
Texas Center for the Judiciary, 108
Thatcher, Margaret, 158
This Week (ABC news program), Roberts, Cokie, 139
Thomas, Clarence, confirmation hearings of, 24, 136
Thunderbolt Thinking (McGartland), 208
Tiernan, Kip, social change by women, 57–64

Tillotson, Mary, women in journalism, 166
Todhunter, Marcia C., women as lawyers, 126
Tolliver, Melba, women in journalism, 146
Toretti, Christine, women in business, 197–198
Torre, Adam (son of Marie), 149
Torre, Marie, women in journalism, 148–153
Torre, Roma (daughter of Marie), 151
Total Quality Management (TQM), 221
Totenberg, Nina, women in journalism, 135–137, 149
toxic shock syndrome, 161
Tracy, Brian, tapes by, 220
Tribbitt, Sherman, governor of Delaware, 26
Truman, Harry S.
    administration of, 20
    Harry S. Truman Scholar, 15
Truth, Sojourner, social change by women, 93
Tucker, Marna, women as lawyers, 118
Tullio, Louis J., mayor of Erie, Pennsylvania, 44
Turner, M. Caroline, women as lawyers, 128–129

United States Congress
    marginalization of women in, 4
    women in 106th Congress, 30–31
United States Department of Defense, Jones, Anita K., 8–9
United States Department of Labor, Dominguez, Cari, 10
United States Supreme Court, 151
    appointments to, 103
    Ginsburg, Ruth Bader, 110

Unwanted pregnancies, 76
    see also Nurturing Network
Up From Poverty, 61–62
Urban Coalition, 113
Urban Meditations (Tiernan), 63
USA Today
    Bullard, Marcia, 159
    Lloyd, Wanda, 159
    Reynolds, Barbara, 153–155

venture capital industry, Davis, Susan, 175–176
veterans' preference in governement jobs, 26
Vietnam War, 143
    draft deferments, 115
    draft interferences, 59
    veterans of the, 31, 240
Violence Against Women Act, 18

Wald, Patricia M., women as judges, 103–105
Walker, Liz, women in journalism, 155–157
Walsh, Alice C., women in arts management, 225–227
Walsh, Holiday, women as lawyers, 122–123
Walters, Barbara, women in journalism, 157
Washington Post, Overholser, Geneva, 159–161
Weister, Linda, women in business, 202–205
Welch, Joseph N., 151
Western Industrial Contractors, Grogan, Barbara, 218–221
White, Father Jack, 59–60
Whitman, Christine Todd, women in politics, 30
Widnall, Sheila E., women in politics, 4–7, 37
Wilson, Betsy, social change by women, 81–87
Wilson, Marie C., social change by women, 65–68
Wolfe, Lois Lauer, women in journalism, 159

The Woman Warrior (Kingston), 233
women
    in 106th Congress, 30–31
    and cancer, 157
    discrimination against in law careers, 99, 133–134
    issues in Congress, 31–32
    as newspaper editors, 159
    rights of, 111–112, 115–118
    see also business, women in; journalism, women in; judges, women as; lawyers, women as; politics, women in; social change by women
Women Owned Law Firms (WOLF), 123
Women's Institute for Housing and Economic Development, Davies, Susan, 92
Women's Lawyers Network, 127
Women's Legal Defense Fund, 112, 113, 118
women's movement
    and African Americans, 21, 35
    appointments to office, 104
Women's Rights Project, Center for Law and Social Policy (CLASP), 17, 116
The Women's Room (French), 219
Woods, Harriet, women in politics, 8, 24–25
Woods, Sandra, women in business, 192–194

Yancey, Jean, women in business, 245–246
Young Presidents' Organization, 197

Ziegenmeyer, Nancy, rape victim, 159–161